## DATE DUE

| 10·28-10 | | |
|---|---|---|
| | | |
| | | |
| | | |
| | | |
| | | |
| | | |
| | | |
| | | |
| | | |
| | | |
| | | |
| | | |
| | | |

# The Words and Music of Bob Marley

THE PRAEGER SINGER-SONGWRITER COLLECTION

# The Words and Music of Bob Marley

David Moskowitz

*James E. Perone, Series Editor*

PRAEGER

**Westport, Connecticut**
**London**

**Library of Congress Cataloging-in-Publication Data**

Moskowitz, David, 1969–
    The words and music of Bob Marley / David Moskowitz.
        p.   cm. — (The Praeger singer-songwriter collection, ISSN 1553–3484)
    Includes bibliographical references (p.   ), discography (p.   ), and index.
    ISBN-13: 978–0–275–98935–4 (alk. paper)
    ISBN-10: 0–275–98935–6 (alk. paper)
    1. Marley, Bob.   2. Reggae musicians—Jamaica—Biography.   3. Reggae
music—History and criticism.   I. Title.
    ML420.M3313M67   2007
    782.421646092—dc22          2006039611
    [B]

British Library Cataloguing in Publication Data is available.

Library of Congress Catalog Card Number: 2006039611
ISBN-13: 978–0–275–98935–4
ISBN-10: 0–275–98935–6
ISSN: 1553–3484

First published in 2007

Praeger Publishers, 88 Post Road West, Westport, CT 06881
An imprint of Greenwood Publishing Group, Inc.
www.praeger.com

Printed in the United States of America

The paper used in this book complies with the
Permanent Paper Standard issued by the National
Information Standards Organization (Z39.48–1984).

10  9  8  7  6  5  4  3  2  1

# Contents

# Series Foreword

Singer-songwriters. While the term might most frequently be associated with a cadre of musicians of the early 1970s such as Paul Simon, James Taylor, Carly Simon, Joni Mitchell, Cat Stevens, and Carole King, the Praeger Singer-Songwriter Collection defines singer-songwriters more broadly, both in terms of style and in terms of time period. The series includes volumes on musicians who have been active from approximately the 1960s through the present. Musicians who write and record in folk, rock, soul, hip-hop, country, and various hybrids of these styles will be represented. Oh yes, and so will some of the early 1970s introspective singer-songwriters named above.

And, what do the individuals included in this series have in common? Although some have never collaborated as writers, while some have, all have written and recorded commercially successful and/or historically important music and lyrics. And, all the musicians included in this series have been active not only as singers but also as instrumentalists to some degree.

The authors who contribute to the series also exhibit diversity. Some are scholars who are trained primarily as musicians, while others have such areas of specialization as American studies, history, sociology, popular culture studies, literature, and rhetoric. The authors share a high level of scholarship, accessibility in their writing, and a true insight into the work of the artist(s) they study. The authors are also focused on the output of their subjects and how it relates to their subject's biography and the society around them—biography in and of itself is not a major focus of the authors of books in this series.

Given the diversity of the musicians who are the subject of books in this series, and given the diversity of viewpoint of the authors, volumes in the series will differ somewhat from book to book. All, however, will primarily be organized chronologically around the compositions and recorded performances of their subjects. All of the books in the series should also serve as listeners' guides to the music of their subjects, making them companions to the artists' recorded output.

James E. Perone
Series Editor

# Acknowledgments

I thank my wife, Jen, and my children, Heather, Lucas, and Katie, for all of their wonderful support during the completion this project. Without their kind patience and support I would never have had the time for such a large undertaking. Thanks always go to Dr. Walter Aaron Clark for his encouragement as I began my study of Jamaican popular music. I also thank Rob Kirkpatrick, who originally brought me in to the singer-songwriter series for Praeger Publishers. In addition, I thank Daniel Harmon, the acquisitions editor, and James Perone, the series editor, for their help in completing this book. Thanks also go to Photofest for its kind permission to use the images that appear in this volume.

# Introduction

Bob Marley's overall importance to Jamaica, Caribbean popular music, and pan-Africanism is difficult to overstate. While he is generally heralded as the first third-world superstar, the contemporary conventional wisdom is that he is also the only such star of his caliber. Marley's influence, both during and after his life, is staggering. It is known that during his life, his music was listened to by groups of people as diverse as the Hopi Indians living in America's Grand Canyon and the Maori people of New Zealand. Even twenty-five years after his death, Marley's name is known internationally, and he is heralded as a prophet, a peacemaker and peacekeeper, a mystic, and a universal symbol of brotherly/sisterly love.

Musically, Marley was able to achieve more in his abbreviated life than most long-lived singer-songwriters. He was not only prolific but imaginative in his music and lyrics, which cling with amazing cohesion. The sound of Bob Marley and the Wailers was the sound of roots reggae. His rhythm section's characteristic one-drop style, coupled with his penchant for high vocal harmonies, made Marley's music unique and attractive. Marley's own vocal presentation was difficult to match. He seemed to draw the meaning and the emotion out of each word as he swung his thick dreadlocks around the stage. Further, his lyrics speak at once of his own life and of the shared existence of all disenfranchised black people. Much of his universal appeal is based on the fact that, as he spoke for himself, he simultaneously spoke for all downtrodden people everywhere. One might think that this was achieved through some distinctive and new songwriting approach, but most of Marley's songs are in standard verse-and-chorus form, with extra weight often afforded to the chorus material.

Marley's place in history has already begun to be established. Although he is memorialized in countless international shrines, his actual gravesite (in St. Ann's Parish, Jamaica) is a place of pilgrimage for all who are struck by his message of "one love." His house at 56 Hope Road, Kingston, Jamaica, has been converted into a museum where an international audience visits annually to learn more of the man. The upstairs bedrooms have been converted into gallery space that contains a world map with all of his concert tour destinations marked with pushpins. Another upstairs room houses a small library and archive, along with the business office. Also on the second floor is the bedroom that Marley once used. It is preserved in the condition in which he left it and allows viewers a glimpse into the private life of a very public person. The main floor of the house contains the remnants of Tuff Gong recording studios (the official location of the studios is now 220 Marcus Garvey Drive). There are now many additional outbuildings that house things such as the Queen of Sheba Restaurant, the Bob Marley Theatre, and the Things from Africa Boutique. Both the house at 56 Hope Road and Marley's ancestral home in St. Ann's Parish remain destinations for an international host of visitors.

In addition to his musical prowess, much has been made of Bob Marley's personality. He has been alternately described as open and welcoming to all, quizzical, and even harsh. The fact is that Marley was all of these things and more. Although he was a private person, he understood his role as a public figure. Thus, when in public, he could be often open and effusive. However, when he grew tired of an interview or conversation, he was able to quickly adopt a serious look (or screwface) and sink into an unintelligible Jamaican patois that was impenetrable to anyone who was not a longtime island dweller. These various personality facets also were manifested on stage, where Marley would alternately strike a prophetic pose, fall into a deep trancelike state, or bound around with reckless abandon, legs and locks flying wildly through the air.

The combination of all of these elements has kept people's attention rapt since Marley came on the scene. An indication of his impact and his legacy is the sheer number of records sold. Since 1991, Bob Marley and the Wailers have sold in excess of 21 million records (these statistics did not begin to be collected until 10 years after his death). Further, Marley has a star on the Hollywood Walk of Fame, he was inducted into the Rock and Roll Hall of Fame, he has received the Grammy Lifetime Achievement Award, and he was awarded the Jamaican Order of Merit. Regardless of these (and many other awards), the true test of Marley's worth is time. Twenty-five years after his death, the music of Bob Marley and the Wailers is as popular, important, and pertinent as it was the day it was released.

## THE SCOPE AND ORGANIZATION OF THIS BOOK

Like its companion volumes in this series, this book focuses on the life of Robert Nesta Marley as told through an in-depth exploration of his music, lyrics, and major recordings. The content is heavily weighted toward the recordings, and many of Bob's lyrics are often autobiographical. Of note, Bob frequently wrote his lyrics in a manner that left the meaning veiled. Here the attempt is to uncover these veiled meanings and apply them to his biography. Further, he often functioned as the spokesperson for black people in Jamaica and around the world; as a result, many of his songs are about the suffering of a group, not just his own pain.

The biography of his life is discussed as it relates to his music, and additional details are supplied as a framework in which to place his musical output. Because we do not have documentation of Bob as a commercial singer until his teenage years, the material at the beginning of this volume is straightforward biography. However, once the early singles are issued and Bob is ultimately picked up by the Island Records label, the discussion focuses more directly on the music itself.

During Bob's 36-year life, he issued several hundred songs. Many he wrote alone. However, Bob's first group was a vocal trio that shared the writing duties. Also, during his mature career, much of Bob's music was written with the assistance of various members of his band, the Wailers. The year 1973 was a watershed for the young singer. It was marked by his signing onto the Island Records roster and by the beginning of the release of his 11 most significant albums. There are now 16 Island/Tuff Gong releases (plus the deluxe editions) as the result of several posthumous greatest-hits and remastered releases. This study focuses on the 11 Island/Tuff Gong albums released during Bob's life and the circumstances that surrounded their creation and release and Bob's subsequent tours. Also included is discussion of early singles, several early non-Island releases, and various posthumous collections. However, the emphasis remains on the Island/Tuff Gong material.

Inconsistency is a feature of much of Bob's biographical material. There is little documentation of his life from his birth, in 1945, until his rise to stardom, in the early 1970s. Christopher Farley's book *Before the Legend* has now done much to fill in the large gaps. Regardless, much of what is believed about him is conjecture, and there are numerous published accounts that conflict. Additionally, there are disputes (most recently involving Aston "Family Man" Barrett) about the credits for some songs.. This study attempts to counter the informational inconsistency by relying on contemporary accounts, interviews, and the most accurate and up-to-date publications. Even with this effort, there remains information that is simply unknown or impossible to verify.

Like its companions in the singer-songwriter series, this volume is meant to be a guide to the recordings it discusses. As a result, I have included a selected discography and an index of the songs discussed. The song index includes all of the songs mentioned in the text, specifically those written, cowritten, or recorded by Marley.

# Origins: The Trench Town Years, 1945–1960

## BOB MARLEY: THE ROOTS OF A REBEL

Although Bob Marley became known as an international superstar and the voice of the underprivileged and oppressed around the world, he came from quite meager beginnings. As Marley's musical popularity grew, so did his influence, first in Jamaica and then internationally. To better understand the musical and cultural importance of the first third-world superstar, one must trace Bob's life back to its roots.

Nesta Robert Marley was born at 2:30 P.M. on February 6, 1945, in the rural Jamaican parish of St. Ann. Bob's mother was an 18-year-old Jamaican named Cedella Malcolm, and his father was Captain Norval Sinclair (or St. Claire) Marley, a white Jamaican, "born in the parish of Clarendon, enlisted in the British army."[1] The child was named Robert after Marley's brother and was given the name Nesta by his father but without any explanation as to its origin.[2] According to Bob's mom, Nesta meant "messenger." As an adult, Bob described his father as a "ship's captain, an adventurer, and a rebel."[3]

Bob began life on his maternal grandfather's farm. Bob's grandfather's name was Omeriah (also spelled Omariah) Malcolm, and he was a land-owning black man who lived in a one-story house known as the "Big House," in the village of Nine Miles. The Malcolm family lived on a farm in the style of a colonial English planter's residence. This area of Jamaica was home to several prominent families, including the Malcolms, Lemoniouses, Lewises, Davises, and a dozen other closely related families who had "been farming in the region since two-hundred years before the abolition of slavery in 1838."[4]

Bob's mother and father met and began their relationship on the family farm. They were married on Omeriah's farm on June 9, 1944. On the register, Cedella was listed as 20 years old, although she was 18, and Norval was listed as 50, although he was actually 63.[5] Rather than being a happy occasion, however, the wedding day brought the news that Captain Marley was to leave the next day for Kingston and that he had no intention of returning. He had decided to take a different government job, as a foreman on a bridge-building project in Kingston, that required less work. This also paid a smaller salary. In addition, when Captain Marley informed his family that he and Cedella had been married, they reacted by "denouncing and disinheriting him."[6] As a result, the Captain was barely able to support himself and could do very little for Cedella and his then-unborn son. When Captain Marley left his pregnant wife the next morning, he promised to visit every weekend until the baby arrived; yet, "during the course of her pregnancy he paid only two brief visits."[7] Bob was born at 2:30, Wednesday morning, February 6, 1945, weighing six-and-a-half pounds. After Bob's birth, Captain Marley visited for one week, after which his correspondence dwindled and eventually stopped.[8]

Cedella continued to try to contact Bob's father, but soon letters were being returned unopened because the Captain had moved and not supplied a forwarding address. These developments left Cedella with little means to care for her son. With Omeriah's help, Cedella opened a small grocery store, where she sold produce from the family farm.

In Stephen Davis's book on Marley's life, Cedella is quoted as saying that Captain Marley visited every month or so after Bob was born. Further, he gave Omeriah money to dole out to Cedella as she needed it for various household staples. Davis states that "he gave Omeriah the money to build a tiny cabin for Cedella and the baby, and eventually set Cedella up in a little grocery shop of her own."[9]

Cedella and Captain Marley's relationship was suffering by virtue of distance and the pressure brought by the Captain's transient lifestyle. However, Captain Marley did not want to leave Bob behind. While Bob was still a baby, Captain Marley came to Cedella and said that he wanted her to release Bob to allow him to be adopted by the Captain's nephew. Cedella reacted with horror to this idea, even though it was very difficult for her to raise Bob without the Captain's assistance. The subject was dropped and the Captain returned to Kingston, but this attempt to separate Bob from his mother foreshadowed events to come.

At age four, Bob began attending a rural Jamaican school called the Stepney School. Here, according to Cedella, Bob led the class in reciting numbers and letters. His teacher, "Mrs. Isaacs, praised him so much . . . she always used to tell us [Cedella and her family] how bright he was and how helpful he was to her."[10] When Bob was six, his father reappeared in St. Ann's parish with another plan to remove him from his mother. This time, Captain Marley wanted Bob to move to Kingston in order to receive a better education in the city's school system. Cedella discussed this with Omeriah and then decided that it would be in Bob's best interest to attend a school in Kingston. His teacher, Mrs. Isaacs, was opposed to the change, saying that, although Bob was bright, he might already be behind the other children his age who had always had the benefit of the city's schools. There were also financial issues that troubled Cedella. According to Bob himself, "I find my mother works for fifty shillings a week and on this she has to send me to school, buy me shoes and lunches."[11]

## MOVE TO KINGSTON

Still just six years old, Bob relocated to Kingston to live with his father and attend public school. For months his mother sent him letters, since she felt that she could not visit given that the Captain's family did not accept her and she had little money. She would periodically receive word from the Captain saying that Bob was doing well and that he was advancing in school. After being separated for six months, Cedella planned a trip to Kingston to visit her son; however, when she told the Captain of her plans, he responded that Bob was on vacation with his teacher in St. Thomas Parish. Discouraged, Cedella delayed her plans and waited for a better time to visit her son.

Cedella received no further word from the Captain for a year and became increasingly worried about Bob. She continued to write, but now her letters went unanswered, and she grew nervous about the wellbeing of her boy. Cedella eventually got a report concerning her son from a friend who had just returned from Kingston. She learned that Bob was not living with the Captain's family at all; instead, he had been living with an elderly woman named Mrs. Grey in an arrangement set up by the Captain. Further, the friend reported that Bob did not like the arrangement and wanted his mother to come to his assistance.

The news shocked Cedella, and she was soon on her way to find her lost son. In early 1952, Cedella arrived in Kingston with the daunting task of finding Bob. While her friend had told her that she had seen Bob, she was unable to provide an address, just the street name, Heywood Street. Once on Heywood Street, Cedella began asking people if they knew of her boy. She quickly learned that he had just been playing in the area. "Then suddenly, running from around the corner, was Robert!"[12] Bob took Cedella to meet Mrs. Grey, the woman who had been caring for him. During this visit, Cedella learned that after the Captain had brought Bob here, he had never returned. The Captain's idea was that Mrs. Grey would adopt Bob and that when she died, all that was hers would be passed on to the youngest Marley. This was an important issue because the Captain knew that he would never have anything to give Bob himself. Reunited, Cedella and Bob returned home to their rural parish.

It took some time, but Bob gradually readjusted to rural life and the Stepney School. He returned to Mrs. Isaacs's class and a job in his mother's grocery store. In an interview, Cedella reported that it was at his job in the grocery store that Bob began to sing. He would frequently sing to customers as they came to inspect the produce available that day. There are numerous classic Jamaican vendor songs, and Bob had apparently learned them in the market district adjacent to Kingston.

At age 10, Bob learned that his father had died in Kingston, in 1955. It was also in this year that Bob was again separated from his mother. Rural life in Jamaica was (and is) extremely hard and, despite emancipation (which took place on August 1, 1834), still has undertones of slavery. Because of this, when Cedella was offered the opportunity to move to Kingston herself and work as a housekeeper for a time, she decided to move to the city in pursuit of greater financial security. Leaving Bob in the care of Omeriah, Cedella took the bus to the city, where she had previously spent very little time.

While his mother was away, Bob worked on his grandfather's farm, where his main duty was tending a large herd of goats, in addition to collecting firewood and cooking. At age 11, Bob and his cousin (and constant companion) Sledger were moved "fourteen miles down the road to live with Cedella's older sister Amy in the village of Alberton."[13] Without much adult supervision, Bob and Sledger were mischievous and invariably caused some trouble. As a result, the pair was returned to live with Omeriah on the family farm. Meanwhile, Cedella was still trying to earn enough money to allow Bob to come to Kingston. Finally, after two years, Cedella was able to afford a big enough apartment to allow her to send for Bob, in 1957.

The west Kingston ghetto where Bob and Cedella lived was not a good place to raise a child. Although Kingston is the capital of Jamaica, its west side was a testament to the difficulties of the third world. Oppressed members of Jamaica's lowest class inhabit crowded back roads filled with wood and tin shacks. This was where Bob grew into an adult, living in "smoky and reeking ghetto conditions of destitution, malnourished children, typhus, polio and the violence of caged people."[14]

Before Jamaica achieved independence from England, in 1962, there was a time when it was much more a Caribbean paradise than a third-world ghetto. Prior to 1938, the island country maintained a fairly equitable and peaceful tenor throughout, with active banana and sugarcane industries. However, the cane cutters' strike in 1938 forever changed the Jamaican working-class climate. At that time, the first Jamaican trade unions were formed, and from these two unions sprang the two dominant political parties. They were called the Jamaican Labour Party (JLP) and the People's National Party (PNP). The JLP was founded by the right-wing labor organizer Alexander Bustamante and represented the white British and Anglo-Jamaican colonial class, the mercantile middle class composed of Chinese and Lebanese businessmen and storeowners, and the elite black Jamaicans who worked for them.[15] Conversely, the PNP, begun by the socialist Norman Washington Manley, represented the rest of the island's population, including both rural and urban peasants. These two parties have run the Jamaican government since the 1940s. Unfortunately, violent protests over the extreme disparity in wealth between the few at the top and the great masses of the poor mark each election year.

As a result of the Jamaican political system, Cedella had a difficult time finding a good-paying job that did not involve manual labor. However, like Cedella, rural Jamaicans considered, and still do to this day, the city to be the land of opportunity where one can rise out of the backward rural communities. Those who came to the city but were unable to find work rarely returned to the country. Instead, they created enormous squatters' camps where violence was the only means of survival. Bob and his mother were spared the harshest of Jamaica's realities by living in the public housing projects referred to as the "government yard." The Jamaican government had built many of these low concrete units in west Kingston after a hurricane destroyed this area in 1951 (commonly called Trench Town).

At the time of Bob's arrival in Kingston, he and Cedella shared a room on Nelson Street. However, a few months later, they relocated to the back room of a friend's house on Regent Street. In 1959, Cedella's older brother Solomon informed her that he planned to immigrate to England and offered her his apartment at 19 Second Street. Cedella had a job as a housekeeper and was just able to afford the rent and Bob's necessities for school. During this time in Trench Town, Bob attended several different schools. They included Ebenezer, Wesley, and St. Aloysius schools. However, Bob was becoming increasingly disinterested in school, so at age 14 he terminated his formal education. At this age, Bob was more interested in playing soccer and spending time with his fellow "ghetto youths." According to Cedella, Bob's friends were "older, and most were on the edge of juvenile delinquency and incipient rude-boy-ism." According to Rebekah Mulvaney, the term "rude-boy" "refers to rough and rebellious youths who reacted to Jamaica's negative political and economic situation in the 1950s and 1960s by emulating Hollywood gangster characters."[16] The core of a rude-boy was a Jamaican youth who was a criminal or a tough guy.

Living on Second Street in Trench Town, Bob began to make musical connections that would affect the rest of his life. Another family that shared Bob's tenement yard was the Livingstons. One of their children, Bunny (born Neville O'Riley Livingston on April 23, 1947), quickly became Bob's closest friend.[17] Together the boys would handcraft makeshift musical instruments out of anything they could find. They fashioned a guitar out of copper wire, a sardine can, and a piece of bamboo and began to sing together. In 1960, Bob and Bunny took the first step toward what would become their singing group.

Jamaican culture was about to begin to carve out its own identity. Four hundred and fifty years of colonial control were coming to an end, and a new independent spirit was being created on the island. "Kingston was developing a new Jamaican sound based on the confluence of mento music, a kind of ragged Jamaican calypso descended from the quadrille music with which Bob was raised, and American rhythm and blues that was pumped without mercy into the culturally vulnerable Caribbean islands nightly by fifty-thousand watt clear-channel stations in New Orleans and Miami."[18] Ska, the new Jamaican sound of the 1950s, was marked by a fast shuffling rhythm that was similar to that of mento but also contained elements of American rhythm and blues and boogie woogie; it was the first commercially viable music produced in Jamaica.[19] The word itself was a vocal representation of the music's offbeat rhythm, which was played either on guitar or on piano.[20] An aspect of ska was the dance associated with it, marked by a charade type of performance. The dancers would act out daily domestic activities, such as cleaning or washing clothes or recreational activities that included sports.

At this time, Bob and Bunny were most influenced by the American rhythm-and-blues sound that they were able to pick up on Bunny's radio. They particularly liked the New Orleans sounds of Fats Domino, Huey Piano Smith, and Earl King. They were also influenced by the jump band style of the Arkansas-born saxophone player Louis Jordan. Because both Bob and Bunny wanted to sing, they paid extra attention to the black vocal groups like the Drifters, whose singles were popular in Jamaica in the late 1950s. Even more influential than the Drifters were the Impressions, a Chicago-based harmony trio started by Curtis Mayfield and Jerry Butler. Bob would later incorporate one of Mayfield's songs into a Wailers hit, "One Love/People Get Ready." These vocal groups were very important to the ghetto youths simply because vocal-harmony groups did not need instruments; thus, Bunny and Bob could imitate their favorite groups without having to scrape together all the instruments needed for a band. Bob said that in early times "my greatest influence was the Drifters—'Magic Moment,' 'Please Stay,' those things. So I figured I should get a group together."[21]

Bob's decision to leave school worried his mother because she knew first-hand how difficult it was for ghetto residents to procure good-paying jobs in Kingston. Fortunately, Cedella was able to arrange for Bob to go to work in a welding shop east of the Parade near South Camp Road and Emerald Street. At the shop, Bob became a welder's apprentice and began to learn the electrical welding trade. He soon discovered that one of the others welders was a fellow musician named Desmond Dekker, who was a singer for the group the Aces and who would become famous in England and the United States with his 1969 release "Israelites."[22]

# Birth of the Legend, 1960–1970

## FORMATION OF EARLY GROUPS

Although Bob acceded to his mother's wishes to learn a trade, he did not forget his dreams of becoming a singer with Bunny. He had realized that in order for his singing to improve, he needed someone to teach him the rudiments of music, such as how to harmonize and project with his voice. Trench Town, although a ghetto, provided Bob with his much-needed teacher in the form of Joe Higgs.[1] Higgs had been part of the "pre-ska singing duo Higgs and Wilson, whose first record—'Manny O'—was produced by the fledgling Kingston recording mogul Edward Seaga in 1960. . . . Joe Higgs resided on Third Street, around the corner from Bob and Bunny's Second Street yard."[2] Higgs's yard was always filled with aspiring vocalists interested in learning the art of singing. Possessing perfect pitch and an acute sense of close vocal harmony, Higgs not only taught interested parties his secrets but also did so without thought of payment. Although love songs were most popular in Jamaica at this time, Higgs preferred to write on the taboo subjects of Rastafarianism and smoking ganja (marijuana). With Higgs, Bob and Bunny not only were taught close harmony but also were influenced by the lyrics of his new songs. Further, in Higgs's tenement yard classroom, Bob and Bunny met a tall, slightly older ghetto youth who would become the third member of their trio. Peter Tosh, born Winston Hubert McIntosh, in Grange Hill, Westmoreland, on October 19, 1944, possessed the only other factory-made guitar in the yard besides Higgs's.[3]

With the union among Bob, Bunny, and Peter established, the three formed a vocal group called the Teenagers that also included two female singers

(Beverley Kelso and Cherry Smith) and another ghetto youth named Junior Braithwaite. Livingston sang high harmony in a natural falsetto, Marley sang tenor, and Tosh provided the harmonic base with his low baritone voice. The group sang covers of songs by Sam Cooke, Ray Charles, Jerry Butler, and the Impressions. In an interview, Bob was asked what type of music he liked, and he replied, "Me listen to almost everyone but me no remember names . . . me love Stevie Wonder, Curtis Mayfield, and Marvin Gaye."[4] Soon Tosh was able to borrow another guitar, and he spent time teaching Marley and Livingston some basic chords. Performing in their Third Street yard, the group was considered to be quite talented. However, Marley aspired to be more than a member of a locally talented vocal group and approached Higgs about learning to be more musically skilled. Higgs taught Marley to accompany himself on the guitar and showed him how to write the three main parts of a popular song: the chorus, the verse, and the bridge.

By 1961, Bob had begun writing his own songs and was looking for a recording studio. He approached the Chinese entrepreneur Leslie Kong (d. 1971), who owned a recording studio called Beverley's, and was promptly turned away. The Jamaican recording industry had started only in the 1950s, but already there were several studios. Ken Khouri (Federal Studios), Duke Reid (Treasure Island Studios), and Clement "Coxsone" Dodd (Studio One) all had fledgling studios and were quick to discourage anyone who did not fit the mold of the new ska singers. Jamaican studios wanted to record local musicians playing for the local audience, not those who wanted to imitate the English or American sounds. In the early 1960s, studio owners were looking to establish a new autonomous Jamaican cultural identity, and Bob wanted to be involved.

After being turned away at Beverley's, Bob went back to work in the welding shop. A coworker at the welding shop, Desmond Dekker, had auditioned for Leslie Kong at his Beverley's imprint and was then able to record his song "Honor Your Mother and Father," which went on to become a hit on the island. Dekker took Bob back to Beverley's in early 1962 to meet Kong's latest sensation, a 14-year-old singer named Jimmy Cliff.[5] Once Cliff heard Bob sing, he immediately took him in and introduced him to Leslie Kong. Of his experiences with Dekker, Bob said,

> me did sing in school and love singing, but when me really tek *[sic]* it seriously is when I go and learn a trade name welding. Desmond Dekker used to learn trade same place and we used to sing and him write songs. Then something happened to Desmond's eye, a little teeny piece of iron fly into it and him go to the doctor and have some days off. The days him have off him go and check out Beverly's and him do a thing name "Honour Your Mother and Father" which was a big hit in Jamaica. After that him just say come man and me go down there and meet Jimmy Cliff and him get me audition and me record a song for Beverly's. It never really do nothing but it was a good song still name "Judge Not."[6]

Bob sang a couple of ska-inflected spirituals and then his own song "Judge Not," all without accompaniment. Kong liked what he heard, and within a few days Marley had recorded "Judge Not" on the Beverley's label, in addition to two other ska songs, "Terror" and "One Cup of Coffee." A month later, Bob's first record, a 45-rpm single of "Judge Not," was released in Jamaica on the Beverley's label. Unfortunately, because he was unknown, Bob received no radio airplay, and the record sold poorly. Kong then released "One Cup of Coffee" and "Terror" as singles, with the same result. Bob had his first records at age 16, but his proceeds from his first big break totaled only 20 pounds sterling.

"One Cup of Coffee" was released under the name Bobby Martell to try to superimpose a little 1960s swagger on the release. However, it was a commercial failure. Additionally, it has widely been believed that Bob wrote the song "One Cup of Coffee." However, Christopher Farley recently discovered that Bob had copied most of the song from the "1961 hit by American singer/songwriter/guitarist Claude Gray."[7]

In 1962, Marley's career continued with both trouble and triumph. He had some musical successes singing in talent contests and in the tenement yard. However, his family life was about to change dramatically. Cedella had an affair with Bunny's father, and together they had a daughter, Pearl Livingston, born in 1962 as half-sister to both Bob and Bunny. Once their little half-sister was weaned, Cedella decided to marry a dependable man, Edward Booker, who was already established in a small Jamaican community in Wilmington, Delaware. Cedella wanted to take both Bob and Pearl with her to live in the United States, but due to lack of money she was able to procure passage only for herself. She did get Bob a passport, though, and it was at this time that his name was changed from Nesta Robert to Robert Nesta. Bob and Pearl lived with Bunny's father until a dispute in the house caused Bob to find a new place to live. At age 18, Bob was homeless, living on the streets, in squatter's camps, or in the Rastafarian enclaves at Darling Street, Back O' Wall, or Denham Town.

By early 1963, Bob's living quarters consisted of a corner of a kitchen on First Street. Also inhabiting the kitchen was his friend Vincent "Tartar" Ford. The two men were always hungry and frequently sang duets to keep their minds off the lack of food. It was at this time that Bob abandoned his dreams of becoming a solo artist and went back to rehearsing with his friends. He again sought additional help from Higgs on the technical aspects of group performance. Although Bob was the leader and driving force of the band, Junior Braithwaite was the lead singer.

In the west Kingston ghetto, one's friends were extremely important for safety, shared food, and, frequently, connections. Bob's close friends included those in the group, in addition to Ford, a ghetto youth named Georgie, and Alvin Patterson. Patterson, also known as Willie, Pep, Franseeco, or Seeco, was a Rastafarian hand-drummer in the Afro-Jamaican *burru* tradition, and he coached Bob's group on the intricacies of rhythm. Patterson had been a professional musician and was becoming the group's spiritual mentor. Further, Patterson had connections in the Jamaican record industry, one of whom was Clement "Coxsone" Dodd. Dodd owned Sir Coxsone's Downbeat sound system (a large portable amplifier and speaker setups for use at street parties) and was preparing to open his own recording facility. Dodd knew the Jamaican music business and had saved enough money by the early 1960s to open his own studio. In early 1963, Dodd's studio opened on the north edge of Trench Town at 13 Brentford Road. Called the Jamaican Recording and Publishing Company Limited but better known as Studio One, Dodd's new studio was primitive, with only one-track recording capability. Regardless of its lack of refinement, Studio One "quickly became the creative center of the Jamaican recording business as well as the laboratory where Jamaican ska, rock steady, and reggae music were researched and developed."[8]

In August 1963, Patterson took Bob's group to Dodd's new studio on Brentford road and got them an audition.

## DAWN OF THE WAILERS

Patterson had built the band up to Dodd, who was aware of, if unimpressed by, Bob's singles released by Kong. At the audition, the band (which also went by the names the Teenagers or the Wailing Rude-Boys; Dodd recalled their using the name the Juveniles) played one original song of Bob's and three covers of songs by the Impressions. "Peter played acoustic guitar and the group sang four songs, 'Straight and Narrow,' 'I'm Going Home,' 'Do You Remember,' and 'I Don't Need Your Love,' Bob's latest composition and the tune that was expected to 'reach' Coxsone and become a hit."[9] After the audition, Dodd told the group that they had talent but that they were not ready for recording. He suggested that they go and rehearse for three months and then return for another audition.

Disappointed, the group prepared to leave, but Tosh, being the most assertive member of the group, exclaimed that they still had another song to play, "Simmer Down." The rest of the group protested, claiming that the song was not complete, but Dodd told them to play it anyway. "Simmer Down" was a band warm-up song written by Bob. It marked the beginning of his use of biography and contemporary commentary in song lyrics. The song was a direct admonition by a ghetto youth to the rude-boys (criminals or tough guys) to control themselves or the violence in the west Kingston ghetto would only escalate. There had been serious violence in the ghetto during Jamaica's struggle for independence in 1962. This song was Bob's plea for peace so that there would be no more lives lost in the ghetto.

After the performance, Dodd told the group to return to Studio One the next Thursday to record the song. For the Studio One recordings, the band needed to decide on a name, and it settled on "the Wailers, in part because of all the people they had read about in the Bible (particularly in Jeremiah 9) who were 'wailing for their freedom.'"[10]

Returning to the studio, the group found that it was going to be backed by some of the best musicians in Jamaica, the Skatalites.[11] Also performing in the session were the guitarist Ernest Ranglin, the trombonist Rico Rodriguez, the drummer Arkland "Drumbago" Parks, and the bassist Cluett Johnson (all of whom would go on to legendary status in Jamaican music history). The collected musicians rehearsed all morning, with "Simmer Down" being recorded in two takes. The product was a fast ska tune dominated by horns, with Bob singing the lead vocals. Listening to the track on the studio playback, all involved believed that the song would be a hit.

## EARLY SINGLES

Released on Dodd's Downbeat label in the final weeks of 1963, "Simmer Down" came out in time for the Christmas market rush. By January, the song had reached number one on the Jamaican Broadcasting Company charts, and it held that spot for the next two months. Without consultation, Dodd had released the single with the name of the group changed to the Wailing Wailers. But regardless of the group's name, its members were immediate stars.

In the wake of the success of "Simmer Down," the Wailing Wailers began to record regularly at Studio One. Dodd even invited Bob to stay in a small shed in the back of the studio, knowing that the aspiring young singer was living in squalor. Dodd said of Bob, "Bob Marley was more or less like an adoption 'cause he used to stay by [with] me, you know."[12] In 1964 and 1965, two more hits quickly followed "Simmer Down" but were much different in character. "It Hurts to Be Alone" was "a slow, plaintive ballad with a brilliant, penetrating lead vocals sung by Junior Braithwaite, who sounded almost exactly like Anthony Gourdine (of Little Anthony and the Imperials)."[13] "Lonesome Feeling," written by Bob and Bunny, was composed as a follow-up to "It Hurts to Be Alone" and again deals with the emotions of loneliness and despair. These early songs were laying the groundwork for the autobiographical lyrics of Bob's mature songs. He often sang of the pain of being alone and the hope for a brighter future.

The next Wailing Wailers hit came in 1964 with the Impressions-style ballad "I'm Still Waiting." The song contained close harmonies, with Bob taking the lead vocals in a doo-wop style. A mainstay of Wailing Wailers music at this time was rewriting existing songs and giving them a Jamaican-ska inflection. Bob did this with the Drifters' classic "On Broadway," even changing the name to "Dance with Me." Reproduction rights were never procured for this type of song covering, and had the Wailers broken in the United States, they would have been open to serious legal action. Another remake that became one of the Wailing Wailers' greatest harmonic masterpieces was the

1964 version of Aaron Neville's "Ten Commandments of Love." The group also released many remakes of old spirituals such as "I Am Going Home," "Swing Low Sweet Chariot," "Let the Lord Be Seen in You," and "Down by the Riverside." Dodd even gave the Wailing Wailers a ska arrangement of the song "Nobody Knows the Trouble I've Seen" with the shortened name "Nobody Knows."

Living on the studio grounds, Marley was able to spend a great deal of time working on his guitar playing and listening to the American rhythm-and-blues and soul records that Dodd had shipped to him from the States for use on his sound system. Bob spent hours listening to Motown recording artists like Marvin Gaye, Stevie Wonder, and the Marvelettes. When not at Studio One, he continued to frequent Higgs's Third Street yard or spent time down at the beach with the Rastafarians. In 1964, Bob's life was filled with learning the music business, playing soccer, discussing current events in Jamaica, and dealing with the rapidly changing Jamaican music scene.

It was during the mid-1960s that the rhymes and rhythms of ska were slowing and transforming into the steady, heavier, rock-and-roll influenced-sounds of rock steady. In rock steady, the beat speed was less than half as fast as in ska. Also, the horn line was largely replaced by a keyboard player, and the texture was thinner. The guitar played on the second and fourth beats of a four-beat measure, and the bass emphasized the first and third. However, the music written early in this style was identified with the portion of society that was writing its lyrics. The transitional style was rude-boy music, and the Wailing Wailers were its most vocal proponents.

During the mid-1960s, the Wailing Wailers played numerous live shows in many local venues. Some of the earliest were for the "Opportunity Hour" at the Palace Theatre on South Camp. A talent scout named Vere Johns ran the show and included in it music, dancing, comedy, and acrobatics. Another venue for the group was the Ward Theatre's "Battle of the Bands." It was at one of these shows that Bob exhibited his rude-boy mentality and showed why he had recently earned the street name "Tuff Gong." After giving a lackluster performance and losing the battle of the bands to a group called the Uniques, Bob flew into a rage and challenged a member of the winning band to a fight.[14] The other Wailing Wailers held him back before anyone got hurt, but the altercation enhanced his reputation as a tough man who ruthlessly achieved his goals.

At the height of the rude-boy era, in 1965, Kingston became embroiled in race riots between the poor black ghetto dwellers and the Chinese merchants who controlled most of the small ghetto businesses. These riots helped to change the attitude in the ghetto from one of group suffering to an "us against them attitude." Out of this oppressed rude-boy mentality grew the Jamaican rude-boy songs.

Lyrics of the rude-boy songs were filled with images of mock court hearings, looting, shooting, stabbing, and robbery—all couched in the ghetto sentiment of taking what one is not allowed to earn. Although the Wailing Wailers had a tough reputation, their music approached the rude-boy situation from a different perspective—a more Rastafarian perspective. Bob's band, like his old friend Desmond Dekker's group the Aces and other groups such as the Clarendonians, was obsessed with rude-boy stories and used them for the lyrics of their songs. However, from the start, Bob was always trying to defuse urban tensions instead of glorifying violence. The rude-boy lifestyle was beautifully illustrated in the 1973 movie *The Harder They Come.*

"Simmer Down" was an example of Bob's telling the ghetto youth that if they did not try to control their temper, things would only get worse. Other songs followed in that vein. "Put It On" was written in a ska/rock style and contained lyrics that identified with the rude-boy spirit without advocating violence. One of the musical elements that separated rudie (rude-boy) music from its predecessor, ska, was the bass and drums that began to dominate the horns. This emphasis on the rhythm section was a key to the stylistic shift from ska to rock steady and a foreshadowing of the reggae beat. Verena Reckord notes that the decline of the earlier horn-driven styles was both economic (horn sections were expensive to maintain) and a result of the death of Don Drummond.[15]

The Wailing Wailers' song "Rude Boy," recorded in 1965, was a ghetto-youth anthem and established the group as the leaders of the movement, both musically and in the ghetto. Recorded as an up-tempo ska, "Rude Boy" had lyrics filled with Jamaican slang, rudie slogans, and "an utterly timeless Jamaican country aphorism: Wanty wanty cyaan getty/Getty getty nuh wanty."[16] This saying encapsulated the rude-boy mentality of wanting what one cannot have and squandering what one does have. The song was a huge hit for Bob's group and did much to further its popularity. Other Wailing Wailers songs that dealt with rude-boy images were "Jailhouse," "Rule Dem Rudie," and Tosh's "I'm the Toughest" and "Stepping Razor."

Even with their original compositions selling well, the Wailing Wailers continued to cover American and English groups. Their song "Play Boy" was a reworking of the Contours' hit "Do You Love Me," and "Ska Jerk" was the remade Junior Walker tune "Shotgun." An interesting crossover was the use of Tom Jones's "What's New Pussycat," which was redone with Bob singing over a piano ska with a club-band-sounding horn section. In addition to covering songs by other bands, Bob constantly studied and learned from other people's music. He was an avid Beatles fan who listened to the albums to acquire the group's craftsmanship and song-writing skills. The Wailing Wailers even covered some Beatles material, such as "And I Love Her" and a remade version of "I Should Have Known Better" that was released under the new name "Independent Anniversary Ska." Bob had the occasion to meet the Beatles in the early 1970s, and he identified with their skill and sense of camaraderie. He said of them, "they're bredrens. . . . Jah just love roots [and] those guys are roots."[17]

These early band years were filled with more than covers, remakes, and rude-boy songs. They also produced several Wailers classics that were released repeatedly by the three original members over the course of their careers. These songs included "Love and Affection," cowritten by Bob and Bunny, which discussed relationship difficulties over a ska beat, and also the seminal "One Love," which espoused redemption through unity in a fast-bubbling ska tempo. It was in this rude-boy era that one begins to find Rasta-encoded Bible references in Marley's lyrics. In "Jailhouse," Bob stated, "What has been hid from the wise and the prudent is now revealed to the babes and sucklings." This lyric was a paraphrase of a passage from Matthew 11:25, "thou hast hid these things from the wise and the prudent, and hast revealed them unto babes." This biblical imagery foreshadowed a more pronounced use of quotation in his later career as he adopted the Rastafarian lifestyle and beliefs. In fact, Bob later confined that his musical inspiration was Jah and his teachings when he wrote, "me dream some melodies. But when you wake up you can't hear them. Inspiration come from vision. Young man say dream; old man say vision. Any time something happen Jah show me the vision."[18]

The end of 1965 marked a turning point for the members of the Wailing Wailers. The band was again reduced to its three-man core of Bob, Bunny, and Peter. Junior Braithwaite's role began diminishing when Bob surfaced as the band's true leader. Thus, Braithwaite left the band during the summer to move to the United States with his family, and they settled in Chicago. Braithwaite's departure from the group coincided with the band's shortening its name from the Wailing Wailers to the Wailers. Bob had asserted himself as the front man with his singing skills and his ability to craft songs and compose lyrics. After Braithwaite departed, the group decided to let go of the two female backup singers. They were able to do well in the studio but frequently had difficulties harmonizing live, when mistakes could not be fixed with overdubbing.

Shortly after the Wailers had restructured, Bob met a new girl who would prove to be important to the group, as well as to him personally. Her name was Rita Anderson, and, like Bob, she fronted a vocal trio, the Soulettes.[19] Rita's group was composed of her cousin Constantine "Dream" Walker, her friend Marlene (also called Precious), and herself. Anderson was a Sunday-school teacher, church singer, and respected member of the ghetto community. Through a friend, Anderson gained access to Dodd's studio, where she met the Wailers and introduced herself. She told Peter that she also had a group, and an audition was set up with Dodd. After hearing the girls sing, Dodd took them in on probation and assigned Bob to them as manager, singing coach, and general protector.

At first Bob was a very strict teacher, and the girls were scared of him and his discipline. Gradually, he softened and admitted to Bunny that he had begun to have feelings for Rita. When Bunny told Rita this, she was amazed in light of his strictness and his harsh treatment of the girls. Eventually, Bob wrote love notes to Rita, with Bunny acting as the intermediary. Soon a love affair began between this unlikely pair that would last the rest of Bob's abbreviated life. The two spent time together in his little corner of the studio and got to know each other better. He showed her the large stack of letters that his mother had been mailing him from Delaware, asking him to join her in the States. He also admitted to being lax in replying to them, and Rita volunteered to act as his secretary. She began taking over the responsibility for answering mail from Bob's mother in Wilmington.

Bob's miserable living conditions were not suitable for him any longer, and he resolved to find a better place to stay. Rita, seeing no other good solution to the housing dilemma, took Bob in to live with her and her aunt and uncle (her parents were working in Europe). Another member of the household was Rita's infant daughter, Sharon, who was the result of a brief relationship the previous year. Unfortunately, Rita's aunt and uncle were very strict, and the young couple had to sneak in and out of the house through a back window. The crying of Rita's infant child soon foiled their plan, and, once discovered, the pair was thrown out for the night. The situation was soon remedied after Rita and her aunt had an opportunity to discuss the matter. It was decided that a small shack would be built behind the main house that Bob, Rita, and her daughter would use as their sleeping quarters.

In Wilmington, Bob's mother, Cedella, had managed to save enough money to afford to pay her son's way to the United States. The timing was bad for Bob; however, and when he received the tickets he was already modestly successful in Jamaica and was living with Rita and Sharon. Bob hoped that the Wailers would soon be successful enough to rise out of the ghetto; therefore, he postponed his plan to relocate to the United States for the time being.

The rest of 1965 was spent working at Dodd's studio, managing the Soulettes, and composing new songs with lyrics inspired by the day-to-day life of the ghetto. The Wailers were poor but always hoping to become more successful, and they knew that there were royalties coming in from their previously released singles. At Christmas, they went to Studio One to demand their proper share of these royalties. Dodd attempted to put them off, saying that their weekly allowance took the place of any additional royalties. After hours of haggling and shouting, Dodd gave the Wailers "sixty pounds in cash, to be split among the group."[20] Although Dodd had helped the Wailers achieve fame in Jamaica, he was the only one making any real money from their efforts because he had been wily enough to record and release the group's material without a royalties contract. Because of this, Bob and Rita decided that he should go to the United Stated to live with his mother and save enough money to return and start his own record company. The Wailers had learned one of the most difficult lessons in the Jamaican recording industry: one must create, record, press, label, and distribute one's own product in order to make any money.

Marley put one stipulation on his plan to move to Delaware. He told Anderson that he wanted to marry her before he left so that if he stayed it would be easier for her to gain access to the country. Anderson replied that she could not marry him because her father was in Sweden, her mother was in England, and her aunt would never give permission for the union without Marley first meeting her parents. Marley swore to Anderson that he would not leave for the States without marrying her first, and eventually he wore her down and she agreed. Next, Marley needed to get Anderson's aunt to allow the marriage. He approached her about it, and she refused him at first, but, after much arguing and discussion, she finally relented. On February 10, 1966, Bob Marley and Rita Anderson were married. Rita wore a white, above-the-knee wedding dress, and Bob had on his black Wailers stage suit. The Marleys' friends all heralded the marriage as the union of two of the most talented and promising singers in the ghetto. Sadly, Marley left for the United States to find work in Delaware the day after the wedding, much as his father had done the day after marrying Bob's mother back in St. Ann.

Marley arrived in Delaware in 1966 and was met at the airport by his mother, her niece Enid, and Enid's husband. Cedella had been told by friends that Bob had gotten married but could not believe that he had done so without consulting her first. Upon his arrival, she learned that her son had married Anderson so that it would be easier for him to bring her to the United States should he decide to stay. Late on the night of his arrival, Marley confided to his mother that he had not married Anderson just for convenience; he had married her because they were in love.

Bob remained in Delaware, living with his mother for seven months. During his stay, he took several different jobs. One was with the Du Pont Chemical Company, where he worked as a laboratory assistant under the alias Donald Marley. In addition, he took part-time jobs as a parking lot attendant, a forklift driver, and a dishwasher. When he was not at work, Bob spent his time playing guitar and writing new songs. He disliked the fast pace of work in the United States, but he was thankful for his break from constant contact with Dodd.

Another conflict arose in Bob's life at this time, a religious struggle between him and his mother. In the four years since Cedella had been away, her son had gradually been shifting his religious affiliation away from the Christian church and toward Rastafarianism. Cedella was amazed at Bob's conversion, for she had bought him up just as she had been raised, as a conservative Catholic. Now he was with her in Delaware letting his hair grow into dreadlocks while telling her stories of Haile Selassie and Ethiopia.[21] Cedella's greatest fear was that Bob would return to Jamaica and become an aimless Rasta who did nothing but smoke ganja all day.

Bob remained in Wilmington until October, when he decided to return to Jamaica and rekindle his music career. There may also have been another reason behind his decision to leave. After returning to his island home, Bob mentioned to a friend that "he had applied for social security in Delaware, and a local draft board then became interested in him as cannon fodder for the war in Vietnam."[22]

When Bob returned to Kingston, he moved back in with his new bride at 18 Greenwich Road. In his absence, Jamaica had changed dramatically. On April 21, 1968, Haile Selassie I of Ethiopia had visited the island and initiated a great deal of change. The Rastafarians, and ultimately the Marley family, viewed Selassie's trip to Jamaica as the coming of the Redeemer. Rastafarians from all over the island had walked for days to see his arrival at the airport. Rita had managed to see the emperor as he rode by in his motorcade and told her husband that she had been able to see scars on his hands from hanging on the cross. It was after glimpsing these stigmata that Rita had come to believe Rastafarian doctrine.

Musically, things had also changed in Bob's absence. Bunny had released a single called "Rude Boy" that had been a big hit on the island. Rita and the Soulettes scored a hit with their Dodd release "Pied Piper," and the Wailers had continued to record, filling Bob's vocal position with Rita's cousin Constantine "Dream" Walker. While Bob was in Delaware, the Wailers released Bunny's "Who Feels It" (released later as "Who Feels It Knows It"), "Dancing Shoes," Rock Sweet Rock," "The Toughest," "Let Him Go," "Dreamland," and several others.

Another significant change in the Jamaican music scene had taken place during the extremely hot summer of 1966. The up-tempo frantic pace of ska had slowed, and the musicians were calling the new, more relaxed tempo rock steady. Rock steady was characterized by a much more sensual and slower beat. The ska sound was marked by the use of horns, fast-paced dancing, and frequent lack of lyric substance. Rock steady arose as a style in opposition to this; it had a slower beat, emphasized the bass instead of the horns, and placed more importance on the lyrical content in the style of the rude-boy songs.

The summer of 1966 was not hot only in temperature; the Jamaican political climate was also turning hot, with ghetto violence again rising and extreme tension developing between the JPL and the PNP. The party leaders "began pressing the previously anarchist rude boys into goon squads along lines of party loyalty."[23] Early 1967 was filled with ghetto violence, turning the once placid neighborhoods into dangerous, politically controlled areas ruled by guns and goon squads. This dramatic political change was mirrored in music in the move away from ska and toward rock steady, which allowed the singer to voice protests and concerns about the Jamaican political climate. In the wake of Bob's return from the United States, the group adopted the changes in musical style.

Like the constantly evolving American jazz scene, no existing Jamaican musical style was abandoned as new styles emerged. Jamaicans continued to write ska-style tunes after the development of rock steady, but they decreased in number.[24] The emergence of rock steady in Jamaica cleared the way for many new musicians to gain prominence. Ska had been controlled by a small number of highly talented professional players and required a large group with a horn line, but with the emergence of the new style another generation of performer emerged. The new performers and groups included Alton Ellis and the Flames, the Maytals, Stranger Cole, the Heptones, the Gaylads, the Melodians, and the Paragons.

At this time, the Wailers changed not only their musical style but also their spiritual identity. Bunny had been interested in Rastafarianism for several years, Bob returned from Delaware already letting his hair grow and knot up, and Peter had stopped shaving and cutting his hair. The new Wailers emerged as the first Jamaican vocal group to outwardly adopt the Rastafarian esthetic of strict diet (called Ital), Bible reading, and copious ganja smoking. In addition, the Wailers began writing more songs with religious and socially consciousness themes.

Tenets of the Rastafarian doctrine, in addition to direct and paraphrased biblical quotations, began appearing in Bob's music with increasing frequency. This put the band in opposition to Dodd at Studio One, where things still operated according to the old-school rules. The conflict had long been building, and with Bob's return the Wailers split with Dodd. Before the separation, they recorded "Bend Down Low," a song that Bob had been working on while in Delaware.

"Despite recording over one hundred songs for Coxsone, and having five of the top ten songs on the Jamaican charts at the same time, the Wailers were not seeing any financial rewards for their efforts."[25] Dodd had brokered a deal to send dozens of Wailers hits to England for re-release, but the band did not see any financial remuneration. Even with their successes, the Wailers remained poor and uncompensated for their music. When "Bend Down Low" became a hit and Dodd again refused to pay the band its proper share, the Wailers broke their contract.

# Rebel Music, 1970–1975

### CATCH A FIRE

Once Marley ended his relationship with Dodd, he sought the guidance of a Rastafarian elder named Mortimer (or Mortimo) Planno. Planno became Bob's spiritual adviser, as well as the manager of the band. Under Planno's guidance, Bob's faith in Rastafarianism grew and his Bible studies increased. When Rita became pregnant with their first child, the Marleys decided to move back to Omeriah's farm in St. Ann (Omeriah had died in 1965). They moved into the cabin that had been built for Bob's mother 20 years earlier. Once settled in St. Ann, Rita gave birth to a girl, whom they named Cedella. Returning to Kingston only on periodic business trips, the Marley family stayed in St. Ann until 1970. While in the country, Bob returned to the farming life that he had known as a child. He and his cousins cultivated corn and a little ganja on the family farm, as had been done for decades. During this time, Bob continued to let his hair grow and form knots (i.e., dreadlocks). He delved deeper into Rastafarianism and the Bible while he continued to write music. Together with Rita, he wrote "Nice Time," "Stir It Up," and "Chances Are" while living on the family homestead. He also began work on two more new songs, "Belly Full" and "Trench Town Rock."

With their contract with Dodd terminated, the Wailers started their own record label, Wailin' Soul Records (the name appears on some singles as Wail'n Soul'm or Wail'n'Soul). Bob said of this experience, "I thought I wasn't going to work for anyone again, so we split Coxsone to form Wail'n'Soul. But I don't know anything about business and I got caught again. 'Bend Down Low' was number one in Jamaica but they were pressing and selling it in a black market type of business."[1] Early releases from the new label included "Selassie Is the Chapel," in which Bob asserts his Rastafarian faith, and "This Man Is Back," which announced Bob's return from America.

Sonny Til and the Orioles set "Selassie Is the Chapel" to the tune of "Crying in the Chapel," and it was Bob's first song dealing with Rastafarianism. The original song had recently been a worldwide hit for Elvis Presley; however, Mortimer Planno had rewritten the words and recast the tune to a slow Nyabinghi drumbeat and had given the song to Marley to sing as a testament to his new faith.[2] The Wailers' experience with Planno and their increasing interest in faith made them "the first really strong Jamaican groups to adopt the abstemious, continually testifying life of the Rastafarian, incorporating elements of Rasta drumming into their music long before it became fashionable for reggae groups to do so."[3]

In the studio, the Wailers employed the producer Clancy Eccles, and at first their new label seemed to be a success.[4] The early releases included the 45-rpm single "Nice Time," with "Hypocrite" on the B-side, and an early version of Bob and Rita's love song from their time in St. Ann, "Stir It Up." Unfortunately, the Wailers did not have the business experience or connections to last in the Jamaican recording industry. The existing labels conspired against them, and their products lacked radio play to boost sales, promotions, and distribution. The label folded at the end of 1967 when they were informed that the stamping machine that actually made the records had broken and production halted. Bob said, "we fight hard, man (to make Wail'n'Soul a success.) But when Christmas came and we go to collect money, the man say the (record) stamper mosh (was destroyed) and alla that."[5]

The closing of Wail'n'Soul Records foreshadowed the difficulties that the Wailers would have in 1968. Peter was arrested for taking part in a street demonstration against the white-supremacist government that had been founded in Rhodesia, Africa, and Bob and Bunny were both jailed for ganja possession. Bob served a month-long sentence, during which he contemplated his captivity and further identified himself with the captive sufferers in the Bible and in slavery. Bunny had been caught with a large enough quantity of ganja that he was jailed for a year in the General Penitentiary. Later in his sentence, he was moved to a work camp called Richmond Farm. These events effectively stopped any progress that the Wailers had been making musically. However, this additional suffering would become fodder for the next round of songwriting. Bob spent the year that Bunny was incarcerated playing soccer and "listening intently to the Jimi Hendrix Experience and the new funk modes of Sly and the Family Stone [with whom the Wailers would eventually tour] and working on songs."[6] Although he was struggling in 1968, Bob was overjoyed when Rita gave birth to his first son during that year. David Marley, the newest member of the ever-growing Marley family, was nicknamed Ziggy early in his life and is known by that name today.[7]

The last two years of the 1960s were a difficult and confusing time for the Wailers. They began identifying with the black power movement in the United States, even going so far as to cut off their dreadlocks and comb their hair out in Afros. Although sympathetic to the movement, Bob was still intensely interested in Rasta doctrine; Planno told him of the Rastafarian sect in Jones Town called the Twelve Tribes of Israel. These Rastas were Christians who believed that the second coming of Christ had taken place in the person of Haile Selassie. Therefore, they revered his words and speeches and spent long hours discussing their meaning at sessions called "grounations." These meetings also included prayers, drumming, chanting, and ganja smoking. Another aspect of the Twelve Tribes sect is its belief in astrology. Members are assigned tribes according to the month of their birth, and frequently they adopt their tribal name and cast off their "slave name." The Rasta philosopher who founded the sect, Vernon Carrington, went by the name Gad the Prophet and was the leader of the 1970s peace movement in Jamaica. Bob was born in February, and, as his association with the Twelve Tribes grew, he learned that he was from the tribe of Joseph. Part of Marley's experience with these Rastas in 1968 was meeting a black American singer named Johnny Nash. Nash was an African American pop singer and actor who gained international recognition with his worldwide hit "I Can See Clearly Now" and was influenced in his later career by American soul and Jamaican reggae. It was Nash who helped the Wailers reorganize musically and who ultimately ushered them onto the world stage. In 1975, Bob said of Nash, "he's good, I like him."[8]

Johnny Nash and his friend Danny Sims had begun a record label in 1964. Called JoDa, for Johnny and Danny, the label released several hits but eventually had the same fate as many other small labels and filed for bankruptcy two years later. However, Nash and Sims did not leave the entertainment business; instead, they began promoting American singers in Jamaica. At this time, it was possible to bring American artists to Jamaica to record very inexpensively. With lowered overhead, it was more likely that the recording venture would be able to remain profitable. Sims sold off all of his original entertainment assets in New York and paid to move both his and Nash's family to Jamaica. He also financed the move for his producer, Arthur Jenkins. Living in the mountain suburbs above Kingston, Sims reopened his music-publishing business in Jamaica. Called Cayman Music, Sims's new company was set up in this tax haven and banking center between Jamaica and Cuba.

Their idea was simply to profit from the relatively inexpensive recording location and to ignore the Jamaican music scene, which did not apply to their business. However, Nash began writing songs that had a Jamaican feel to them and eventually released an album recorded at Federal Studio, in Kingston, that contained "Hold Me Tight," which had a distinct Jamaican influence, and a remake of Sam Cooke's "Cupid," which was heavily influenced by the rock steady style. The effect of the worldwide success of this record on Nash and Sims was that they began to take Jamaican popular music more seriously as a product that could be exported and sold. Beyond this, Nash had become interested in Rastafarianism, and when a disc jockey friend, Neville Willoughby, offered to take him to a grounation, he agreed. The Rasta meeting that they attended was one of the Twelve Tribe's Sunday afternoon gatherings called *Satta Amassagana,* which means "give thanks and praises" in the Ethiopian Amharic language. At this meeting, Nash was introduced to two promising young Jamaican singers, Bob and Rita Marley.

The next day, the Marleys were brought to Sims's house by Willoughby, and together they performed "Nice Time," "Chances Are," "Don't Rock My Boat," and "Lively Up Yourself," along with many others. These songs impressed Sims and Nash both, and they told Bob and the Wailers that they were very interested in working with them. Although they were anxious to get back to work, Bunny was still in jail, so Bob and Rita returned to St. Ann for several months to work on existing songs and to compose new material.

Sims wanted to promote the Wailers internationally, and he approached Bob with the idea. Bob sent him to Mortimer Planno, who was still functioning as the Wailers' manager, and after some discussion they came to an agreement. Cayman Music had hired the Wailers as songwriters at a weekly retainer of fifty dollars each. When Bunny was released from custody at the end of 1968, the Wailers began recording the songs that had been written for their new employers. During the following four years, the Wailers recorded more than 80 songs for Cayman Music.

In early 1969, Sims formed a new record company, called JAD Records, again a shortening of the names Johnny, Arthur Jenkins (the producer and new partner), and Danny. During this period the Wailers did not record songs that contained Rastafarian imagery. Instead, they worked out rock steady versions of many songs such as "Mellow Mood," "Put It On," "How Many Times," and "There She Goes." Also recorded were Peter's songs "Hammer" and "You Can't Do That to Me," which was an early version of his seminal "Stop That Train." Later songs recorded for Cayman Music included Bob and Rita's "Chances Are," "Hold On to This Feeling," and "Touch Me." The most significant track from these sessions was Marley's post-rude-boy track "Soul Rebel." Even though the Wailers' output for Cayman Music was marketable, it did not contain the Trench Town sentiments that the Jamaican audience had come to expect from the Wailers, and it seemed to some that the Wailers were selling out for commercial success.

Early 1969 brought another change to Jamaican popular music in which the beat slowed down even further. The new beat was a slow, steady, ticking rhythm that was first heard on the Maytals song "Do the Reggay." Toots Hibbert of the Maytals wrote the song and said that the word really meant "regular," referring to the steady pulse of rhythm. Whatever its meaning, he had given a name to the new style. Also at this time, JAD Records and Cayman Music had scaled back their production and had agreed to let the

Wailers record for other producers with the stipulation that the records be released only in the Caribbean. In response, Bob approached Leslie Kong, who was the hottest Jamaican producer in the late 1960s, and together they recorded enough tracks to create an album. Kong was recognized as one of the best producers on the island and was one of the major developers of the new reggae style and a prime candidate to assist the Wailers. The Wailers used Kong's studio musicians as their backup band on the tracks and benefited from their expertise. Called Beverley's All-Stars, the group consisted of the bassists Lloyd Parkes and Jackie Jackson, the drummer Paul Douglas, the keyboard players Gladstone "Gladdie" Anderson and Winston Wright, and the guitarists Rad Bryan, Lynn Taitt, and Hux Brown.

The tracks recorded in this session illustrated the Wailers' earliest efforts in the new reggae style. Gone are the ska trumpets and saxophones of the earlier songs, with instrumental breaks now being played by the electric guitar. Although the majority of the new tracks were dance songs, some contained lyrics of social consciousness and concern. The majority of the new material recorded in the session was written by Bob, but a few of Peter's compositions were included as he gradually became recognized as an adept songwriter and lead singer in his own right. The tracks included "Soul Shakedown Party," "Stop That Train," "Caution," " Go Tell It on the Mountain," "Soon Come," "Can't You See," "Soul Captives," "Cheer Up," "Back Out," and "Do It Twice."

Kong released almost all of these tracks as 45-rpm singles, both in Jamaica and in England, but they were all commercial failures. Kong later informed the Wailers that he was going to release an album of tracks they had recorded for him, which would be titled *The Best of the Wailers*. This sent members of the group into a rage, because they had not yet had the opportunity, time, or maturity to record their best material. Without the Wailers' consent, the album was released the following year. However, Kong did not live to reap any of its rewards; he died of a massive heart attack at age 38.[9]

Bob was again becoming disillusioned with the Jamaican recording business and felt that the only way to get the best Wailers products to the market was to have complete control over all aspects of the process. To this end, he again left Jamaica in the spring of 1969 and returned to Delaware and his mother to earn enough money to open his own studio. While in Delaware, Bob worked on a truck assembly line for Chrysler and also held several other part-time jobs. He stayed with his mother, played guitar, and wrote new songs in his free time. Bob returned to Kingston in the fall of 1969, having saved little money for his studio dreams. The money that he brought back went to support Rita and his three children, Sharon, Cedella, and Ziggy. The Marleys now lived in a rental house on First Street in Trench Town. The house was small, but it provided a space for the Wailers to get together and rehearse. Although Bob had not earned the money that he needed for his own custom studio, he had returned refreshed and ready to work. Toward this goal, he began a new business and musical relationship with an old friend from the days spent with Coxonne Dodd. The new Wailers producer and songwriting assistant was the sound engineer and musician Lee Perry, who alternately went by the nicknames "Upsetter," "Little," and "Scratch."[10]

Together Bob, Bunny, Peter, and Perry worked in the back room of Perry's Upsetter Records shop at the corner of Beeston Street and Luke Lane. Perry spent long hours with the Wailers trying to completely remake the basic Wailer sound and altering almost all facets of their music. Bob's vocals were changed to make them rougher, more urgent, and more raw. Further, the use of horns was completely dropped, and any sign of Kong's smooth production style was removed. The lead instrument was now the bass, whose rhythms were augmented by offbeat chocked-chord chops on electric guitar. The product was a reinvigorated Wailers sound that was more driven, in the vein of the rude-boy days.

Backing the Wailers for these sessions was Perry's studio band, called the Upsetters. The core of the Upsetters was one of Jamaica's most famous rhythm sections, the Barrett Brothers. Aston Francis Barrett, called "Family Man" or "Fams," played bass in a driving melodic manner that provided both a rhythmic and a melodic anchor for the Wailers. His counterpart and younger brother, Carlton Lloyd Barrett, called "Carlie," had an innate sense of time, and together the Barrett Brothers became the driving force behind the Wailers.

The first sessions of the new and Perry-improved Wailers were held at Studio 17, Perry's record store, in the final months of 1969 and into early 1970. Two early Wailers/Perry collaborations were released on Bob's new Tuff Gong label instead of on Perry's Upsetter label. "Duppy Conqueror" and "Who's Mr. Brown" were both released as 45-rpm singles with their dubs on the B-sides. Dubbing referred to the Jamaican practice of releasing a single with the same song on the B-side with the vocals "dubbed" out so that local deejays could talk, boast, and toast (supply their own words) over the rhythm tracks at the local sound-system dances.

Again, the Wailers' attempt at an independent-label release failed, and Tuff Gong disappeared as quickly as had its predecessor, Wail'n'Soul. Lack of radio play, distribution, advertising, and money had sealed the fate of the new label. Perry, who had wanted the Wailers to record for his label from the beginning, again extended the invitation, and the Wailers began recording for the Upsetter label. During the Wailers' tenure with Perry, he would act not only as producer but also as coauthor and co-lyricist. This resulted in some of the Wailers' most impressive tracks but also created a great deal of difficulty over author attribution. Many of the early collaborations were credited to Perry, but it is likely that these songs were written with Bob, Bunny, Peter, Perry, and the band all contributing in the hothouse environment of Perry's studio.

Tracks from the early Upsetter sessions (now available in a six-CD set, released by Trojan in the summer of 2000) included Wailers masterpieces such as "Small Axe," "Stand Alone," "Don't Rock My Boat," "Mr. Brown," "Corner Stone," and "It's Alright." During the early 1970s, the Wailers/ Perry sessions mixed recording of new tracks and reworking of old songs (the CD set contains 116 tracks, many of which are dub versions). Begun in early 1970, a second Wailers/Perry session contained many more new and power- ful songs. Seminal tracks from this second session included "Lively Up Your- self," "Kaya," and "400 Years." The track "Kaya" reflected on the Jamaican Rastafarian drug culture in 1970. "Kaya," a Rasta term for ganja and the relaxed feeling that smoking it causes, further reflected the early 1970s "herb culture" that dominated artists and musicians in Jamaica at this time.

Also recorded during these sessions were many of Bob's most personal songs about love—not just the love of a man for a woman but also the broth- erly love that he had come to understand in the ghetto. Love songs from these sessions included "Don't Rock My Boat," "Stand Alone," "Put It On," "Keep On Moving," and "Fussing and Fighting." Songs that illustrated the Wailers' Rastafarian faith also surfaced with examples such as "Brain Washing," a track written by Bunny about the Babylonian contamination in Mother Goose nursery rhymes, and "African Herbsman." Perry released several singles from these sessions in Jamaica and England through 1970 and 1971, with encouraging results. However, when "Trench Town Rock" was released in 1971, the Wailers again soared up the Jamaican charts.

Even though the Wailers would achieve success by the end of 1971, the decade began with the band again struggling. Its session work for Perry was complete, but there was as yet little monetary compensation to divide. The group was in a period of stasis in late 1970 and early 1971. Bob had learned that in early 1970, Sims and Nash had liquidated their Jamaican record busi- ness and that Nash was planning to travel to Sweden, where several of his singles had been hits. Nash had been offered the job of writing the music for and acting in a movie to be shot in Sweden. Nash and Sims asked Bob to accompany them and assist in the scoring for the movie. Marley accepted, and on the way he took Rita and the children to live with his mother in Delaware. During the year that Bob was in Europe, Rita worked as a nurse in a Delaware hospital.

Bob's time in Sweden was filled with work on the soundtrack for the movie. He spent time "collaborating with Nash's Texas-born keyboard player, John 'Rabbit' Bundrick . . . [in addition to] two African hand-drummers who played on the soundtrack sessions, Remi 'Rebop' Kwaku Baah and Coffee."[11] Nash and his band had a small tour of Sweden scheduled, and Bob went along before he left Sweden. Once the tour and the movie (neither the movie nor its soundtrack was ever released) were complete, Nash, his band, and Bob went to London, where Nash was working on a record deal with the English branch of CBS Records. With the deal secured, Peter, Bunny, and the Barrett Brothers came to London, where they thought that they would be supporting Nash on a tour of England. The Wailers lived in deplorable conditions in a hotel in Bayswater and rehearsed in the basement of a Surrey-based company called Rondor Music. The group was very disappointed with its situation, but Bob remained optimistic that Danny Sims was working on a recording deal with CBS for the Wailers.

The Wailers began recording at the CBS studio at Soho Square in early 1971. They were working as the backing band for Nash's upcoming album, which contained "I Can See Clearly Now." Also recorded in this session and included on the album were four of Bob's songs: "Stir It Up," "Comma Comma," "Guava Jelly," and "You Poured Sugar on Me." Another of Bob's songs, "Reggae on Broadway," was also recorded at this time, because Sims hoped to sell it to CBS as a single.

The Wailers returned to Jamaica in the spring of 1971 to visit and to do some recording. They were scheduled to return to England in the fall to back Nash on a British tour. While back on the island, the Wailers began recording at Dynamic Sounds and at Harry J's, a new studio on Roosevelt Road built by the producer Harry Johnson. The Wailers spent the next four months creating and recording at a pace they had never before attained. This new energy came about as a result of some new musicians and a new manager, Alan "Skill" Cole. Known as one of Jamaica's most talented soccer players, Cole was a perfect match for Bob and the Wailers, sharing their enthusiasm for music and Rasta culture and having extensive connections thanks to his sports popularity.

The Wailers' core group of Bob, Bunny, and Peter now included the Barrett Brothers but lacked a keyboard player. Tyrone Downie, a 15-year-old who had played in the Young Professionals, the Barretts' club band formed while Bob was in Sweden, was recruited to fill the open position. The first track that Downie played on with the Wailers was the new song "Lick Samba." Engineered by Lee Perry and produced by Bob, Downie's performance on "Lick Samba" cemented his place in the band. In the early summer of 1971, the Wailers and Perry recorded and released "Trench Town Rock," a true reggae standard that not only galvanized ghetto residents but also sent the Wailers to the top of the Jamaican charts for the next five months.

The release of "Trench Town Rock" immediately caused a big demand for the Wailers both in the studio and for live appearances. Additionally, the social and cultural importance of the song made the Wailers into the voice of the ghetto, and they were never to return to songs of less substance. The song was about the deadly 1967 Kingston riot that was a harbinger of the troubled Jamaican political climate that would affect Bob's entire life. Bob sought to move the Jamaican underclass out of its depravity through music. When he sang "one good thing about music, when it hits you feel no pain," it was as an anesthetic to the ghetto. Bob and the Wailers also benefited financially from the popularity of their new single. Bob and Rita were able to establish Tuff Gong Records, first on the Parade and then on Beeston Street, where they sold the Wailers' releases.

Meanwhile, Perry was busy releasing many of the tracks that the Wailers had recorded with him, including "Small Axe," "Kaya," "All in One," and "More Axe." With the increased revenue, Bob was able to establish Tuff Gong Productions to keep up with demand for their new music. There followed an unprecedented period of productivity for Bob Marley and the Wailers. They worked at several studios and recorded "Midnight Ravers," "Craven Choke Puppy," "Satisfy My Soul," "Redder Than Red," and "Mr. ChatterBox." They also recorded Peter's songs "Stop That Train" and "Burial," in addition to Bunny's "This Train" and "Dreamland." Other songs recorded or re-recorded in 1971 were "Guava Jelly," "Screwface," "Natural Mystic," "Concrete Jungle," "Reggae on Broadway," its follow-up "Dance Do the Reggae," "Chances Are," "Mellow Mood," "Stay with Me," "Gonna Get You," and Bob's extremely raw tale of ghetto abandonment, "Hurting Inside."

Although this was the busiest Bob had been in his adult life, he was kept in balance by Alan "Skill" Cole. Cole had Bob on a schedule of exercise and physical activity in addition to his full days of recording. Each evening began with a communal Ital meal (referring to the Rasta diet of organic foods, no meat other than fish, no salt, and no alcohol) and ended with rehearsing and composing new songs. This hectic pace, coupled with their meager financial gain (in comparison with the earnings of American and English rock-and-roll stars who periodically came to Jamaica), began to strain the seams of the once inseparable Wailers. Bob and Bunny, though raised as brothers, frequently stopped speaking due to disputes, and Peter was constantly disappointed when his songs were passed over in favor of Bob's during recording sessions.

In the summer of 1971, Bob began his first foray into politics by allying the Wailers with the People's National Party (PNP). Since the country's independence, in 1962, the Jamaican political climate had remained largely unchanged, with the Jamaican Labour Party (JPL) running the government. The JLP maintained a neocolonial state in which the landed wealthy, the mercantile families, and the middle class always benefited from the blind oppression of an ever-increasing pool of cheap black labor from the ghetto. The leader of the PNP was Michael Manley, the son of the party's founder, who was a union leader and a moral authority.[12] Manley gained a portion of his moral authority from his alliance with both the working class and the Rastafarians. It was Manley who had invited Emperor Haile Selassie I to visit Jamaica in 1966. By virtue of this, the Rastas felt that Manley had been chosen by the Emperor to lead Jamaica. Manley often carried a staff that the Emperor had given him when he arrived on the island and that the Rastas referred to as the "rod of correction."

In preparation for the general elections of 1972, Bob and Rita traveled on the "PNP Musical Bandwagon," playing and singing on the back of a flatbed truck in support of the Manley candidacy. Bob believed that Manley could effect change in the Jamaican political scene that would reflect the interests of the underclass Jamaican. Also, Bob saw in Manley's breed of socialism an inroad for Rastafarianism that would allow it to be viewed as a legitimate island religion and not as one of the fringe sects that the JLP had caused it to become.

Sims again called Bob to England in the fall of 1971 to support the four tracks Bob had written for Nash's new album, which was steadily climbing up the British charts. Also, Sims now wanted to sign Bob to CBS so that they could release "Reggae on Broadway" in the wake of Nash's success.

The Wailers again suffered in England from poor accommodations, staying in the same seedy hotel they had stayed in on the last trip, and there was general discontent among the group members. To placate them, Sims hired a Trinidad-born black Londoner named Brent Clarke to serve as the Wailers' London manager. Clarke's first act was to move the Wailers to a small house with a kitchen so that they could prepare their own Rasta Ital food. This did much to improve the morale of the group, and the members began to immerse themselves in the London music scene. Soon an entourage of other young black musicians, groupies, drug dealers, and fans was surrounding the Wailers. Bob and Peter were adjusting quickly to their new environment, but Bunny resisted, always pining for Jamaica.

By the end of 1971, Nash's "I Can See Clearly Now" was a number one hit all over the world. However, Bob's single "Reggae on Broadway" suffered a very different fate and was ignored by its English audience. Trying to boost sales of both records, Sims convinced CBS to fund a three-week tour for Nash and Bob. For 18 days in November and December, the two toured 72 English high schools, performing acoustic sets at 4 schools a day. The tour ended with a greater English appreciation for Bob, but still no record sales. The group was then left in dire straits when Sims and Nash disappeared unexpectedly. They had returned to New York to try to boost waning sales of Nash's album in the United States. Bob and the Wailers were abandoned in England with no money, no work, and no means of getting back to Jamaica. Bob did the only thing that he knew to do, and, in December 1971, he went to the Basing Street Studios of Island Records to see its owner, Chris Blackwell.

Blackwell, an Anglo-Jamaican, had begun to record Jamaican music under the company name Island Records in 1959, and he knew of Bob Marley and the Wailers before Bob came to see him. For several years prior to their meeting, Blackwell had followed the Wailers' progress. In fact, 10 years earlier, Island had released Bob's single "One Cup of Coffee" in England under a license issued by Leslie Kong. Blackwell was firmly grounded in the music business, having discovered the Jamaican singer Millie Small, whose song "My Boy Lollipop" had sold 6 million copies in 1964. Blackwell also discovered the 15-year-old singer and keyboard player Steve Winwood when he was playing with the Spencer Davis Group and went on to sign Traffic (Winwood's second group) after the Spencer Davis Group broke up, in 1968. With these successes, Island had changed its focus and become a rock-and-roll label, with a large stable of bands that included John Martyn, Fairport Convention, Cat Stevens, Free, King Crimson, Jethro Tull, and Emerson, Lake, and Palmer. Blackwell's rock acts had already made him a millionaire by the time he was approached by Bob.

Shortly after their meeting, Blackwell advanced the Wailers 8,000 pounds to return to Jamaica and begin recording their first album for his record label. Once the Wailers were back in Jamaica, with the money and support of Blackwell, their attitudes improved dramatically. Bob could afford to bring Rita and their children back from Delaware, and everyone was happy to be reunited. Tuff Gong Records was moved to Beeston Street and Chancery Lane, and the Wailers began rehearsing songs for their new album.

The new sessions began in early 1972 and produced the tracks for the album *Catch a Fire*. The words "catch a fire" were Jamaican patois for "catch hell." They were applied to Bob when his friend Mortimer Planno, a Rastafarian affiliated with the Divine Theocratic Temple of Rastafari, in Kinston, told him that he would either grow in his spirituality as he became more famous or "ketch a fire."[13]

Prior to this album, true reggae music had always been released on 45-rpm singles, but Blackwell wanted the Wailers to make the first reggae album. Recording sessions for the album took place at Dynamic Sound, Harry J's, and Randy's, on the North Parade. The product was a mixture of songs of alienation, rebellion, and love that had previously been released in Jamaica, in addition to several new songs. Released on Island Records on April 13, 1973, *Catch a Fire* comprises nine tracks in the following order: "Concrete Jungle," " Slave Driver," "400 Years," "Stop That Train," "Baby We've Got a Date," "Stir It Up," "Kinky Reggae," "No More Trouble," and "Midnight Ravers." Bob said of the album, "*Catch a Fire* was an introduction. Nobody know who Bob Marley and the Wailers were, at the same time maybe you have other group who people were more interested in at the time. It was for people [to] get in and listen."[14]

The lineup for the *Catch a Fire* sessions grew from the Wailers' core. Bob sang and played acoustic guitar, and Peter sang backup vocals and played guitar, piano, and organ. Bunny sang backup vocals and played congas and bongos. The Barrett Brothers supplied the rhythm section on many tracks, with Aston on bass and Carlie on drums. However, several studio musicians were also used during the recording sessions. The legendary Jamaican bassist Robby Shakespeare played on "Concrete Jungle," and Tyrone Downie again joined the Wailers to play organ on "Concrete Jungle" and "Stir It Up." Winston Wright, a veteran Jamaican keyboardist, played organ on other tracks and a longtime friend of Bob's, Alvin "Seeco" Patterson, played hand percussion on *akete* drums for several tracks.[15] The original tracks for the album were recorded at a variety of Kingston-based studios, including Dynamic Sound Studio, Harry J. Studio, and Randy's Studio.

The album also exhibited the first use of the female vocal backing trio of Rita Marley, Judy Mowatt, and Marcia Griffiths that would become known as the I-Threes. With the rhythm and vocal tracks recorded, Bob returned to London to overdub and mix the album.[16] For this, additional players were enlisted, including the guitarist Wayne Perkins (known for his work at Muscle Shoals Studios in Alabama) on "Concrete Jungle" and "Stir It Up." The percussionist Chris Karen overdubbed tabla drum parts on "Concrete Jungle," and John "Rabbit" Bundrick added electric piano, Clavinet, and Moog synthesizer parts to the majority of the songs. Blackwell added his own flavor to the mix by slightly accelerating the tempo of all the tracks to appeal to a larger rock-and-roll crossover audience.

Blackwell's idea of tailoring the sound of the Wailers' first album to help it achieve crossover success was significant. His rock success and sensibilities allowed him to take the original Wailers material and transform it into a product that could generate international attention. Blackwell's decision to overdub rock guitar and keyboard parts on *Catch a Fire* changed the Wailers' sound. This changed the sound of future Wailers' releases and, by extension,

The Wailers: Bunny, Bob, Carlie, Peter, and Aston. Courtesy of Photofest.

reggae music at large. The goal of Blackwell's overdubbed material was to make the Wailers sound more approachable to a wide, rock-centric audience; the result was that it helped catapult Bob and the Wailers to international superstardom. He said of this, "I felt the way to break the Wailers was as a black rock act; I wanted some rock elements in there."[17]

Interestingly, the Blackwell-altered Wailers sound maintained significant Jamaican roots. The lively and rootsy sounds of the rhythm section, coupled with the tight male and female harmonies, were benchmarks of Jamaican popular music in the 1970s. The songs on the album were all original and were written by all of the members of the Wailers. Peppered over what would soon be called roots reggae, the lyrics on this album move from grave reports on life in the Kingston ghetto to lighthearted love songs.

Also unique was the original packaging for this album. The first vinyl release of *Catch a Fire* was fashioned in the form of a large stainless steel Zippo lighter with the album titled engraved on it. Instead of sliding the record out of the right side of the jacket (the usual way of exposing a vinyl LP), the lighter case hinged on the left side to expose the record. Inside the lighter case was a cardboard cutout of the internal workings of the lighter. Included inside were the standard windproof mechanism, the striker wheel, and a flaming wick. In retrospect, these flames seemed to signify how this album would catch on around the world and rocket the Wailers to international fame. While the Zippo concept-album art was unique, it was also expensive to produce. Upon its release, *Catch a Fire* received a favorable review in *Rolling Stone;* the package garnered nearly as much attention in the British press.

Subsequent pressings of *Catch a Fire* were released in a more traditional package. The second incarnation of *Catch a Fire* displayed a large picture of Bob taking a draw from a massive bugle-shaped spliff.[18] The back of the non-Zippo version of the album depicted Bob, Peter, Bunny, and the Barrett Brothers standing on an outdoor staircase. Bob had his hands in his coat pockets, Bunny had one arm in his coat in a vaguely Napoleonic pose, and Peter was wearing an Army surplus jacket that displayed the stripes for the rank of a U.S. Army staff sergeant on the left sleeve.

The album began with the song "Concrete Jungle." The sentiment of this song was inspired by the Jamaican government's urban development plan. The plan resulted in the demolition of vast tracts of the west Kingston ghetto, which were replaced by concrete-bunker-style housing projects, the concrete jungle. Most of the members of the Wailers lived in these housing projects during their formative years. Bob viewed the governmental intrusion as evidence of unwanted political control and references this sentiment in the words of the song. In short, the song described the plight of the Jamaican underclass living in the ghetto.

The lyrics describe a place where the sun does not shine, a place whose suffering residents cannot escape. Images of darkness and despair prevail.

However, each verse does contain at least one reference to gaining some sort of happiness. The words are cast in a loose verse/chorus form in which the chorus does not contain the same lyrics each repetition. Significantly, "Concrete Jungle" was rife with rock-guitar overdubs by Wayne Perkins.

The track was the first example of Blackwell's overdubbed rock-and-reggae hybrid. Much of Peter's usual lead-guitar role was relegated to rhythm guitar, and Wayne Perkins played the lead. Perkins was an American session player affiliated with the Muscle Shoals Sound Rhythm Section, which played in a driving rock-riff style unlike Peter's more laid-back, island-informed style. Blackwell himself described the number as "a song with an urgent, contemporary edge, 'Concrete Jungle' is complex, brilliant."[19]

The relationship of reggae music to the Rastafarian religion has long been misunderstood. Reggae music was not the music of the Rastafarians; there was a separate and distinct type of music specific to the religion. Rastafarian music consisted largely of chanting and drumming. Three drums were used: the bass drum, the *fundeh,* and the repeater (*peta*). The bass drum would move very slowly and keep time. The *fundeh,* or lifeline, carried a steady rhythmic pattern that was faster than the bass drum line. The *peta* was the highest pitched of the three drums and supplied a colorful melody line and embellishments. The role of the *peta* was not just to mix with the patterns of the other two drums but also to move against them in complex counterpatterns. The late Oswald "Count Ossie" Williams was a highly accomplished Rastafarian drummer who was credited with bringing the drums into Jamaican popular music.

Not only the instruments but also the texture of Rastafarian drumming permeated reggae. The typical reggae band consisted of a drum and a rhythm guitar functioning as the Rastafarian bass drum. The more active repeated rhythm of the *fundeh* was comparable to the activity of the electric bass in a reggae band. The function of the repeater was usually taken over by the singer in the contemporary ensemble; however, during instrumental breaks this part was often taken by the lead guitar or the bass. The vocalist could choose either to complement the patterns established by the other players to create a polyrhythm or to move against them in a counterrhythm; either resulted in a highly stylized, rhythmically active product.

The texture of "Concrete Jungle" basically conformed to the crossover just described. The drum set and the rhythm guitar function in the support role of the Rastafarian bass drum. The drum largely accents the second and fourth beat of each measure while the guitar plays eighth-note offbeats. The guitar's role changes at the time of the solo, during which it functions more as the repeater. The rock-and-roll guitar solo was performed in the studio by Perkins but was subsequently played live by Wailers guitarists such as Al Anderson. The electric bass fills the role of the *fundeh* with a fairly active line that complements the rhythms of the drum and the guitar. The vocal line was the most active, with the inclusion of some echoing and phrase-end harmonizing by the band, and occupied the role of the repeater for the majority of this song. Here the vocals did not move against the rest of the group in cross-rhythms; instead, they occupied the role of the most rhythmically active part.

"Slave Driver" was the second song on *Catch a Fire*. Written and sung by Bob, the sentiment of the song was again defiance and discontent with a longstanding oppressive state. The album takes its title from the lyrics of this track, which begin, "Slave driver, the table has turned, catch a fire, you're gonna get burned." Here the Wailers warned the government that the day of reckoning was coming and that when it did, the master and slave roles would be reversed. Evident in the sentiment of the song was the Wailers' groundings in Rastafari, the teachings of Marcus Garvey, and the American civil rights movement.

The song was built on a repetitive bass pattern, which was augmented by offbeat rhythm guitar chords. Layered over this were intermittent high vocal harmonies and Bob's lyrics. Here the standard verse/chorus form was clear and straightforward. Upon his first hearing, Blackwell reported that he was simply blown away. The songwriting, musicianship, and quality far exceeded earlier Wailers material.

"400 Years" was written and sung by Peter Tosh. The song began with a downward turning opening phrase, before the bass and keyboards entered. The drum exhibited reggae's characteristic one-drop rhythm.[20] The vocals entered next and expressed dire statements lamenting Jamaica's extended period of slavery and colonization (this album was written just 10 years after Jamaica declared its independence from England). Peter implored the youth to rise up out of the vestiges of colonial oppression and positioned them as the saviors of the future.[21] The ultimate outcome was the "promise land, the 'land of liberty,' [which] is the hope of Tosh . . . commanding the people to turn from a life of pain and suffering and enter a land of hope and possibility."[22]

The next song, "Stop that Train," was also written and sung by Peter. Faster than "400 Years," this song maintained much of the same sentiment. Here Peter was looking to escape his depressed situation after realizing that he could not change it. The sound of the song was characteristic Wailers. The drum played the one-drop rhythm, the guitar kept time on the offbeats, and the vocals were cast in high male harmonies; however, the bass movement was not as present in the mix. Intermittently during the song, there were breaks in the standard beat, during which Peter sang and was closely accompanied by a lead guitar solo. This was not a standard Wailers band sound, but it was particularly effective in this case. These breaks were in the verse position of the standard verse/chorus alternation. Peter chose to begin this song with the chorus, so there were more statements of the chorus than the verse material.

One of the lighter songs on the album, "Baby We've Got a Date (Rock It Baby)," was written and sung by Bob. In the lyrics of this song, Bob forecast the events of an upcoming date. There was mention of his coming to pick up his girl and them walking in the moonlight (Bob's love songs were always sung to an anonymous lover). However, the real subject was physical love. Bob repeated that they have got to get together and "rock it baby, tonight." This song was again in verse/chorus form, but the form was loose and freewheeling. The chorus music did not have the same words each time and came in statements of varying length. Musically, the song began with a short and repetitive organ part, which was augmented by an active bass part, one-drop drumming, and offbeat guitar chords. The vocals began with Bob's voice in front of alternating female and high-male vocal harmonies. As the song progressed, the lead guitar part became more active. This material was part of the overdubbed lead parts played by Wayne Perkins. His southern rock–influenced guitar style was foreign to reggae but ended up meshing perfectly with Bob's voice.

"Stir It Up" was the sixth track of *Catch a Fire*. The words and music for this song were both credited to Bob. It had already been a hit for Johnny Nash on the CBS label the year before Bob released it on *Catch a Fire;* incredibly, it was not released as a 45-rpm single until 1976. The track again contained rock-inflected overdubs by Wayne Perkins on guitar.

The song began with a distorted guitar line that was underpinned by an active walking-bass pattern. The drum played the one-drop rhythm but was buried in the mix. The form of the song was protracted and involved, making use of five chorus statements and a keyboard solo. It was, however, symmetrical. The song began with a statement of the chorus, which was followed by standard alternations of verse and chorus. The chorus was sung in high male harmony and was the same for each repetition. During the verse sections, Bob repeatedly referenced a love interest whom he implored for physical contact. Although the chorus statements were straightforward in their message, the verses contained more metaphorical references to lovemaking, such as "quench me when I'm thirsty." Bob wrote this song while he and Rita were living back in St. Ann's parish in 1967, and the vivid love descriptions applied to his life with Rita.

"Kinky Reggae" was written and sung by Bob. The song began with the rhythm section establishing the characteristic Wailers groove. Added to the texture were offbeat chords on the organ, which played an active role throughout the song. The form was an interesting alternation of short verses and extended chorus statements. The two statements each came in three parts, and the middle section was different from chorus one and chorus two. The only two sets of lyrics that can be described as verses were short, referenced places (downtown and Piccadilly Circus), and mentioned people (Miss Brown and Marcus).

Kwame Dawes noted that Bob's choice of lyrics position the song in two distinct realms. First, he observed that in Jamaica the word "kinky" did not have the sexual connotations that it does in the United States. In Jamaica, the word has the meaning "insane, strange, or different."[23] Further, the location associations Bob made in the lyrics place it in London, as opposed to Jamaica. Like "Reggae on Broadway," Bob used place names in his lyrics to separate Jamaican and foreign concepts. He took this separation one further step by stating that he "just can't settle down" and that he is "leavin' . . . today." Thus, Bob remained separate from these foreign references.

Track eight was another politically motivated song. "No More Trouble" was written and sung by Bob. It began with a distant sounding chorus of the title words, which led into the first chorus. The form alternated chorus and verse with the song being chorus-heavy. An interesting feature was that the chorus sections highlighted the female background vocals. The verse sections were sung by Bob, with the female vocals adding emphasis to phrase ends by repeating the last word of each line. Distinct in the Wailers' songcraft approach on this album was that, while the songs were in verse/chorus form, there was little use of instrumental solos toward the end of any given song. The general message of the lyrics was similar to that of "Simmer Down," a general call for love to overcome conflict and for peace to reign.

The final song on *Catch a Fire* was "Midnight Ravers." Again the song began with the rhythm section establishing the standard Wailers reggae groove. The lyrics began after a short introduction, and Bob began singing. Unlike other examples on this album, "Midnight Ravers" was not in verse/chorus form. Instead, it was built in two large sections that were lyrically related. The first four lyrical statements constituted section one. Section two was a repetition of section one, with all of the pronouns changed to first-person statements. Thus, the line "They become the midnight ravers" in section one becomes "I've become a night-life raver" in section two. The music of both sections was the same and quite static. The raver reference spoke to the 1960s and early 1970s party culture. Interestingly, when Bob descended into the raver culture, in the second half of the song, he pleaded for help to escape. The possible remedy was found in the biblical reference to "10,000 chariots." Maybe the armies of God can save the singer from the ravers.

The biblical reference that Bob made, "10,000 chariots," echoed the language of Psalm 68.[24] Old Testament language is found throughout Bob's output and his use of it intensified as he matured. This illustrated his deep religious roots and strong Old Testament convictions. There were several iconic images of Bob reading the Old Testament to children, and in that same vein he was passing these religious convictions on in his lyrics. Bob's connection to Rastafari and Marcus Garvey and his association with Joseph bear witness to his interest in connecting his faith and his music.

Timothy White's take on Bob and "Midnight Ravers" dates to something that happened to Bob in 1972. At that time, the Wailers were sleeping outside in the yard of the house at 56 Hope Road. Various hangers-on were free to approach the band members as they relaxed in the evening. According to the story, on one such occasion Bob met a woman named Patricia Williams. This meeting yielded a child named Robbie. Bob reportedly wrote about the meeting the day after it occurred. His account yielded the song "Midnight Ravers."

Late in 1972, Bob was in London working with Blackwell on overdubs and mixing the album. Sims and Nash were also in London at this time for a short tour to promote "I Can See Clearly Now," which had finally broken in the United States, selling 2 million copies. Bob agreed to be the opening act for the tour, with Nash's band, the Sons of the Jungle, backing him. Sims did not realize yet that the Wailers had established a business relationship with Island, and he informed Bob that he was negotiating with CBS to release another Wailers single and to back an English tour. For this purpose, the rest of the Wailers were brought to London to rehearse for the often-postponed tour. At Nash's London concert, the Wailers informed Sims of their desire to abandon CBS and to record exclusively for Island. Sims put the Wailers off, saying that he had already given CBS five tracks toward an eventual album and that they had already agreed to release a follow-up to "Reggae on Broadway."

After the tour, Sims and Nash again immediately returned to New York, leaving the Wailers in London. Shortly thereafter, CBS sent Blackwell documentation that the Wailers had indeed been signed to them though their agent, Danny Sims. Anxious to avoid a lawsuit with Cayman Music, Blackwell sent Bob to New York to ask Sims to release the Wailers from their contract. Sims agreed but informed Bob that the group owed CBS for advances and expenses and that Blackwell was expected to pay 5,000 pounds for the Wailers' contract. Further, he insisted that the Wailers sign a new songwriting agreement with Cayman Music and grant Sims a 2 percent override on the first six Wailers albums to be released by Island. Bob informed Blackwell of the terms, and he agreed to buy the Wailers from CBS, Sims, and Cayman Music.

While in New York, Bob spent an evening with his label mates in the band Traffic, who were there on their last American tour. After the show, the band invited Bob back to the Windsor Hotel for a party, where he met a harmonica player named Lee Jaffe. An immediate friendship began between Bob and Jaffe that lasted for the rest of Bob's life. For the following three years, Jaffe accompanied Bob almost everywhere, acting as road manager for the Wailers and becoming the only white musician to regularly perform with the group. After returning to Jamaica, Bob contacted Jaffe and invited him to join the Wailers on the island.

When Jaffe arrived, he eventually found Bob in the Wailers' new rehearsal space, in an outbuilding behind a large house at 56 Hope Road. Blackwell had just purchased the house, called Island House, as the Jamaican headquarters of Island Records. Bob had use of the house for the Wailers' rehearsals and various band activities; eventually he took up residence there and ultimately took complete possession. Soon after Jaffe's arrival, Blackwell chartered a DC-3 and took the Island Records contingent to Carnival in Trinidad. Flying from one Caribbean island to the next, Blackwell would periodically "notice a nice beach somewhere below, [and] he'd tell the pilot to land so everybody could swim."[25]

In early 1972, Rita had given birth to Bob's second son, named Stephen, and moved to a small house at Bull Bay, west of Kingston. Bob slept either at 56 Hope Road or at Bull Bay. While Bob was staying at the Hope Road house, he was having an extramarital affair with Esther Anderson, a beautiful Jamaican actress he had met in New York. Through the course of his life, Bob had several childbearing relationships with women other than Rita. As noted, early as 1970, Bob had a son named Robbie with a Trench Town girlfriend named Patricia Williams (thus White's theory on "Midnight Ravers"). About that same time, an affair with a woman named Janet was about to produce another Marley son, Rohan. It was common in Bob's adult life to periodically spend a night with "the mothers of his babies." On his second trip to London, an affair with a black English girl, also named Janet, produced a daughter named Karen.

During this time in Bob's life, a typical day began just before sunrise with a chalice full of ganja that was passed among those in attendance.[26] Cole, when not out of town playing soccer for Santos Brazil, had put himself in charge of Bob's fitness training, which consisted of eating a regimented diet, running and jogging, and playing soccer. Part of being a Rastafarian, which Bob considered himself regardless of hairstyle, was submitting to a strict diet that excludes meat, salt, and shellfish. Thus, in addition to Cole's workouts, Bob limited his diet primarily to fruit, fish, and rice. Once awake, Bob, Cole, and friends drove to Bull Bay for an hourlong run on the beach. Frequently, they ran up the hill to the Cane River waterfall to bathe and wash their hair. While in Bull Bay, Bob visited Rita and his children and checked the progress Rita was making rebuilding the house that they owned. Next, the group went to the Tuff Gong Record Shop, in Kingston, where Bob took an accounting of sales and spent time as part of the downtown reggae scene.

The Wailers retained the Caribbean rights to all of their Island Records output and sold new Wailers releases at the Tuff Gong shop, along with many of their own singles and those of Peter, Bunny, Rita, and the Barretts. After spending the morning at the record shop, Bob frequently got back together with Cole for an afternoon drive into Trench Town in search of fresh ganja. On these trips into the ghetto, Bob was now treated as a hero. He was immediately recognized and had to carefully navigate the throngs of children that gathered around his car. Once he and Cole had purchased some fresh ganja, they traveled to the ball fields at Boy's Town to play pickup soccer games against all comers into the late afternoon. Finally, they returned to 56 Hope Road for Wailers rehearsals, which often continued long into the night.

Two events occurred in 1972 that had lasting effects on Bob and on Jamaica. First, Michael Manley was elected the new Prime Minister, and under his socialist government Jamaica began to change from its days of post-colonial servitude to a nation preoccupied with equal rights and justice for all on the island. Second, *Catch a Fire,* the first-ever full-length reggae album, was released in December in Jamaica and in January 1973 in the United States. Regardless of the album's sales and reviews, the release of *Catch a Fire* changed reggae both in the way that it was played and in the way that it was sold. Bob and Blackwell had made it possible for a reggae artist to compile enough material to generate a whole album and had infused the reggae style with so many other elements (funk, rhythm and blues, and soul) that the music now had international appeal.

The release of their first album had an effect on the Wailers, as well. They were now professional musicians with all of the associated responsibilities, such as regularly releasing new recordings, touring, and sitting for interviews. Blackwell had informed Bob just as *Catch a Fire* was being released that he wanted the Wailers to create another album as soon as possible. In addition, Island would back the Wailers on a promotional tour of England in the spring and on an American club-date tour in the summer and fall. The Wailers began rehearsing new songs for the tour, in addition to holding auditions for a keyboard player to take on the road.

As a result of these auditions, the Wailers hired a keyboardist named Earl "Wya (or Wire)" Lindo. Born in Kingston in 1953, Lindo was well known on the island for playing in the band the Now Generation. He took the place of the young Tyrone Downie, who had opted to stay in Jamaica through the tour and work in the resorts on the North Coast. When Lindo agreed to join the Wailers on tour, he took a leave of absence from the Now Generation until that group got back together for its next album.[27]

The tour rehearsals were held behind the 56 Hope Road headquarters of Island Records. The Wailers also worked on new songs for the next album, which had been tentatively titled *Reincarnated Souls,* after the title of a new song by Bunny. Like its predecessor, the new album contained remakes of several older songs, along with new tracks. Blackwell arranged for the sessions to take place at Harry J's studios in Kingston. The old songs were updated and included "Put It On," "Small Axe," and "Duppy Conqueror." They also recorded three new tracks written by Bunny: "Reincarnated Souls," "Hallelujah Time," and "Pass It On." Peter contributed a new song called "One Foundation," and the *burru* meditation song "Rasta Man Chant" was updated and recorded. The songs that Bob supplied for the sessions were militant and reflected the new Jamaican political climate more than any of the other tracks on the album. Bob contributed three new rebellious songs, "I Shot the Sheriff," "Burnin' and Lootin'," and a track he had cowritten with Peter, "Get Up, Stand Up."

## *African Herbsman*

The first official Wailers tour began in April 1973 when the group arrived in London for the three-month British leg. On the way, Bob had made a stop in Delaware to visit his mother. Once in London, the group was amazed to find a Wailers album called *African Herbsman* available in local record stores. Released on the Trojan label, *African Herbsman* contained the best tracks from the Wailers' sessions with Lee "Scratch" Perry; however, the Wailers themselves knew nothing about it. Perry had sold the license for these tracks to Lee Goptal, an Anglo-Indian accountant, who had founded Trojan with Blackwell. Blackwell and Goptal had dissolved their partnership in 1972, but Goptal retained Trojan and its holdings. Together with Perry, Goptal released *African Herbsman*, which increased the Wailers' audience even though they did not benefit from it financially.

*African Herbsman* was released in 1973.[28] The album contained the following songs: "Lively Up Yourself," "Small Axe," Duppy Conqueror," "Trench Town Rock," "African Herbsman," "Keep On Moving," "Fussing and Fighting," "Stand Alone," "All in One (Medley)," "Don't Rock My Boat," "Put It On," "Sun Is Shining," "Kaya," "Riding High," "Brain Washing," and "400Years." Although the album was a respectable collection of early Wailers material, it was not generally taken as seriously as the Island releases. Its release did come at a good time for the Wailers in that it parlayed the success of *Catch a Fire* and kept the Wailers audience satiated while the group toured and recorded *Burnin'*.

The first show of the tour was held in a London club called the Greyhound. The Wailers had been scheduled to play two shows a night, travel in a small van without a road manager, and set up and tear down their own equipment at each show. Many of the audiences at the shows were initially shocked, having never heard music from the Caribbean before, but soon people were coming backstage after the show to express their pleasure at the new sound.

Returning to London at the end of the tour, the Wailers were in peak performing condition. However, they were struggling in all other respects. Bunny, a strict Italist, had spent days on the tour without food, since he did not allow himself to eat anything that had been processed. In addition, Bunny and Peter were having difficulties with Bob's ever-increasing control over the band while they struggled for equality.

While still in London, where their following was the largest they enjoyed outside Jamaica, the Wailers played a club date at the Speakeasy that garnered some significant media attention. Also, on May 20, 1973, the Wailers appeared on the BBC program *Old Grey Whistle Test,* performing "Concrete Jungle" and "Stop That Train." Another television appearance quickly followed when the Wailers played at the BBC's Paris Theatre for the pop music series *Top Gear.* The set that the Wailers played on *Top Gear* was almost flawless, with sizzling performances of "Rasta Man Chant," "Slave Driver," "Stop That Train," "No More Trouble," "400 Years," "Midnight Ravers," "Stir It Up," "Concrete Jungle," "Get Up, Stand Up," and "Kinky Reggae."

The band returned to Jamaica exhausted and in bad need of rest. Bunny immediately left the band, never to tour with the Wailers again. He told Bob that he would record and perform in Jamaica but that he was not interested in touring. This presented a problem for Bob because the Wailers were now scheduled to go on a short North American tour. Bob consulted Peter about the problem, and together they decided to invite their old teacher Joe Higgs to tour with them and cover Bunny's high-harmony parts. Higgs agreed, and the Wailers resumed rehearsals at Island House.

With the great increase in Wailers activity, coupled with touring, the band was in dire need of a manager, both on and off the road. Blackwell had been fulfilling this role, supervising recording sessions, acting as artistic director, and promoting and booking Wailers shows. He also knew from his experience that in order for *Catch a Fire* to sell well in the United States, the band needed to book some high-profile shows and thus generate interest in their recordings. To this end, Blackwell enlisted Lee Jaffe to fly to New York to promote the record and to book shows for the upcoming tour. Jaffe was able to secure a date for the Wailers to play at one of New York's premier pop club, Max's Kansas City, on Park Avenue South. The show was booked for the second week of July 1973, as the opening act for a young New Jersey–born singer named Bruce Springsteen. Jaffe then arranged for the Wailers to play at a Boston jazz club called Paul's Mall. Gradually, Jaffe arranged other tour dates, and soon the Wailers embarked on their first American tour. The tour included shows all over the United States, with concerts in Florida, Kentucky, New York, Massachusetts, Illinois, and California.

## BURNIN'

Released in October 1973, the Wailers' second album was called *Burnin'*, after Bunny's song "Reincarnated Souls" failed to make the final cut. The album revealed a more organic roots sound than its heavily produced predecessor, *Catch a Fire*. The tracks on the new album were on a mixture of topics that ranged from the political protest sentiment of "Burnin' and Lootin'" to direct Rastafarian content in "Rasta Man Chant." The cover art was a depiction of the heads of the six core Wailers (Bob, Peter, Bunny, Lindo, and the Barrett Brothers) burned into the side of a wooden box. According to Ian McCann, this crate-and-brand imagery recalled the type of tools used to mark and transport slaves in the colonial era.[29] The rear sleeve had a picture of Bob taking a drag from a large spliff. *Burnin'* was released just six months after *Catch a Fire* and was indicative of Bob's prolific songwriting ability.

The band lineup for this second "official" Wailers and Island project included the original trio of Bob, Peter, and Bunny, each in their traditional roles. To this was added the Wailers' rhythm section: Aston on bass and Carlie on drums. Additional players were Earl "Wya" Lindo, on keyboards, and Alvin "Seeco" Patterson, on percussion. The album was recorded at Harry J's Studio in Kingston and mixed at the Island Studios in London. Production credits were shared by the Wailers and Blackwell.

The songs that made the final album were a tight collection of the Wailers at their full post–*Catch A Fire* potency. The music was rootsy and hard hitting and revealed an increasing religiosity and militancy. The 10 tracks that made up the album—"Get Up, Stand Up," "Hallelujah Time," "I Shot the Sheriff," "Burnin' and Lootin'," "Put It On," "Small Axe," "Pass It On," "Duppy Conqueror," "One Foundation," and "Rasta Man Chant"—were an interesting blend of old and new and included songs written by each of the three core members.

The first song on the record was credited to Bob and Peter. "Get Up, Stand Up" featured Bob on lead vocals, with a heavy dose of Peter and Bunny on backing vocals. In addition, Peter took over the lead vocal role for the third verse. The song began with a drum and bass lead-in that went directly into the first chorus, sung in male harmony. The instrumentalists assumed their usual role as a rhythm-section underpinning with one-drop drumming, active and increasingly present bass, and demure keyboards. The song alternated chorus and verse, with three verse statements.

The essence of the message was that if those living in the Kingston ghettos and black people internationally would "get up and stand up" against corrupt and oppressive political systems, then change can begin. Bob began the first verse by admonishing the "preacher man" for selling the underclass a bill of goods that kept them in a disadvantaged condition. This preacher reference was one that Bob used in a derogatory manner, and it was pointed at the Pope and the Catholic Church. Rastafarians felt oppressed by Catholicism and believed that Catholic popes had waged a longstanding battle against the black race through their tacit acceptance of slavery. This sentiment was continued in the second verse when Bob warned listeners not to bank all of their earthly time for prosperity in heaven. Peter echoed this sentiment in the third verse. Here, he declared that "almighty God is a live man," a reference to Haile Selassie I. He continued with warnings against trying to continue to fool the righteous. The song was a testament to Bob's life. He was fed up with the treatment of the Jamaican underclass, and he had finally attained enough success to start commenting on it in an honest, and fairly militant, manner. In 1975, Bob said of this song "that song say man can live."[30]

The harmonies used were static and meant to highlight the presentation of the lyrics. The result was an unsettled feeling that could be what Bob was intending in this message to the people of the ghetto. Further, his singing was not lyrical; instead, he was intoning a direct call to action. In the verse sections, where he was furthering the text of the song by chanting the lyrics rapidly, he did so without consideration for melody. There were many repeated notes, and the range of any individual phrase was very small, generally limited to only two or three notes.

The precedent for this type of chant-style vocal presentation can be found in both the African *akete* tradition and many religious rituals. (The *akete* drum is an African drum with a high pitch that is sometimes used in Rastafarian and reggae music; it is also called the repeater, as mentioned previously.) This drumming and chanting style descended directly from the mystic *burru* tradition. The *burru* tradition was an African-derived drumming style played by African-Jamaicans in the parish of Clarendon, in the center of the island, in the 1930s and later in the west Kingston ghettos. Living on and off in the ghetto while growing up, Marley was exposed to this type of chanting and drumming from an early age, and it had a strong musical influence on him.

The roles of the instruments in this song can again be defined within the Rastafarian drumming model. Here the drum set and the guitar function in the slow-moving support capacity. The electric bass, moving step-wise, fills the role of the slightly more active *fundeh*. The most active line is held by the vocals that fill the role of the repeater.

> After the *Burnin'* had been out for five years, Bob commented about "Get Up, Stand Up": How long must I protest the same thing? I sing "Get Up, Stand Up," and up 'til now people don't get up. So must I still sing "Get Up, Stand Up"? I am not going to sing the same song again. . . . I do not want to be a prisoner. I don't want too see people suffer and sing as if I'm glad to see people suffer and to make money off of that. I want people to live big and have enough.[31]

As a testament to the staying power of this song and its unfailing popularity in the United States, in 2005, "Get Up, Stand Up" was played in the NASA control room as confirmation images proved that the Spirit launch had landed on Mars.

The second song on the album was written and sung by Bunny, although it was credited to Jean Watt.[32] The song itself began with a short bass and guitar lead-in. The end of the introduction was signaled by the first stroke of a gong. There followed a male harmony lead in that created a call and response with Bunny's voice. The opening lyric was telling, with the words "hear the children crying." However, Bunny immediately responded that "they cry not in vain." This opening led into the first full verse, which furthered the suffering and toiling allusions. Under this material, the Wailers played a medium-tempo reggae groove with one-drop drum, active bass, and guitar offbeats. The chorus followed, and the sentiment changed from despair to jubilation. The song's two chorus statements were the same, and each described the turning of the tables from the verse material. Instead of crying, the children were singing.

Bunny's singing voice was markedly higher than Bob's and Peter's, and he used it to excellent effect. Additionally, Bunny was careful to sing in standard English and not to obscure his words with the heavy Jamaican patois that he was capable of talking in (as Bob often did). Kwame Dawes noted, "'Hallelujah Time' unfolds with clarity and grace. Yet both [Bob and Bunny] shared a seriousness of purpose in the writing of songs, one that was matched by Tosh's work."[33]

Song three on *Burnin'* was "I Shot the Sheriff." The song was markedly faster than most of Bob's others. It began with a short introduction of chorus material that was sung by Bob, Peter, and Bunny in high male harmony. The drumming was a more straight-ahead rock beat, the bass was active and present in the mix, and the guitar maintained the reggae role of playing offbeat chords. In the transition material from the verse to the chorus, the bass and keyboard played a unison descending line that drove into the chorus. The song structure was verse heavy, as the song was a narrative story told by Bob.

In 1974, Bob said of the song: "I want to say 'I shot the police' but the government would have made a fuss so I said 'I shot the sheriff' instead . . . but it's the same idea: justice."[34] The song quickly became the most popular on the album. Also, in 1974, Eric Clapton's version of the song went to number one on the charts. The general tenor of the lyrics was self-defense but also defiance. While Bob admitted remorse over taking the life of the deputy, he said that he was simply defending himself against "Sheriff John Brown [who] always hated me [Bob]." Bob went on the record in 1975 this way: "'I Shot the Sheriff' is like I shot wickedness. That's not really a sheriff, it's the elements of wickedness. The elements of that song is people been judging you and you can't stand it no more and you explode, you just explode."[35]

"Burnin' and Lootin'" followed "I Shot the Sheriff" and continued the defiant attitude of much of the album. Whereas "I Shot the Sheriff" was faster than most of Bob's songs, "Burnin' and Lootin'" was slower. It began with a winding, distorted guitar part underpinned by one-drop drumming. Bob entered on the opening verse and began his story of imprisonment and brutality. The mood was one of despair, but there was an escape plan. The chorus elucidated the plan for "burnin' and lootin'" the way out of the negative circumstances. The original story behind the song was that the police had cordoned off Bob's Trench Town neighborhood in response to violence perpetrated by ghetto youths. Thus, when Bob awake, he was literally locked in and surrounded by the police.

The song began with two verses, followed by a chorus statement. The third verse was then presented, followed by the return of the chorus. Next, the third verse was repeated, seemingly for emphasis, and the song ended with a return of the chorus material. Bob described the song in March 1976: "Dat song about burnin' and a-lootin' illusions. The illusions of the capitalists and dem people with the big bank accounts."[36] This declaration was a window into Bob's growing discomfort with the white-run record industry in England and in the United States. This sentiment intensified as Bob's popularity grew. This growing uneasiness was expressed in both the lyrics and the sound of this song.

The serious tone of the first four songs on *Burnin'* was defused by the playful feeling of "Put It On." The song was in an up-tempo reggae groove that began with a vaguely doo-wop-sounding male chorus statement. The song itself was written earlier in the Wailers' career and exhibits their early influences. The bass was not as present in the mix as was the usual Wailers custom. The drum played a more standard offbeat heavy second- and fourth-beat rhythm, and almost all of the minimal lyrics were presented in tight harmony. The message of the lyrics seemed to be a call to the faithful to "feel the spirit" and "thank the Lord." Unlike much of Bob's material, this song did have an instrumental solo between the alternating verse and chorus statements. Two-thirds of the way through the tune, an electric organ solo interrupted the presentation of the lyrics. Garth White and Kwame Dawes were careful to point out that this song may not have been as innocuous as it seemed. The phrase "put it on" was a term of violence in period street language. "When a man used a ratchet knife to cut another man, he would be said to be 'putting it on' the other fellow. Thus, the spiritual song of piousness becomes something more ominous and disarming."[37]

"Small Axe" was another of the early Wailers songs that made it onto the album. The song began with an organ and distorted guitar introduction that drove into the first verse. Here, Bob returned to his role as biblical prophet. He sang in biblical parlance and quoted from Proverbs. "Small Axe" was originally recorded for Clement "Coxsone Dodd," at Studio One, in 1971. It appeared on the unauthorized *Best of the Wailers* album. However, its inclusion on *Burnin'* was the first official release of the song. The song itself was a collaboration between Bob and Lee "Scratch" Perry. It was an oddity on the album since it was recorded for Dodd but appears courtesy of Upsetter Records (Perry's imprint), which places the genesis of this track about five years prior to the rest of the album.

An interesting aspect of Bob's music was that, although he had a growing global fan base, it was surprising how the myriad meanings behind his songs frequently were lost on his loyal followers. "Small Axe" was one of Marley's songs that had several messages, both obvious and obscure. On the surface, the song is about a woodsman who is informing a large tree that he is about to chop it down; however, according to Timothy White, it is actually a three-pronged assertion that "is readily understood by all Jamaicans but is utterly obscure to almost anyone else."[38] The first underlying meaning is a warning to colonial powers from the Third World, which is conveyed in Old Testament imagery. The warning comes in the form of a boast that the people of the Third World will one day rise up and cut their oppressors down to size.

The second is a warning from the Wailers and their then-producer Lee "Scratch" Perry to the big three studios in Kingston. Perry complained to the Wailers about the "big t'ree," referring in Jamaican slang to Federal, Studio One, and Dynamic Studios. According to the lore of this song, Peter commented at the time, if they are the big t'ree, then we are the small axe, meaning that, regardless of the power of the three companies, the Wailers could (and did) cut them down to size and prevail in spite of them. The irony of this was that the song appeared on a Clement "Coxsone" Dodd–produced Studio One release. The third, and possibly most important, message was a direct condemnation of all who held down God's chosen ones, the followers of Rastafari.

The song setting was quite complex. In addition to the surface and veiled meanings of the words, there were several instances of word painting. This centuries-old technique was defined as the literal portrayal of the meaning of the words in the motion of the music. Thus, when Bob sang, "whosoever diggeth a pit, shall fall in it" and "we are the small axe, ready to cut you down," the melody descends. On the words "fall" and "down," the melody of each phrase descended, tying the meaning of the text to the motion of the music.

Beyond these examples, this song also contained several examples of the lyrics taking the cross-rhythm role with regard to the Rastafarian three-drum texture. The highest pitched drum (repeater), frequently analogous to the vocal line in reggae music, can choose to act in either a syncopated manner to create cross-rhythms with the other two drums or to add another rhythmic layer that maintains the expected accents. In this song, the vocal line moves almost exclusively against the rhythms being created around it.

The form of the song was fairly symmetrical: a verse and chorus with a short guitar solo about two-thirds of the way through. As was the case in "Burnin' and Lootin'," the words of the third verse are repeated as the fourth verse. This emphasis on certain lyrics was not by mistake. In this case, Bob was adding further emphasis to texts with biblical connotations. The biblical content in this song appeared in the opening verse: "you're working inequity to achieve vanity," which paraphrased Proverbs 22:8. The reference in the third and fourth verses was "whosoever diggeth a pit shall fall in it," which paraphrased both Proverbs 26:27 and Psalm 7:15. Emphasis was given to this passage when Bob preceded them with the lyric "these are the words of my Master."

In addition to quoting the Bible, Bob made use of language that was specific to his Rastafarian faith. Specific words were loaded and had meaning that Rastas identified with immediately. The words "I-doreth" and "I-ver" were purposeful mispronunciations specific to the Rastafarian context. Rastafarians frequently manipulated the spelling and pronunciation of words to make them begin with the letter "I." This was done as a sign of respect for their deity, Haile Selassie I. Rastafarians interpret the Roman numeral one after his name as the letter "I." This led to the use of phrases such as "I and I," referring to one's self and one's god collectively.

"Pass It On" was another song written and sung by Bunny and again credited to Jean Watt. An opening organ solo led into Bunny's singing alone in his high male vocal range. After he presented the first verse, he was joined by the other Wailers as backup singers for the second verse. Next, the chorus entered for the first time, sounding like a slow gospel choir. The texture was sparse, and Bunny's lyrics were emphasized. The third and fourth verse statements then followed, and Bunny moved quickly through the lyrics. The song ended with other chorus statements that repeated the first chorus before the song faded out.

At first listen, the song seemed to contain a few basic messages. First, Bunny advised to keep one's actions pure, as one's conscience was the judge. Second, he pushed the message that the wise man lived for others. Finally, he warned that these truths were universal and could not be escaped. Kwame Dawes described Bunny's song as "typical of his carefully constructed hymning style and . . . manner of offering of truth . . . the lyrics [are] filled with personification and a careful literary style."[39]

The third of the older songs on the album was "Duppy Conqueror." Bob wrote and sang this song. Interestingly, as Bob continued to emphasize the message in his music, the form of the songs increasingly became verse heavy (more verse statements than chorus statements). That was the case here. The song began with a short drum, organ, and guitar introduction that led into three consecutive verse statements before the chorus finally entered. Next, the first verse was repeated, followed by a return of the chorus. The first verse was again repeated, and the song faded out to end. A feature of this song that was quite uncommon was the inclusion of approximated bird cooing by one of the male vocalists.

The word "duppy" was Jamaican patois for a ghost or spirit that descended on a living person to do him harm. In the song, Bob has not only slain the evil spirit but gone on to reach Mount Zion. There was a degree of autobiography to this song. Bob was on record as fearing that he was being taken over by a duppy when he lived in the back room of Dodd's studio. He relayed the story to Rita, who often visited him during his residency in the studio. However, as the song attested, Bob was too tough to be taken by an evil spirit.

Peter was credited with the authorship of the epic "One Foundation." The song opened with a dense layering of bass, keyboards, and guitar woven into a distorted cacophony (vaguely reminiscent of the more psychedelic work of the Beatles). This was then replaced by Peter singing the first chorus statement with minimal accompaniment, save the medium-tempo reggae groove. The first verse was similar to the first chorus, except that the phrase endings were punctuated by wordless female harmonies. The chorus then repeated with instrumental accompaniment reminiscent of the introduction. Verses two and three were not interrupted by a chorus statement in between, but, once verse three was complete, the chorus returned and faded out to end the song.

As was typical of songs written and sung by Peter, the message here was serious and dire. The sentiment of the verses boiled down to the idea that unity is necessary to achieving success and love. The single foundation was the root on which everything must be built. Kwame Dawes speculates that this "'one foundation' is an allusion to the New Testament teaching that Christ is the foundation of the church."[40] Christ as the one foundation was a sentiment that Bob also put into song with "Corner Stone." Ephesians 2:20 contains the line "and are built upon the foundation of the apostles and prophets, Jesus Christ himself being the chief corner stone." All three of the original Wailers core members believed these biblical prophesies and infused their lyrics with this sentiment.

"Rasta Man Chant" was described in the original *Burnin'* packaging as a traditional song that had been arranged by the Wailers. The original version of the song was meant for performance at Nyabinghi, but, as customized by the Wailers, the song was transformed into a medium-tempo reggae song. Here the traditional Rastafarian Nyabinghi drumming was present. There was a low-pitched heartbeat drum and two higher pitched and more active drums. The only other added instruments were the bass and the organ. Layered on top of this was Bob singing the lead lyrics and Peter and Bunny providing high male harmony.

The song did unfold in verse/chorus form, but not in strict alternation. After a shorthand drumming introduction, the bass and the organ entered to usher in the opening chorus. Bob led the vocals but was closely shadowed by Peter and Bunny. The first chorus was followed by a repetition of the same material with the words of the first line altered. This happened again as the chorus was repeated a third time and the words were again altered. The changing words moved from "rasta man" to "higher man" to "angel with the seven seals." There followed a verse made up of several repetitive phrases and more repetitions of the last line of the verse. This repetition continued until the song ended.

The song structure might be atypical, but the messages delivered in the song were clear and present. The initial invocation of the Rasta man was followed by the destruction of Babylon's throne. Here Bob was at once introducing the world to Rastafarian religious chanting and calling for the end of an oppressive system. The religious ramifications of the "higher man" and "angel with the seven seals" lyrics served to heighten the religiosity of the opening three statements. The "fly away home" language of the verse linked this song to songs of freedom from the slave days. Thus, in this wedding of the traditional and the modern, Bob was also joining the concepts of slavery and the Babylonian captivity.

The group and the label were disappointed by their record sales in the United States, and, in an effort to promote *Burnin'*, the Wailers again went on tour. At the end of October 1973, the Wailers joined an in-progress, 17-city tour by Sly and the Family Stone as the opening band. Because Bunny refused to leave Jamaica, Joe Higgs was again recruited to fill Bunny's high-harmony role. The tour was a great opportunity for the Wailers thanks to Sly Stone's popularity and expansive audience at the time.

On the fourth date of the tour, the Wailers were fired because they had been outplaying the Family Stone and were not generally accepted by Stone's audience. When the tour moved on, it left Bob Marley and the Wailers stranded, broke, and without management in Las Vegas. The Wailers had an in-studio performance date with KSAN-FM and somehow managed to get to San Francisco, where they had already established an enthusiastic audience on the previous tour. Broadcasting from the Record Plant, in Sausalito, the band began with an acoustic version of "Rasta Man Chant." The performance brought to bear the ties between Rastafarian traditional drumming and reggae. Peter, Bob, and Joe Higgs sat in front of three mikes and laid down the heartbeat reggae rhythm on *burru* hand drums. Higgs played the *fundeh,* Bob played the repeater, and Peter supplied support on the large bass drum. The Wailers' performance continued with full electric-band versions of "Bend Down Low," "Catch a Fire," a new song by Peter called "You Can't Blame the Youth," "Stop That Train," and "Burnin' and Lootin'." The Wailers continued with "Kinky Reggae," "Get Up, Stand Up," and "Rude Boy," and the show ended with the first live performance of "Lively Up Yourself."

During the last two weeks of October 1973, the Wailers returned to Jamaica to rest before leaving for England for a brief tour to promote *Burnin'*. Higgs did not accompany the Wailers on this tour, which left Bob and Peter to front the band. The British dates included shows in Bradford, Birmingham, Stafford, Blackpool, Liverpool, Doncaster Outlook, Leeds Polytechnic, and Manchester. The shows were poorly attended and the reception unenthusiastic. In Northhampton, at the end of November, Bob and Peter got into an argument that led to blows. The Wailers were all miserable, and Earl "Wya" Lindo announced that he was leaving the band to join the American folk singer Taj Mahal. The final 10 dates of the tour were canceled, the official explanation being that Peter had become ill and could not continue. Lindo embarked for San Francisco, and Peter and the Barrett Brothers left for Jamaica. Bob remained in England briefly to meet with Blackwell and discuss the fate of the Wailers. In the wake of the loss of Peter, Bunny, Joe Higgs, and Lindo, a new Wailers band was about to emerge from the rubble.

## NATTY DREAD

Bob spent the rest of early 1974 at Harry J's studio, in Kingston, working on songs for the upcoming album. These sessions produced the first recording of "No Woman, No Cry," in which Bob discussed difficulties in his past as a comfort for the present and future. The Wailers of that time consisted only of Bob and the Barrett Brothers, together with a 16-year-old keyboard player named Bernard "Touter" Harvey, brought in to play organ. The harmonica parts on "Talkin' Blues" and "Road Block" were played by Lee Jaffe, and the traditional Wailers three-part harmony was supplied by the female vocal trio of Rita, Marcia, and Judy (commonly referred to as the I-Threes). The guitar parts were not overdubbed until later in the year when Bob and Aston "Family Man" Barrett were in London.

In May 1974, the Wailers were asked to open for the American Motown singer Marvin Gaye, who had come to the island with a 40-piece orchestra to perform at the Carib Club. The concert was to benefit a new sports facility in Trench Town and sold out quickly due to Gaye's popularity. Everyone in attendance the night of the concert was dubious about the Wailers' performance, since the group had not performed in Jamaica for several years. However, when it was time to go on stage, all three of the original Wailers were ready, as were the Barrett Brothers. There was a dispute backstage before the show because Touter was thought to be too young to perform live with the Wailers, and at the last minute Tyrone Downie was substituted to cover the organ parts. The performance was a success, and the Wailers impressed the crowd with their new, harder reggae sound.

After the show, Marvin Gaye's manager, Don Taylor, approached Bob and offered to manage the Wailers. Although born in Jamaica, Taylor had immigrated to the United States and claimed to have significant connections in the American music business. During their conversation, Taylor guaranteed to make Bob a hit in the United States. Although this excited him, Bob did not accept the offer immediately. Opening for Marvin Gaye was the final performance of the original Wailers trio; from then on Peter and Bunny went on to record solo albums.

Bob, Aston "Family Man" Barrett, Cole, and Lee Jaffe went to New York in June 1974 with the understanding that they were being invited to work with Taj Mahal, the American singer who now employed Earl "Wya" Lindo. Lindo had made an arrangement of Bob's song "Slave Driver," and Taj was preparing to put it on his next album. "The Taj Mahal/Wailers connection might have been wonderful, because Bob and Family Man were prepared to play music; but Taj Mahal had already recorded his album by the time they arrived, and could only invite them to help him mix."[41] Disappointed with the missed opportunity, the group returned to Kingston.

Back in the studio, Bob went to work on the tracks that would become *Natty Dread*. Work on recording new versions of "Bend Down Low" and "Lively Up Yourself" progressed. Several new militant songs were also recorded, including "So Jah Seh" and "Revolution." Bob (who was credited as L. Cogil) and Carlie Barrett collaborated in the studio to write "Them Belly Full," and a demo of "Am-A-Do (Do it to Your Bad Self)" was recorded but not released. The group had a continuing problem finding a keyboard player. Touter was frequently used in the studio but was generally considered too young to go on tour, and Downie was a full-time member of the Caribs, the house band at the Kingston Sheraton. Because of this situation, "Family Man" stepped in to cover the keyboard parts on the recordings of "Road Block" and "Bend Down Low."

The album captured Marley at a critical point. It reflected the fact that the Wailers, as they had existed, had unofficially disbanded by early 1974. However, Bob spent the year working on and recording the next album, *Natty Dread*. The album was originally meant to be titled "Knotty Dread," which was notoriously mispronounced in Jamaica. The result was the name change from "knotty" to "natty," which effectively changed the intended meaning. The original meaning referenced the dreadlocks of the devout

Rastas. The unintended meaning change was to someone with a smart appearance in dress and manners. The pronunciation confusion yielded the opposite meaning of the original intent.

The *Natty Dread* sessions employed Bob on lead vocals and rhythm guitar. The Barrett Brothers continued on the bass and drum, respectively. Bernard "Touter" Harvey was the keyboard player of record, and Al Anderson was credited with lead guitar parts (overdubbed). The original high male harmony of the Wailers was replaced by the female harmony of the I-Threes. Lee Jaffe supplied uncredited harmonica parts. Other uncredited performers were the horn players Glen da Costa, David Madden, and Tommy McCook. The album cover reflected Marley's new role as a solo artist. The cover art was an airbrushed picture of Marley standing alone. This was in stark contrast to the previous album, *Burnin'*, which pictured the whole band on the cover.

Recorded at Harry J's studio and mixed in London at Island Records' Basing Streets Studios, the album listed both Bob and Chris Blackwell in the production credits. An interesting feature of the recording process for this song was that it was a very early example of the use of a drum machine in reggae music. Bob and Carlton Barrett had been experimenting with the drum machine from the mid-1970s, and it was used for the drum track on songs on this album. The use of a drum machine in Marley's recordings did not persist, however; they were used extensively in the style that came after reggae, called dancehall.

The songs included were again a mixture of new and old. The album cover was an airbrushed picture of Bob's face and dreadlocks over an abstract jungle background. Musically, the new material was the next logical step after *Burnin'* and *Catch a Fire,* with Bob acting as a Rastafarian preacher over the steady reggae grooves of the Wailers. Anderson's guitar playing infused the Wailers sound with a distinct blues quality that fit perfectly. The horn section returned on some tracks on *Natty Dread* with well-placed punches to add weight to the end of certain phrases.

The album began with Bob letting out an enthusiastic Yoruba lookout call that seemed to herald a new beginning for Bob Marley and the Wailers.[42] This call led directly into a rousing version of "Lively Up Yourself." Eight more tracks follow, including "No Woman, No Cry," "Them Belly Full," "Rebel Music," "So Jah Seh," "Natty Dread," "Bend Down Low," "Talkin' Blues," and "Revolution." The general sentiment of the album was a militant Rastafarianism that culminated in the last two songs. "Talkin' Blues" discussed bombing a church as an extension of the Rastafarian belief that the Catholic Church and the Pope were part of the Babylon system that oppresses the black race. This militant sentiment was continued in "Revolution," in which Bob stated that in order for the situation of Jamaican blacks to change, a revolution would be required. In 1974, Bob said of the track "So Jah Seh" that it "really mean is progress. People a fe [to] start live together. I don't know so much the big people, but the youth must get together."[43]

The album was produced by Blackwell and the Wailers. In 1974, Bob said of the new album that "the *Natty Dread* album is, like one step more towards [for] reggae music. Better music, better lyrics, it have a better feelin'. *Catch a Fire* and *Burnin'* have a good feelin', but *Natty Dread* is improved."[44] When reading direct quotations of statements made by Marley, one must bear in mind that it is typical for Rastafarians to purposely misuse English. This was done as a means to separate themselves from those that they viewed as their Babylonian oppressors. It was also a form of reverse acculturation. Although the diasporic blacks were trained to speak English by their slave ship or colonial oppressors, this did not mean that they had to speak it in the recommended way. By purposely misusing English, black Jamaicans turned the language against its teachers and thus took ownership of it.

The first track on the new album was the already recorded "Lively Up Yourself." New material was being written by Bob that included "Road Block" (also called "Rebel Music"), "So Jah Seh," "Talkin' Blues," and "Knotty [or Natty] Dread." Many of the new songs were inspired by the Jamaican political climate of the time as Michael Manley continued to immerse Jamaica in his brand of socialism. The political situation was quickly getting out of control, with factions that reflected class and political affiliation taking sides and refusing to change. The conflict got worse in the early spring of 1974 when several ghetto neighborhoods were under the control of gun-wielding thugs and violence was widespread. Manley had lost control of the situation and declared a state of emergency. The capital was held by government tanks and troops and a 6 P.M. curfew was implemented. It was at this time that the Gun Court, a barbed-wire-enclosed concentration camp, was established in Kingston. Anyone convicted of possessing an illegal handgun was sentenced to mandatory life in prison. The two warring political parties were responsible for the unrest as they fought for territorial dominance. However, the battlegrounds were the west Kingston ghettos where gunmen and political goon squads entered into frequent skirmishes.

Track one on Marley' first "solo" album was the perfect new beginning, "Lively Up Yourself." The song was written, credited to, and sung by Bob. The song began with a heavy bass rift that was augmented by a guitar during the introduction. The first statement of the chorus followed and conveyed the song's languid reggae beat. Unique here were the intricate lead guitar overdubs over Bob's call to "lively up yourself, and don't be no drag." The song does not seem to have formal verse and chorus sections. Instead, Bob took the listener on a long and winding tour through lyrics that were occasionally reminiscent of James Brown's "brand new bag"; an example was the line "'Cause reggae is another bag."

Song two on the album was "No Woman, No Cry." Oddly, the song was credited to Vincent "Tartar" Ford. Despite this, a great deal of debate has taken place over this issue. Several explanations have been posited concerning the authorship of the track. First, it is possible that Ford, who was a friend of

Bob's from Trench Town and who also spent time with Marley at his house on Hope Road, actually wrote it. According to McCann, Ford was a paraplegic diabetic who was capable of writing the song, except that it sounds too much like a Marley track to have been entirely written by someone else.

Another possibility that McCann posited was that, because of their long-standing friendship, Bob wanted to thank him for befriending him as a Trench Town youth. Ford's physical handicaps left him unable to work. Therefore, it was possible that Bob wanted to make sure that Ford would be taken care of financially. He may have taken care to do this because, as a young man, Ford had reportedly run a soup kitchen that fed hungry ghetto youths (such as Bob). Assigning authorship to him gave Ford the right to royalty checks that would keep coming to the present day because of the extreme popularity of this song. The last possibility that McCann noted was that Bob may have worked collectively with Ford while they spent time together, and Ford could have written some lyrics while Bob strummed the guitar.

The fourth possible explanation for the attribution mystery was that *Natty Dread* was released in 1974, during the time that Marley was under contract to Danny Sims's Cayman Music Company. Marley had split with Sims in 1972, and their previously signed contract may have been the cause of resentment. The altered attribution could allow Bob's own company, Bob Marley Music, to collect royalties for the song. This story gained credence when one looks at the other attributions on the album. Of the nine tracks included, five were credited to people other than Marley. A desire to avoid royalty payments, coupled with the knowledge that the author credited on "So Jah Seh," Willie San Francisco, was a known Marley pseudonym, begins to seem like the most logical explanation.

The introduction of the song was a brief organ-led statement. Next, Bob entered with the first chorus, which then alternated with two large verses. The lyrics of the first verse advised the female subject not to cry because Bob was able to make everything all right. They also discussed time spent in the government yard in Trench Town, the place where ghetto youth grew up. The initial statement of the lyric "no woman, no cry" was sung tenderly. However, the restatement was delivered as a command, and, to add gravity to the repeated text, it was presented at a higher pitch, with a rest after the word "no" in order to establish the desired tone.

After the third statement of the chorus, Al Anderson performed a short guitar solo that was executed over the same chord progression as the chorus. The song ended with an eight-measure coda that again used the chord progression from the chorus. The general tenor of the music fits well with the text that Bob was presenting in this song. He was trying to bridge his experiences in the past with optimism about the future. He also marveled at the generosity of the poor as he observed the hypocrisy and stinginess of the rich. The song became one of Bob's most famous, and he embraced its popularity.

In 1974 he said, "Me really love 'No Woman, No Cry' because it mean so much to me, so much feeling me get from it. Really love it."[45]

Track three of *Natty Dread* was credited to L. Cogil and Carlie Barrett. Regardless of attribution, "Them Belly Full (But We Hungry)," was sung by Bob with special militant fervor. The song began with an extended wordless chorus by the I-Threes, which led into the first texted chorus. Here Bob made clear that the hungry in the ghetto were being left unfed. The only remedy offered was to dance to Jah music to try to forget the circumstances. The chorus unfolded in two sections, the second of which had different words with each repeat.

The second verse bemoaned the high cost of living over a standard Wailers groove. The sound of this song was similar to many of Bob's most famous; it was a medium-tempo reggae tune with one-drop drumming, active and melodic bass playing that sometimes doubled the voice, offbeat rhythm-guitar chords, and meandering overdubbed lead-guitar parts. After a short guitar solo by Anderson, the song wound to a close with repetitions of the second half of the chorus music with progressively different words. The parting sentiment was simple: a hungry man was an angry man, and angry men create angry mobs.

One of Bob's more straightforward songs was actually credited to Aston "Family Man" Barrett and H. Peart. "Rebel Music (3 O'clock Road Block)" was a personal and harrowing account of Bob's own experiences in the violence-filled period that led up to the Jamaican national elections of 1972. The sound of the song showcased Bob, with the three-part harmony of the I-Threes as background. It was an immediate hit, and "Road Block" went to number one on the charts in Kingston. Despite its local popularity, the single received no radio airplay on the island. The rebellious nature of the song's lyrics made it dangerous, and both the Jamaican stations played very little indigenous music anyway. In response to the censorship, Bob and Cole, along with two of Bob's friends who were notorious killers, went down to the studios of JBC Radio and threatened the disc jockey on duty. With his life in his hands, the disc jockey played the single, and it remained number one all summer.

The song was actually an account of an experience Bob and several of his friends had had. It told of Bob and friends running into a Kingston roadblock while returning from Negril. Rounding a corner at three o'clock in the morning, Bob, Lee Jaffe, Sledger (Bob's cousin), and Esther Anderson (one of Bob's girlfriends) encountered an army-run roadblock. The officers searched their car for illegal firearms and ganja. Fortunately, the group had disposed of its large spliff before it was noticed, but all of them were all searched, and Bob and Sledger were reprimanded for their dreadlocks. The lyrics of the song recount the events of that meeting with the police, which culminated in Bob's talking the cop: "ain't got no birth certificate on me now."

The song began with a repeated drum and harmonica statement over which the I-Threes intoned wordlessly. The first chorus statement began next, with questions about freedom on the island. The first verse began the confrontation with the police. The roadblock was spotted, and the ganja was ejected from the car. The chorus then repeated, followed by another verse. Verse two ended with Bob talking about his lack of identification directly to the police. Next came a guitar solo that led back into two more chorus statements. For emphasis, Bob repeated verse two, and the song ends with him again directly addressing the police.

In contrast to the militant sentiment of "Rebel Music," "So Jah Seh" offered a message of religious salvation. Begun with what sounds like a drum machine beat, the song included horn lines that added considerable depth to the musical texture. The song unfolded in a manner that became increasingly common for Bob, opening alternations of chorus and verse that culminated in two statements of the second verse before the song ended. Here the lyrics are admonitions from Jah about the treatment and activities of his faithful, channeled through Bob. Jah's children shall no longer go hungry, and unity of all shall reign. The language Bob used was telling for his choice of words from Psalm 100: "Ye are the sheep of my pasture." The overall meaning of the psalm was that of praise and glad servitude. Another interesting feature of the lyrics was Bob's use of numbers in the second verse. By numbering the streets that he walked down in the verse, he effectively made "Natty Dread" into a counting song. Also, Bob made repeated use of the I and I language to associate himself fully with his God: "I and I hang on in there, I and I naw leggo [not let go]."

"Natty Dread," the album's title track, was credited to A. Cole (Alan "Skill" Cole) and R. Marley (Rita Marley). The song was in an upbeat reggae tempo that implored the listener to dance. Again, Bob enlisted the help of his horn players to assist on this song. The horn line introduction led into the first chorus, and the song alternated chorus and verse statements, with the verses being much larger than the choruses. The instrumental accompaniment to the song was the standard one-drop drumming, offbeat guitar chords, and active and melodic bass part. The sentiment of the song was the claiming of black and Rastafarian cultural history despite the Babylonian captivity. One formal oddity was that in the position where the guitar solo should be, there was instead a vocal and instrumental passage that was neither verse nor chorus. The lyric meaning of this section was encapsulated in the line "Natty 21,000 miles away from home."

Rita Marley was credited with writing "Bend Down Low." Begun by organ, guitar, bass, and cowbell, the song was an up-tempo burner that Bob wrote early in the Wail'n'Soul days. The bass was the real driving instrument in the song, with its ascending walking parts. The I-Threes sang the first chorus, followed by Bob quoting the Bible sentiment about reaping what one sows. The song then alternated choruses sung by the I-Threes and verses sung by Bob. The third chorus led into an organ solo, and the second and third verses used the same words. The final verse was unique in that a flute was introduced to the texture. Overall, Bob was drawing in a female love interest, asking her to "bend down low" so she could "let me [him] tell you what I know."

"Talkin' Blues" was also credited to L. Cogil and Carlie Barrett. Slow and languid, the introduction sounded like a rock and roll song. The first chorus came in two sections and described sleeping on the ground with a rock for a pillow. The lore of this was that, as a youth in Nine Mile, Bob would lay outside at night with his head on a rock and dream of a more prosperous future As Bob's childhood home has become a tourist attraction, the rock that supposedly inspired the song has been identified and painted red, gold, and green. Not to be missed was the association of the title and the situation of black American blues musicians in the rural South.

The song contained only one verse, but Bob made the most of the short statement. He described being on the "rock" for so long, with the rock being slang for Jamaica. This usage made Jamaica sound like a prison, not a tropical paradise. He also talked of wearing a permanent screw. The term "screwface" has several meanings in Jamaican urban patois, but the most likely meaning here is a scowl or angry face. The middle of the verse talked of bombing a church, which again referenced Bob's and the Rastafarians' distrust of the Catholic Church. Finally, Bob ended the verse with talk of joining the freedom fighters.

The final track on *Natty Dread* was the most incendiary on the album. Opening horns heralded Bob's warning to all listening to seek a "Revolution." On the track, Bob was supported by the horn section and the I-Threes. His vocal style was altered in that he spoke many of the opening words, instead of singing them in his usual manner. In the lyric, he urged people to rise up from the oppressive prison of poverty, spoke of lack of trust for politicians, urged death to deceivers, and invoked the righteousness of Rasta. The scathing commentary culminated in biblical images of fire, brimstone, and lightening. The song was received with dread by members of the JLP. They interpreted the messages of revolution to mean that Prime Minister Manley (the leader of the PNP) was in fact being backed by Bob.

The Jamaican daily newspaper profiled the Wailers in its Sunday magazine as the *Natty Dread* recording sessions ended for the new album. The photograph for the interview was taken by a Kingston-born U.C.L.A. graduate in design named Neville Garrick, who would later become the Wailers' art director. The story came out in the August 11, 1974, but did not mention that the original Wailers had disbanded. Instead, Bob discussed the need for touring in support of the new material, his desire to go to Africa, and his seven children (another son had been born recently, named Justin Marley, to an Englishwoman Bob had met on the most recent tour).

Bob and Aston "Family Man" Barrett took the *Natty Dread* master tapes to London in August 1974 so that Chris Blackwell could supervise the mixing. While working in London, Bob and Aston found the man who would become the next Wailers guitarist, Al Anderson.[46] Born in New York, in 1950, Anderson was a young black rock guitarist who had played in bands that copied Jimi Hendrix and Jeff Beck. Anderson was a bass player when he met Chris Blackwell and began to work for him as a studio player. He had learned about reggae from a fellow Island musician, Paul Kossoff, a guitarist for the rock band Free. Kossoff had played *Catch a Fire* for Anderson to illustrate an aspect of reggae bass playing, and it was his first exposure to the style. Through Kossoff and Chris Wood, of the rock band Traffic, Anderson met Blackwell and ultimately played with Bob. The following day, Blackwell contacted Anderson to ask him to do some session playing on Bob Marley's next album. Anderson agreed, having already given up the bass in favor of playing lead guitar for an Afro-rock band called Shakatu, which was led by the Nigerian-born master drummer Remi Kabaka.

Anderson's first performance for Bob was to provide overdub guitar parts for "Lively Up Yourself" and "No Woman, No Cry" (overdubs previously discussed in the description of the album). The session was not going well because Anderson was playing in an unfamiliar style. Bob advised him to simply play the old-style, 12-bar blues pattern, and soon the overdubs were complete. Anderson was set to leave London and visit Nigeria with Shakatu, but Blackwell called him again and offered him the job as the Wailers' lead guitarist. At first, Anderson was skeptical, since he was accustomed to much greater freedom playing with Shakatu. However, he met with Bob one evening at Bob's apartment in Chelsea and quickly learned of the reggae star's huge potential.

Anderson agreed to join the Wailers, becoming the only non-Jamaican member, and made plans to meet with Bob back in Jamaica. He arrived ready to play but soon learned that there had been complications with the new album and that the release date had been delayed. For six months, Anderson lived in Jamaica as the new Wailers guitarist but without a single rehearsal. During this time, Anderson spent long sessions with Aston "Family Man" Barrett, practicing and learning the reggae guitar style of offbeat chord strumming.

The Wailers spent the majority of 1974 working on their music in a fairly low-profile capacity. However, it was an important year for their music, and its dissemination brought the group even greater notoriety. Taj Mahal covered "Slave Driver" on his new album *Mo' Roots*. Barbra Streisand included a cover of "Guava Jelly" on her album *Butterfly*. The greatest cover was a version of "I Shot the Sheriff" by Eric Clapton (the guitar god from the 1960s rock band Cream), which held the number-one position around the world in the late summer of 1974. Not only did these covers give the Wailers extraordinary exposure on the world stage; it also gave them serious legitimacy among rock critics and listeners. Clapton's version of "I Shot the Sheriff" gave the Wailers something that they had never enjoyed before— radio play on both of the Jamaican radio stations.

At the end of 1974, the relationship between Bob and Chris Blackwell was disintegrating. The tension escalated, and soon the Wailers were told to leave the house at 56 Hope Road, which was still owned by Island Records. The band packed all of its equipment into a truck and took it to Rita's house in Bull Bay. The difficulties that the two men were having served to delay the release of the new album for several more months, during which time Bob contemplated changing labels again, in favor of the black-music company Motown Records. Ultimately, Bob realized that the only producer that he trusted was Blackwell, and gradually their conflicts were resolved. However, part of their new deal was that official ownership of the house at 56 Hope Road would be transferred to Bob's company, Tuff Gong, thus ensuring Bob that he would not be evicted again.

## THE ORIGINAL WAILERS DISBAND

In January 1975, the original Wailers officially broke up because of Bunny's refusal to tour and Peter's disgust at the secondary role he was forced to take in the band. While Peter was angry with Bob because he felt that Bob did not support him musically, Bunny still treated Bob as a brother. Bunny had long been aware that Bob's songs of protest did not fit with his own songs of religious activism and brotherhood. Always philosophical, Bunny approached the end of the Wailers as an opportunity to produce even more music, not as a negative breakup. Bunny's idea was soon realized as Bob and the Wailers continued to release new music, Peter started his own label (called Intel-Diplo, short for Intelligent Diplomat) and began releasing singles in Jamaica, and Bunny began work on his album *Blackheart Man,* which Island released in 1976.

In early 1975, the new Bob Marley and the Wailers made their official debut as the opener for a Jackson Five concert in Kingston. Bob was now able to officially assume his natural role as the front man for the band and stood at center stage singing, dancing, and playing rhythm guitar. Rita, Judy, and Marcia (the I-Threes) provided vocal support and the trademark Wailers three-part harmony. The Barrett Brothers continued to provide the reggae rhythms on drum and bass, and Al Anderson took over the role of lead guitarist.

In early February 1975, *Knotty Dread,* the third Island Records Bob Marley and the Wailers album, was officially released. The title had been taken from the single that had been released several months earlier by Tuff Gong. However, when the album came out, the title had been altered by Island to *Natty Dread.* This caused Bob some consternation regarding the control that the label exerted over his music; however, he remained stoic about the label's influence. The music press in England and the United States accorded the release high praise and *Natty Dread* was an international success.

In the spring of 1975, the Wailers were rehearsing in preparation for a summer tour. Bob had decided to allow Don Taylor to become the manager of the Wailers but only after seeking advice about this from his Jamaican lawyer, Diane Jobson. Bob knew that the Wailers were making substantial amounts of money, and he was concerned that Taylor was just trying to take a cut of the Wailers' earnings. Additionally, Bob was worried that Taylor did not have the professional connections or management skills that the Wailers now required. The two met and talked about the situation, and Taylor told Bob that he did not even want a contract between the two of them; he simply wanted to manage the band. Largely because of Bob's previous bad experiences with every contract that he had signed, he decided to take a chance on Taylor and hired him to manage the Wailers.[47]

Taylor began organizing a North American tour for the Wailers that was scheduled to take place in June and July of 1975. This was to be followed by a brief tour of England in support of the new album. Bob began work lining up the Wailers touring group, which included the I-Threes, the Barrett Brothers, and Al Anderson. To this, Bob added his old rhythm teacher from Trench Town, Alvin "Seeco" Patterson, on supplemental percussion. However, the Wailers still lacked a keyboard player, which they all knew was a crucial role in their music. Earl "Wya" Lindo was still working with Taj Mahal, and Touter was still generally regarded as too young to go on the road. Al Anderson and Lee Jaffe both wanted Bob to hire Tyrone Downie away from the Sheraton Kingston cocktail band the Caribs. Bob eventually agreed, and Tyrone was given the new name "Jumpy" as he was brought into the Wailers.

By early 1975, Bob Marley and the Wailers had taken up permanent residence at 56 Hope Road. Island Records had moved out and Tuff Gong Records had moved in, with Don Taylor taking the role of foreman as the house was modified to accommodate the band and its entourage. The outbuildings that surrounded the house were changed into the Wailers' official rehearsal space. The façade of the house was altered, and the inside was completely remodeled. Also, plans were made to transform part of the ground floor into a Tuff Gong recording studio.[48]

Bob's personal life was about to come into the limelight just as his musical career was flourishing. Another one of his girlfriends, Anita Belnavis, the Caribbean women's table tennis champion, had just given birth to Bob's eighth child, a son named Ky-Mani, on February 26, 1976. However, Bob was already beginning a relationship with a Jamaican beauty queen named Cindy Breakspeare. Bob and Cindy quickly became close, and their relationship was immediately turned into a scandal in the press, which dubbed them "Beauty and the Beast." When asked about Cindy in an interview, Marley responded, "I-man [referring to himself] is a saint. My only vice is plenty women."[49]

With Bob's increasing popularity came opportunities for new and different musical developments. Sire Records had contacted him and sent him a tape of one of its artists to see if Bob would be interested in negotiating a production deal. Intrigued by the offer, Bob and Don Taylor flew to New York in April 1975 to strike a deal. The artist was Martha Velez, a talented rock singer based in Woodstock, who was interested in having Bob produce her new album. During the meeting with Sire Records executives and Velez, Bob let Taylor handle the conversation. The group agreed on a production deal, and Bob and Taylor returned to Jamaica.

Velez arrived in Kingston a month later, and Taylor was sent to the airport to meet her. Upon arriving at 56 Hope Road, Velez became nervous when exposed to the group of Rastafarians. However, Bob soon removed her from the group, and together they went to an empty room and began their collaboration. Bob played several songs on acoustic guitar for Velez and told her that he wanted to create an international sound on her record. They began writing a song together that was called "Disco Night." Three weeks passed, and work on Velez's album was progressing slowly, having resulted in only two recorded songs. Disheartened by the working conditions and the lack of productivity, Velez returned to New York to consult with her record company.

Shortly thereafter, she returned to Jamaica and was pleased to find that Bob was ready to get to work. Velez and the Wailers went to Negril and began rehearsing at a resort called the Sea Grape. When they returned to Kingston, the remainder of the album was cut at Harry J's uptown studios. Bob and Lee "Scratch" Perry acted as co-producers, while Tyrone Downie and Aston "Family Man" Barrett worked out the musical arrangements. Velez benefited from years of Wailers' experience in the forms of Bob, his band, his facilities, his connections, and his backup singers. The album was released in 1976, titled *Escape from Babylon,* and contained four Bob Marley songs: "Bend Down Low," "Get Up, Stand Up," "Happiness" (a remake of "Hurting Inside"), "There You Are" (a remake of "Stand Alone"), and the song that they had cowritten, "Disco Night."

Having fulfilled his obligations to Velez and Sire Records, Bob refocused on the Wailers. In June 1975, the Wailers embarked on the North American tour that Taylor had arranged. They flew to Miami, accompanied by Neville Garrick, the new Wailers art designer and lighting director. Staying in the Attaché Motel in Hollywood, Florida, the Wailers began rehearsing while Garrick worked to create red, green, and gold (the colors of the Ethiopian flag) Lion of Judah backdrops that would hang behind the band during concerts. "To relieve the dietary problems that the band had suffered on past tours, the Wailers brought along their own cook, Mikey Dan, a patriarchal Rasta who specialized in Bob's favorite foods—fish, stew beans, peas and rice, cornmeal or oatmeal porridge, and vegetables and Irish moss, a Jamaican health drink prepared with seaweed, linseed, and milk."[50]

Completing the Wailers' entourage were Don Taylor; their equipment manager, Dave Harper; and Tony Garnett, a Jamaican-born disc jockey and the group's road manager. Bob also appointed Garnett their master of ceremonies, sent on stage to warm up the audience and introduce the Wailers at each show. The tour generated a great deal of media attention, and everywhere the Wailers went they were hounded by the press. Thus began the media's love-hate relationship with Bob Marley. Bob very rarely refused an interview, regardless of the interviewer's employer. However, he was often difficult to question, frequently turning the questions on the journalist. Nonetheless, during the tour, interviews with Bob appeared in *Rolling Stone,* the *New York Times,* and New York's *Village Voice.* Bob never missed an opportunity to discuss his faith in Rastafarianism during these interviews, often quoting from the Bible and frequently leaving the interviewer confused.

The first tour date was at the Diplomat Hotel, in Hollywood, Florida (smaller venues were chosen for the tour because the Wailers were gaining popularity but could not sell out larger arenas). Next, the Wailers traveled to Canada to begin the North American tour in earnest. After the Canadian shows, which were mostly held in nightclubs, the Wailers returned to the United States. They played in Philadelphia and then returned to Paul's Mall, in Boston, for a sold-out show. A crowd of 15,000 was in attendance for the outdoor show as part of the Schaefer Music Festival, in New York's Central Park. In its review, the *New York Times* reflected the newness of reggae to the American audience. John Rockwell, the reviewer, described Bob as "handsomely fine featured, rapt, even crazed, with those lurching movements and all that wild hair."[51] However, he went on to question whether music that is so heavily rooted in a particular culture can translate to others. Such interest was generated by the Wailers' performance that a follow-up show was booked and immediately sold out at the Manhattan Center. The standard set list for the tour was "Trench Town Rock," "Burnin' and Lootin'," "Them Belly Full (But We Hungry)," "Road Block," "Lively Up Yourself," "Natty Dread," "No Woman, No Cry," "I Shot the Sheriff," and "Kinky Reggae." The shows closed with an encore extended version of "Lively Up Yourself."

From New York, the tour progressed to Cleveland, Detroit, and then Chicago, where the Wailers played a club called the Quiet Knight. While in Chicago, Bob was reunited with Junior Braithwaite, the original Wailers lead singer, who had immigrated to the United States 10 years earlier. Although this Wailers tour was more successful than previous attempts, there were still many problems. The band clashed openly with the manager, Don Taylor, who refused to show respect to anyone other than Bob. Also, there were logistical difficulties. Travel plans were frequently mishandled, and only one roadie had been hired to drive the truck, unpack, set up, and tear down the equipment for each show.

The Wailers reached California by mid-July and played San Francisco's Boarding House to a sold-out crowd. "Impresario Bill Graham was so impressed [with the Wailers' live show] that he quickly promoted a last-minute Wailers show at the large Oakland Paramount Theater . . . the hall came within a hundred tickets of selling out."[52] The final date of the U.S. leg of the tour was in Los Angeles, at the Roxy Theatre, on the Sunset Strip. The show at the Roxy was the highlight of the American tour. The Rolling Stones were in Los Angeles on their own tour, and they attended the Wailers' show. The Wailers were building an impressive reputation throughout the rock-and-roll community. Also at the Roxy show were George Harrison and Ringo Starr of the Beatles, the Band, the Grateful Dead, Billy Preston, Herbie Hancock, Joni Mitchell, Cat Stevens, Buddy Miles, and several movie stars. The Wailers were gathering momentum in the United States, and their audience was growing exponentially, largely as a result of the fervor caused by their live performances.

## LIVE!

With the completion of the North American tour, the Wailers flew to London on July 16, 1975, for a four-date British tour in support of *Natty Dread*. The dates were set for performances at the Odeon in Birmingham and the Hard Rock in Manchester and two sold-out shows at the Lyceum in London. Although Bob was nervous about the shows, having learned on arrival at Heathrow Airport that *Natty Dread* was no longer on the British charts, he rehearsed the band vigorously, and the British leg was a success. Chris Blackwell was in attendance at the first of the Lyceum shows and took particular notice when the crowd erupted with emotion at the opening chords of the fifth song, "No Woman, No Cry." Blackwell decided to record the second show, on July 18, 1975, and this recording turned into the *Live!* album that was released in November 1975. The album opens with Tony Garnett's voice introducing the band to uproarious applause from the audience.

The *Live!* album was a pared-down version of the set that the Wailers played that night, which comprised only seven songs: "Trench Town Rock," "Burnin' and Lootin'," "Them Belly Full," "Lively Up Yourself," "No Woman, No Cry," "I Shot the Sheriff," and "Get Up, Stand Up." However, the energy exuded by Bob and the heavy reggae rhythms of the Wailers was readily apparent on the album. Several of the songs performed that night were taken at a speed just slightly faster than their studio versions, which made them even more danceable and energized. The recording created a lasting record of Bob and the Wailers at a potent and powerful point in their career. The album art was a mixture of color pictures taken during the show by Adrian Boot, Bob Ellis, and Dennis Morris. The cover photograph was of Bob swinging his dreadlocks, dancing, and holding his signature Les Paul guitar.

Also in November, the original Wailers reunited for their last public performance ever. They joined forces in support of a benefit concert given by Stevie Wonder at Jamaica's National Stadium for the Jamaican Institute for the Blind. The show culminated with Wonder joining the Wailers on stage for renditions of "Superstition" and "I Shot the Sheriff." This experience would lead Wonder to write a song about Bob called "Master Blaster (Jammin')."

James Perone, the author of *The Sound of Stevie Wonder: His Words and Music* described "Master Blaster" as a "tribute to Bob Marley and the Pan-African politics expressed in some of Marley's songs." Perone noted that Wonder gave a nod in the direction of Jamaican popular music by pairing down his usually lush orchestrations to the sound of a ska band and enhanced the vocals with the echo effect familiar from Jamaican recordings. Wonder's song went on to hit number five on the *Billboard* pop charts and number one on *Billboard Magazine*'s R&B charts.[53]

After the London shows, Bob and the Wailers began the trip back to Jamaica, but on the way Bob stopped in Delaware to visit his mother. While in Wilmington, Bob began to work on several new songs that would soon be recorded, including "Cry to Me" and "Rat Race." At this time, he was also working to set to music a text by Haile Selassie I that the Ethiopian emperor had delivered to the United Nations assembly at Stanford University, in California, in 1968. The text dealt with war, struggle, and inequality, all issues that were very personal to Bob. The product of this work eventually became the song "War."

Upon returning to Jamaica in mid-August, Bob and the Wailers went back into the studio, working on the material for the next album. It was recorded at Harry J's studio and the studio owned by his old friend, singing coach, and mentor Joe Higgs. During the recording process, on August 27, 1975, Haile Selassie I died in his palace in Addis Ababa at the age of 83. This event sent the Rastafarians in Jamaica into a whirlwind of confusion. Many began to doubt the divinity of Selassie, but the devout pointed to Revelations and disbelieved what they had heard.

At 56 Hope Road, the sentiments were mixed, but Bob never wavered in his faith. He and Lee "Scratch" Perry took over Harry J's studio one night in September, and, as the evening progressed, Bob laid down the vocal track to a prerecorded Barrett Brothers rhythm that articulated his position on the Rastafarian situation. The song, titled "Jah Live," was Bob's response to the death of the Ethiopian emperor. Next, Al Anderson overdubbed the guitar part, and the I-Threes filled in the backing harmonies. Released as a 45-rpm single on the Tuff Gong label in Jamaica and on Island in England, "Jah Live" was one of Bob's most poignant statements of his faith in Rastafarianism.

# Uptown Skankin', 1976–1977

## RASTAMAN VIBRATION

The year 1976 marked the beginning of Bob's career as the first third-world superstar. He was in demand for concerts and interviews, and his records received advance orders for the first time. *Rolling Stone* magazine voted Bob Marley and the Wailers "Band of the Year," and Bob appeared on the cover of *Rolling Stone* issue 219, photographed by Annie Leibovitz. It was also an extremely difficult year in Jamaican politics. The Manley government hosted a meeting of the International Monetary Fund, and the opposition JLP responded by inciting riots in the ghetto to shame and destabilize the socialist government. Manley responded by instituting a 7 P.M. curfew and sending troops to quell the rioters. The result was that thug groups and political goon squads took over the streets at night, and even the normally tough Kingston police were reluctant to travel after dark.

Bob and the Wailers continued to work at Harry J's on new music through this period. When not in the studio, Bob spent most days of early 1976 at his house at 56 Hope Road, frequently pestered by journalists and photographers from magazines such as *Time, Rolling Stone, Melody Maker,* and the *New York Times Magazine.* His wealth had afforded him some comforts that he grudgingly accepted. Alan "Skill" Cole had persuaded Bob to buy a silver-blue BMW Bavaria, both because he thought Bob deserved it and because Bob needed a good car for their travels to St. Ann and Trench Town (it did not escape Bob's attention that BMW could stand for either Bavarian Motor Works or Bob Marley and the Wailers). Bob was also able to afford one of his most prized situations: he was able to have his children, from Rita and others, around him at the house on Hope Road.

The sessions for the next album, called *Rastaman Vibration*, continued, and plans were being made for another summer tour of America and Europe. However, the Wailers' lineup was about to change again; Al Anderson decided to leave the group to play with Peter Tosh. Anderson cited problems with the band manager, Don Taylor, as the impetus for his departure. The Wailers lost another member to Tosh when Lee Jaffe informed Bob that he was departing. Jaffe cited dissatisfaction with the end of the previous summer's North American tour as his reason for leaving. The end result was that the Wailers, without Bob and the Barretts, were the backing band, and Jaffe was the co-producer for Tosh's new album, *Legalize It*, released early in 1976.

These new developments left Bob with several important vacancies to fill in the Wailers' organization. Earl "Chinna" Smith, a well-known reggae session player and leader of his own band, Soul Syndicate, soon replaced Anderson.[1] However, Smith opted to fill the rhythm-guitar role, which left open the job of lead guitarist. Chris Blackwell again came to the aid of the Wailers in finding the appropriate lead guitar player. Blackwell had signed an American black-rock power trio called White Lightning to Island Records. The leader of the band was a 23-year-old professional blues guitarist from Gary, Indiana, named Don Kinsey.[2] Don Taylor called Kinsey in March 1976 and invited him to come to Miami, where the Wailers were mixing their new album at Criteria Studios. Kinsey played for the Wailers at the studio and was immediately accepted to play the lead guitar parts on *Rastaman Vibration*. His blues-roots style mixed well with the existing Wailers tracks, and he overdubbed leads onto all songs except "Crazy Baldhead," which Anderson had already done before leaving the band.

The Wailers released their fifth Island Records album in May 1976. The album jacket was simulated burlap and depicted Bob, with long dreadlocks, looking contemplative in army fatigues. The album included two parenthetical statements as well; the first was "This album jacket is great for cleaning herb." The second was the Blessing of Joseph from the Old Testament. Bob was as active as even in the Rastafarian sect the Twelve Tribes of Israel, in which his name was Joseph. The actual quotation is as follows:

Joseph is a fruitful bough, even a fruitful bough by a well;
whose branches run over the wall:
The archers have sorely grieved him, and shot at him and hated him:
But his bow abode in strength,
and the arms of his hands were made strong by the hands of
the Mighty God of Jacob, the King of Israel,
King of Kings, Lord of Lords, the conquering lion of the Tribe of Judah.
Let the blessing come upon the head Joseph, and upon the
top of the head that was separated from his brethren.
*(Genesis 49:22–24, Revelation 19:16, Deuteronomy 33:16)*

Upon release, the album climbed to number eight on the America pop charts and was the top-selling record of Bob's life. Of the new album, Bob said, "it's not music right now, we're dealing with a message. Right now the music [is] not important, we're dealing with a message. *Rastaman Vibration* is more like a dub kinda album and it's come without tampering y'know. Like 'War' or 'Rat Race,' the music don't take you away, it's more to listen to."[3]

Lyric content on this album ranged from songs of Rastafarian faith to an overt call for African independence in "War." The use of Selassie's UN speech forever identified Bob with the new international support movement for African resistance to colonial oppression that would come to a head with the liberation of Rhodesia (now Zimbabwe). Another particularly political song was the final track, "Rat Race." Here Bob's lyrics deal with the impending Jamaican national elections and the violence that always accompanied such elections. Overall, the album was a direct statement by Bob about Haile Selassie's death and a clear and forceful declaration of his Rastafarian convictions.

Musicians on the album included Bob on vocals, rhythm guitar, and percussion. Aston and Carlie Barrett appeared on bass and drums, respectively, and Earl "Chinna" Smith played rhythm guitar. Al Anderson was credited with lead guitar on "Crazy Baldheads," and Don Kinsey supplied the lead guitar parts for the rest of the album. Tyrone Downie supplied keyboard and percussion parts, and Alvin "Seeco" Patterson played additional percussion. The I-Threes were again the female backup vocal trio. The original tracks were recorded at Harry J's and Joe Gibbs's studios in Kingston, and the final mixing was done at Criteria Studios in Miami. Production credits were retained by the Bob and the Wailers.

"Rastaman Vibration" was the first track on the album and immediately reasserted Bob's allegiance to Haile Selassie. Bob said of the song, "It's a Rastaman playing so it must be a Rastaman Vibration! And we're serious about the vibration we're putting into ALL our records, not just this one."[4] This song was again credited to Vincent "Tartar" Ford. The song began with the Barretts establishing a mid-tempo reggae groove, followed by Bob chanting the first chorus. In the first verse, he warned that quarrelling and negative living were no way to exist. He then offered the listener an exit through positive living and basking in Jah's love. The chorus then returned, and again Bob associated himself with his God (Jah) through the use of the "I and I" statements. The song ended with Bob repeatedly asking if the audience was picking up his message.

Track two was "Roots, Rock, Reggae," another Vincent Ford attribution on which Bob did the singing. Drums and organ led into the first chorus, in which Bob demanded that they play "I" some music and said that that music must be reggae to get him dancing. This sentiment pervaded the chorus, first verse, and chorus restatement. The second verse was a window into Bob's mind in which he tipped his hat to R&B, which had influenced him early in his career. Bob mentioned the American style by name with "play I on the

R&B." He also noted that the Wailers were now "bubbling" on the top 100, which was a testament to their growing international fame. In fact, this song charted in the American Top 40.

Rita Marley was credited with penning "Johnny Was," like the earlier song "Simmer Down" a warning to ghetto youth to stop warring with the government and each other or risk ending up dead. The first chorus began with Marley describing a scene in which a woman cried over the loss of her son after he was gunned down in the street by a stray bullet. This scenario became commonplace in the boiling political climate of the west Kingston ghetto. Government influence, both Jamaican and American, exacerbated the situation, and rival gangs frequently clashed in the ghetto, leaving a path of death.

"Johnny Was" retold the death of a ghetto youth blamed on the existing political system. The chorus and verse statements were musically the same, both presented over a one-drop drumming, a melodic bass, and rock-sounding lead guitar overdubs. The "Johnny" in the song was one of the notorious Trench Town gunmen named Carlton "Bat Man" Wilson. Wilson engaged in numerous ghetto gunfights until he was seriously wounded. Others of his ilk did not fair as well; in the years that followed the release of this song, the notorious Trench Town gunfighters (and Bob associates) Claudie Massop, Bucky Marshall, and others were killed. In this song, Bob used a single biblical quotation, "the wages of sin is death, but the gift of God [Jah] is life." The statement was a direct quotation from Romans 6:23. With this quotation, the bad deeds of the gunmen come full circle; chapter six of Romans deals with the removal of earthly sin through death.

"Cry to Me" was credited to and sung by Bob. Begun by a soft organ introduction, the song used lyrics by Bob that implored the subject of the song to cry. This song had no formal sections; it comprised four statements that all started with the same words but ended differently. Kwame Dawes noted that the song was meant to serve as retribution for the pain that a woman had caused Bob. The woman's cheating games would be turned back on her now that Bob was "by the still waters." This lyric was another biblical paraphrase, this time from Psalm 23:2. Dawes concluded that the biblical reference to David's soul being restored applied equally to Bob.[5]

Track five was "Want More," which was credited to Aston "Family Man" Barrett. Again, Bob did not cast his words in a standard verse/chorus form. Instead, he constructed a palindrome (mirror) form, in which the song runs the same both forward and backward. The song began with a short drum statement followed by overlapping guitar parts. Bob entered, singing, "now you get what you want, do you want more." There followed repeated statements about casting off a deceitful foe (a backbiter) who would stab him in the back. The centerpiece of the song was another biblical reference. This time Bob evoked the coming of the Lord from Zion to clean the evil blood of wrongdoers. His paraphrase of the third chapter of Joel referenced the "valley of decision" in which those who were doing harm to Bob (the back-biters) would get their just rewards.

"Crazy Baldheads" was credited to Rita Marley and Vincent Ford but was sung by Bob. It described his problems with non-Rastas. The term "baldhead" referred to one who lacked dreadlocks and, more important, one who worked for Babylon. The song began with Bob emitting a Yoruba yell, followed by the rhythm section locking into a mid-tempo reggae beat and the beginning of the first chorus. The chorus emphasized Bob's desire to run all workers of Babylon out of town. The chorus ended with Bob sliding into several bars of unchar-acteristic scat singing. The first verse put a sharp point on Bob's feelings about the injustice perpetrated by the baldheads. The verse described the work of the Rastas in building and farming for Babylon, only to have the fruits of their labors taken away by those who scorn them. Verse two described the Rastas building schools, only to be brainwashed by the education they received in them. The climax of the song's sentiment was the lyric "hatred your reward for our love, telling us of your God above." "Crazy Baldhead" made clear Bob's feelings about non-Rastas and about his Babylonian captors.

"Who the Cap Fit" was a remake of an early Wailers single, "Man to Man," released on the Upsetter label in 1971. The song reappeared as the seventh track on the *Rastaman Vibration* album. The Barrett Brothers, the Wailers rhythm section, were credited with writing this song; however, it was likely written by Marley and the Barretts. The misattribution was intentional as part of Bob's continued avoidance of royalty payments to Cayman Music, which was laying claim to songs written by him during this period.

The song was built of even phrases that alternate between 16-measure verse statements and an 8-measure chorus. Two-thirds of the way through, there was an 8-measure bridge that was followed by a final abbreviated verse statement and a last chorus that was altered to end the song. The sound of the song was stock Wailers, with the inclusion of ethereal synthesizer parts.

The lyrics of the song contain several interesting references, one specific to Jamaicans and one from the Bible. The central lyric refers to the familiar task of feeding chickens, but with a Jamaican twist. The chorus stated, "I throw me corn, me no call no fowl." The origin of this reference to throwing dried corn kernels to chickens was explained by Timothy White:

> [The references] in the song "Who the Cap Fit" are incomprehensible to the average non-Jamaican listener, who is unaware that the central phrase is actually a rural proverb. It evokes the image of a farmer silently scattering feed who is saying, in effect: "Don't call yourself a chicken just because you eat my feed; I never said I was endeavoring to feed chickens." That is, "You are who you show yourself to be, not who you might say you are."[6]

This ideology pervaded the entire song, with Marley warning the listener to trust what people do and not what they say. "Who the Cap Fit" made use of the Jamaican Creole word "su-su," which was defined in Cassidy and Page's *Dictionary of Jamaican English* as whispering behind someone's back, gossiping, or speaking ill. The sounds "su-su" are meant to mimic the sound of whispering. The biblical reference was to Proverb 25:21, which is a directive to give food and water to your enemy regardless of his status as such. This text reference included not only Jamaican patois but also a biblical paraphrase.

"Night Shift" was credited to Bob and came from the early Wail'n'Soul days. The lyrics were a personal account of his time spent in Delaware working at the Chrysler plant when he was trying to make money to start his own label back in Jamaica. During this period, Bob was living with his mother, working, and writing music. His life was relatively joyless, and he was using the "sweat of his brow" to make a better life for him and his family.

The Wailers backed Bob on this track with a strong, fairly slow reggae groove that had the Barretts locked in, and additional synthesizer parts added to the texture. Bob began the lyrics with a biblical quote from Psalm 121: "The sun shall not smite I by day, not the moon by night." The sentiment of the quote echoed the meaning of the song. Bob was working in a foreign land to help his family and himself, and the psalm verse spoke of turning to the Lord for protection from evil in this type of situation.

"War" was one of the more direct and powerful songs on the *Rastaman Vibration* album. The Barrett Brothers were credited with both the words and the music for this track. However, the majority of the words are actually taken from a speech given by Haile Selassie to the United Nations on February 28, 1968. At the time, Selassie was pleading for civil rights in Ethiopia, and his plea took on even greater strength and immediacy with the addition of driving rhythms and Marley's vocal presentation.

Because this song was really a speech set to music, the form was odd, and Marley made the harmonic motion static. The intent was to recast the speech in a form as close as possible to the original. The song began with a four-measure introduction, emphasizing the drums and horns. The majority of Marley's songs begin with this type of introduction, because it allows for the tempo and the key of the song to be established. The text of the speech was then presented in the following five verse statements. Marley did not break the continuity of the speech by inserting a repeated chorus between the verses, and his singing was not lyrical but rather a direct, spoken chant. Phases were underpinned by the I-Threes singing "war" repeatedly in the background, along with horn-section punches at the end of certain phrases.

All of the verses were different musically, and they varied in length, with the only exception being the third and fourth verses, which are both 20 measures long and use the same music. Interestingly, the original speech began "What life has taught me on the question of racial discrimination, I like to share with those who want to learn." The liner notes of the album contain the following preface to the song: "What life has taught me I would like to share with those who want to learn." The tone of Selassie's speech was quite dire, and, with the added force of Marley's presentation, the words took on even greater force. The lyrics warn that unless everyone can find a way to live in peace, there will always be war both on the African continent and all over the rest of the world.

The final track on the album was "Rat Race," which was credited to Rita Marley. The Barretts maintained a fairly demure presence on this song. There were still horn punches at the ends of some phrases, but the important feature was Bob and the words he was presenting so everyone else stayed out of the way. The song began with Bob chanting the opening chorus, and chorus material punctuated the end of each verse. The verses contained the main message of the song, and the chorus statements were short.

The song was soaked with political commentary, which began in the first few words. Marley declared repeatedly that the Rasta did not want to be involved in any political dealings. Bold statements included "Rasta don't work for no CIA," "Political violence fill your city," and "don't involve Rasta in your say-say." The year 1976 was another election year, and there was increased violence in Kingston and the westside ghetto. Through these lyric, Bob tried to remove the faithful from the dire circumstances.

In June 1976, the Wailers departed on a three-month tour of the United States and Europe in support of *Rastaman Vibration*. The 10-piece touring group was made up of Bob, the Barrett Brothers, the I-Threes, Smith and Kinsey on guitar, Tyrone Downie on keyboards, and Alvin "Seeco" Patterson on additional percussion. The Wailers' entourage included their general manager, Don Taylor, along with Alan "Skill" Cole, their road manager; Tony "Gillie" Gilbert, their cook; Neville Garrick, the art and lighting designer; Dennis Thompson, the soundman; and Tony "Tony G" Garnett, the road manager and general manager's assistant.

The tour again began in Miami, but the first major show was at the Tower Theater in Philadelphia. Bob's mother, Cedella Booker, had been driven to Philadelphia from Delaware and was in attendance for her first live Bob Marley and the Wailers performance. Next, the tour went to Boston and on to New York, where the Wailers sold out the Beacon Theater on Broadway. The tour continued on to Chicago, and in several weeks the Wailers were back in California. They played several soldout concerts on the West Coast, in Los Angeles, Santa Monica, Long Beach, and San Diego. Bob Dylan was present at the Roxy Theatre show, and Bob Marley treated one of his idols to an amazing set. That night the Wailers performed "Trench Town Rock," "Burnin' and Lootin'," "Them Belly Full (But We Hungry)," "Rebel Music," "I Shot the Sheriff," "Want More," "No Woman, No Cry," "Lively Up Yourself," "Roots, Rock, Reggae," "Rat Race," "Rastaman Vibration," "Get Up, Stand Up," "No More Trouble," and "War." This show was recorded and was eventually released as the two-CD set *Bob Marley and the Wailers Live at the Roxy*.

Bob on stage in 1976. Courtesy of Photofest.

After the southern California shows, the Wailers traveled to Europe, where they played in Düsseldorf, Amsterdam, and Paris and at various places in England (including the Hammersmith Palais). After the successful English shows, the Wailers returned home. Back in Jamaica in September, the Wailers immediately noticed the changes taking place in Kingston. Manley had declared another state of emergency four months earlier and was ruling by decree. As noted, there was a tradition of election-year violence in Kingston, and this situation had been exacerbated by an unexplained influx of handguns. In addition to this, Manley had weakened his own political position and begun to take on Communist-influenced positions by declaring it illegal to possess U.S. currency, promoting his militant socialist stance, supporting the revolution in Angola, and highlighting his friendship with Fidel Castro, of Cuba.

As a result of Manley's political maneuvering, the International Monetary Fund forced Jamaica to adopt stricter currency restrictions and import policies. This created additional unrest due to periodic shortages of staples such as rice, cooking oil, and flour. The political situation in Jamaica was quickly destabilizing the island's economy. It was producing a serious drain on the Jamaican intelligentsia as many skilled and educated people fled the island. Across the island there was talk of the political unrest. The leader of the opposition JLP, Edward Seaga, was even accused of allying himself with the American CIA as a means to win control of the island. The situation got so heated that everyone in Jamaica was affected, even the first third-world superstar, Bob Marley.

It was at this time that Bob set into motion his plan to play a concert to thank Jamaica for the support that he and the Wailers had received over the past decade. His plan was to stage a free concert in Kingston's National Heroes Park as a gesture of gratitude. The Prime Minister's office was contacted, and plans were made through the People's National Party minister, Arnold Bertram. A date was set (December 5, 1976), and the aid of other acts was enlisted. The other original Wailers, Peter Tosh and Bunny Livingston, both agreed to play, along with Burning Spear. The concert had a theme, "Smile Jamaica," and was meant to reduce the friction between the warring factions active on the island. Bob and the Wailers recorded a song with this title at Lee "Scratch" Perry's new studio, called Black Ark. "Smile Jamaica" was Bob's most overt statement of Jamaican nationalism.

Once the concert had been scheduled, the government announced the date of the next national election, December 20. This was pure political maneuvering on the part of the PNP and the Manley administration. The timetable made it appear that all the performers at the "Smile Jamaica" concert were endorsing Manley. The anticipated large audience would then be expected to usher in another term for Manley and his socialist regime. Bob had supported Manley in the election of 1972; however, he and his proposed concert were now being set up for use as political pawns in a game of ever-escalating stakes (this was precisely why Peter Tosh referred to politics as "poli-tricks"). Bob's distaste for the government's action was compounded by his Rastafarian faith. In the previous election, the normally apolitical Rastafarians had largely backed the Manley ticket. With the new election now set, the Rastas were coming out in opposition to Manley because he had failed them on the issues of ganja legalization and the facilitation of Jamaican repatriation of Ethiopia.

In addition to the political situations that were weighing on Bob, his name was again in the press when, in October, Cindy Breakspeare was crowned Miss World. Again, the headlines about "Beauty and the Beast" surfaced as Bob and Cindy continued their relationship. The scandal was newsworthy throughout the Western world as a result of Bob's hard-won fame. Further, Bob was called to Delaware at this time to aid his mother as his stepfather, Edward Booker, was dying.

## ATTEMPTED ASSASSINATION OF MARLEY

On December 3, 1976, the Wailers were at 56 Hope Road rehearsing for their upcoming concert. The horn section from the Zap Pow band (Vin Gordon, Glen Da Costa, and David Madden) was present, preparing to back the Wailers in concert, as were the I-Threes. At approximately 8:45 P.M., the group took a break, and Bob went to the main house to get something to eat. Also at this time, Judy Mowatt of the I-Threes, who was pregnant, began feeling ill and asked Bob to have someone take her to her house in Bull Bay. Bob directed Neville Garrick to take Judy home, and at about 9 P.M., Neville,

Judy, and an assistant sound engineer named "Sticko" left 56 Hope Road in Bob's BMW. At the same time, Don Taylor was just arriving at the house, and he could hear the band rehearsing the bridge to "Jah Live."

Taylor had come to the house to meet with Chris Blackwell; Blackwell had not yet arrived, so Taylor waited in the kitchen talking to Bob and the guitarist Don Kinsey while they snacked on some grapefruit. No one was aware that minutes earlier, two white Datsuns had followed Taylor's car into the yard at 56 Hope Road. Six gunmen exited the cars, and, while two men stood guard, the other four opened fire on the house. Rita Marley was shot in the head as she tried to shelter her children. A friend of the Wailers, Lewis Simpson (some sources report his name as Lewis Griffiths), was badly wounded in the melee. In the kitchen, Bob, Don Taylor, and Don Kinsey were surprised by the popping of gunshots as one gunman stuck his head into the kitchen and opened fire with a submachine gun. Don Kinsey jumped out of the way as Bob attempted to jam himself into the corner. Don Taylor was the most exposed of the group and took the majority of the bullets. Eight shots were fired into the kitchen, two of which were wild and ricocheted around the room (one can see the bullet holes in the plaster walls while touring the house even today). Five of the bullets hit Don Taylor, riddling his torso and pelvic area. The last bullet hit Bob, grazing his sternum and lodging in his left bicep. For a full five minutes after the attack, no one moved at 56 Hope Road for fear that the gunmen were still in the area.

Remarkably, no one was mortally wounded during the shooting. Bob, Rita, Lewis Simpson, and Don Taylor were all loaded into cars and taken to the hospital. The police arrived 10 minutes later and secured the area. Everyone who had been at the house quickly disappeared, and within half an hour the only people left at 56 Hope Road were the police. Meanwhile, Neville Garrick and Sticko heard of the shooting on the radio at 9:30 P.M. and, once they had dropped Judy off in Bull Bay, hurriedly returned to Kingston. On the way, they got a flat tire, and as they were fixing it the police arrived and demanded to know why they had Bob's car. Neville explained to the police who they were, and the police gave them an escort back to Hope Road. The police instructed Neville to stay at the house and take control there, but he immediately left for the hospital.

The scene at the hospital comforted Neville to a certain degree. He arrived to find Bob being bandaged around the chest where the bullet had chipped his sternum. Rita was lying on a hospital bed with her head wrapped, because of the bullet fragment that had lodged between her scalp and her skull. Don Taylor, who had been the most seriously wounded, was wheeled past Neville on his way to the lifesaving surgery that was needed to repair his numerous wounds.

Shortly after Neville arrived, Prime Minister Michael Manley came and visited Bob and the other fallen Wailers. PNP finance minister David Coore, who knew Bob because his son Cat was a member of the Third World band,

Bob in the wake of the assassination attempt.
Courtesy of Photofest.

followed closely behind. The Prime Minister placed Bob under the protection of the Jamaican security service, and he was taken from the hospital
to a secret location to convalesce. Ever the political calculator, Manley still
wanted Bob to play the Smile Jamaica concert, and he was determined to
keep Bob alive for that purpose.

Chris Blackwell made his mansion at Strawberry Hill, 3,000 feet above
Kingston, available to Bob that night as a safe house. Four hours later, Bob and
his inner circle of friends arrived at Strawberry Hill and were ushered into the
house. That night a heavily armed police unit, along with a contingent of local
Rastas, watched over the house to ensure Bob's safety. Bob spent the following
day resting, sleeping, and beginning his recovery. However, the concert was
looming, and the Wailers needed to decide if they should still participate.

That night, the Wailers held a long meeting to decide what to do and to
ascertain who had tried to kill them. The reasons behind the assassination
attempt were never uncovered; however, the attempt could have been motivated by the JLP's resentment over the Wailers' unspoken endorsement of
the PNP. Another theory was that someone who was jealous of the Wailers'

success or Bob's romance with the recently crowned Miss World could have engineered the attempt. It was also postulated that one of Alan "Skill" Cole's moneymaking schemes had gone wrong and that the shooting was some type of revenge or retribution. However, Bob was inconsolable, regardless of the reasoning behind the shooting, and was still uncertain what to do about the concert, which was scheduled for the next day. Part of Bob's continued anxiety stemmed from the fact that the gunmen had not been caught. One of the vehicles used in the assault had been found in Trench Town burned and abandoned, but the would-be assassins were still at large.

Sunday, December 5, 1976, brought the encouraging news that Don Taylor would survive his gunshot wounds and was being flown to Miami to have a bullet removed from his spine. Also, the film crew that Blackwell had hired to tape the "Smile Jamaica" concert had arrived and given Bob a set of powerful walkie-talkies to allow him to keep track of the Wailers as they stayed safe in various locations around Kingston. Bob posted several people around town and kept track of events on the day of the concert via walkie-talkie. He sent Cat Coore of the Third World band to Heroes Park and found out that Peter, Bunny, and Burning Spear were no-shows, having learned of the assassination attempt. Cat and Bob together decided that Third World would go on and test the situation to see if it would be safe for the Wailers to appear. Meanwhile, Bob was attempting to locate the rest of the band. Don Kinsey was found, agreed to perform, and was taken to the Sheraton, where the film crew was preparing itself for the concert. Carlie Barrett and Tyrone Downie had returned to 56 Hope Road, which accounted for the core of the group minus the other Barrett brother.

At 4:00 P.M., Cat told Bob that there were an estimated 50,000 people at the venue and that Third World was preparing to open for the Wailers. Still at Strawberry Hill, Bob had not yet decided to perform, and Rita, who was out of the hospital but still in bandages, was now on the scene trying to convince him to cancel. Also at Strawberry Hill was the PNP housing minister, Anthony Spaulding, who had been charged with the job of persuading Bob to go on. Bob continued to vacillate, but eventually Spaulding prevailed and convinced him to perform that evening. Spaulding, Bob, and Rita got into a waiting motorcade and began their descent into the city.

They arrived to find that the crowd had grown to 80,000 people. The stage looked tiny in the midst of such a huge number of spectators. The car containing Bob was ushered into the area, and, upon exiting the car, Bob ran on stage and was greeted by Michael Manley, who had been talking to the waiting audience. As Manley left the stage, Bob checked to see which of the Wailers were present to perform the show. Casting his eye around the stage, he saw Tyrone, Carlie, Cat from Third World, the horn section from Zap Pow, and five hand drummers from the *akete* drumming group Ras Michael and the Sons of Negus. He decided that this would work and called to the crowd for quiet to make the following announcement: "When me decided ta do dis yere concert two anna 'alf months ago, me was told dere was no politics. I jus' wanted ta play fe da love of da people." Bob Marley and the Wailers then dove into the song "War" (part of the way through the song, Don Kinsey, wearing a brown tunic over his bandaged torso, arrived on stage and took over on his guitar part).

At the beginning of the performance, Bob had said that the Wailers would perform only one song; instead, they launching into a 90-minute set. "War" was followed by "Trench Town Rock," "Rastaman Vibration," and "Want More." They also performed "So Jah Seh" for the first, and possibly only, time live. The Wailers' performance came to a climax when Bob pulled up his shirt to expose his fresh bandages from the wounds that he had suffered. After the Wailers set had ended, it was noticed by many that the nervous audience dispersed quickly.

The night of the "Smile Jamaica" concert, Bob returned to Strawberry Hill and was again heavily guarded. The following day, he and Neville Garrick left Jamaica on a private jet chartered by Chris Blackwell and traveled to the island of Nassau, in the Bahamas. Blackwell had moved his Island headquarters to Nassau because of the constant unrest in Jamaica. On Nassau, Bob and Neville were thoroughly searched by customs and immigration officials and asked if they were seeking political asylum. They replied that they were on the island for vacation, but this did not placate the Nassau officials; news of the attempted assassination had spread worldwide immediately, and those in Nassau were aware of the situation. Finally allowed to proceed, Bob and Neville went to Blackwell's house at Compass Point.[7]

After resting for a few hours, the two were rousted by a group of policemen and taken to another immigration interview. The second interview was with higher-ranking customs officials, who granted the two men only provisional visas, allowing them to be deported at the whim of the Nassau officials. A day later, Rita arrived with the children, and in another week the rest of the Wailers were also in Nassau. One outcome of the assassination attempt and the ensuing chaos was that the guitarist Don Kinsey left Bob and the Wailers and returned to Indiana.

Temporarily out of harm's reach, Bob began the process of rest and recovery from his injuries and the whole experience in general. The question of who tried to kill Bob Marley and why has never been officially answered. An opinion that is widely held was that the attempt was made because of a race-track fix at Kingston's Caymanas Park that was supposedly masterminded by Alan "Skill" Cole. This rumor has many variations involving ganja dealing, cocaine, and revenge. The truth may never be known, but an interesting fact was that, at this same time, Alan "Skill" Cole disappeared from Jamaica and did not return for several years.

Regardless of the reason behind the assassination attempt, it did remove Bob from the Jamaican political landscape just prior to the election. On December 15, 1976, the Jamaican public voted Michael Manley and the

PNP to 47 of the 60 possible seats in the Jamaican Parliament. The socialist government had won another election, but in the process approximately 200 people had died. In the wake of the election, the Wailers remained in Nassau for another month. Bob was reunited with Cindy Breakspeare just before Christmas on Paradise Island. They spent time together and rekindled their relationship, and Bob was overjoyed when Cindy told him that she wanted to bear his child. Within the year, Cindy gave birth to Bob's ninth child, a son named Damian.

## EXODUS

In early 1977, the Wailers traveled to London to begin work on their next album. The band stayed in a comfortable apartment at 42 Oakley Street, Chelsea, and the Wailers machine began to roll again. "Gillie," the band's road cook, was again with them, and he prepared Ital meals of ackee, salt cod, vegetables, dumplings, and Irish moss.[8] However, the Wailers were again in the market for a guitar player, and Bob was thinking about trying to entice Al Anderson to return to the Wailers. Anderson had left the group to play with Peter Tosh's band.[9] Bob talked about this with Chris Blackwell, who brought up a young, black blues guitarist named Junior Marvin.

Marvin performed under the names Junior Kerr and Junior Hanson (his given name was Donald Hanson Marvin Kerr Richards Junior). Although born in Kingston, he had been raised in both England and the United States and had apprenticed under the Texas bluesman T. Bone Walker. Further, he had worked with Billy Preston, Ike and Tina Turner, and Stevie Wonder, in addition to having two releases on Atlantic Records with his own band, called Hanson. In early 1977, Marvin was recording a guitar track for a Steve Winwood song at Island Studios when Blackwell asked if he would like to join the Wailers. Marvin agreed and was soon working with Bob and Tyrone Downie to learn the new Wailers material.

In the ensuing sessions, in the winter of 1977, the Wailers recorded more than 20 songs. The earlier recordings produced the next album called *Exodus: Movement of Jah People*. While in the studio, the Wailers paid careful attention to the music being made in Jamaica in their absence. They heard songs by groups including Israel Vibration, the Meditations, the Itals, and a band called Culture. Culture had a big hit in 1977 with its song "Two Sevens Clash," which discussed the millenarian Rasta belief that the year 1977 would bring many judgments, both good and bad.[10]

Halfway through the sessions, Lee "Scratch" Perry appeared in London and moved into the apartment above Island's Basing Street Studios. Upon Perry's arrival, the *Exodus* sessions stopped so that Bob and Perry could spend time together and talk about the future. While the Wailers were off the island, Perry had continued to record various Jamaican artists, one of which was Junior Murvin, who had released a Perry song, "Police and Thieves."[11] Interestingly, while Bob and Perry were together, they heard a version of "Police and Thieves" recorded by the Clash.

Perry asked Bob to record a song that he had written about the shared ideology of reggae and punk called "Punky Reggae Party." Of this song and his affinity for the English punk scene, Bob said, "in a way, me like see them safety pins and t'ings. Me no like do it myself y'understand, but me like see a man can suffer pain without crying."[12] Bob laid down the vocal track with a quickly cobbled-together backing band that contained members of Third World and a new English reggae band called Aswad. Ultimately, members of the Wailers overdubbed their parts on the track.

The Wailers sessions again resumed and produced enough material for more than one album. The 10 most moving and cutting-edge songs made up the *Exodus* album, released June 3, 1977. The other 10 songs from the session were released in 1978 as the album *Kaya*. Although products of the same recording session, *Exodus* and *Kaya* were very different in character, the former being much more militant in character than the latter. Beyond this, the material on *Exodus* also marked a change in the basic Wailers groove. The fifth song and title track of the album used a more militant drumming style, which had been popularized by the Jamaican studio player Sly Dunbar. Here, the drum was more active and accented all four beats in the measure (frequently called "rockers") instead of the typical one-drop style that accented only the third beat of each measure. This feel was compounded by Junior Marvin's tendency to rush the beat on the guitar and the use of a three-piece horn section, composed of Vin Gordon, Glen Da Costa, and David Madden (often referred to as the Zap Pow horns because they played together in a band with that name).

Although *Exodus* was recorded at Island Record's Basing Street Studios, in England, Bob said that the change of location was not responsible for the change in the groove: "positive vibrations man. That's what makes it work. That's reggae music. You can't look away because it's real. You listen to what I sing because I mean what I sing, there's no secret, no big deal. Just honesty, that's all."[13] *Exodus* began with the song "Natural Mystic," which was powerful in its simplicity; Marley himself was sometimes referred to as the "natural mystic." The three songs that followed were a programmatic story of the assassination attempt on Bob. "So Much Things to Say," "Guiltiness," and "The Heathen" all dealt with themes of rising against oppression, unavoidable guilt, retribution for persecutors, and one of Bob's favorite topic—that a man will reap the wickedness he sows. These messages were expertly couched in biblical quotations and language that invoked Marcus Garvey and Paul Bogle.[14] The next track, "Exodus," repeated Garvey's sentiments about African repatriation, either mentally or physically.

The second half of the album was very different in character, composed of dance and love songs. "Jamming" was a joyous, danceable track, and "One

Love" was a wonderful makeover of the Curtis Mayfield song "People Get Ready." "Turn Your Lights Down Low," "Waiting in Vain," and "Three Little Birds" were all love songs either about or directed to Cindy Breakspeare. The *Exodus* album offered an interesting look into Bob's life at this time—his horror over the attempt on his life and his Garvey-influenced call for African repatriation, mixed with the relatively relaxed dance and love songs. The content of the record was so strong that seven of the tracks were released as singles. This depth of release was not repeated until Michael Jackson's *Thriller*, released in 1982.

Performers on the recording were Bob on lead vocals, rhythm guitar, and percussion. Aston "Family Man" Barrett and Carlie Barrett made up the lock-step rhythm section on bass and drums, respectively. Tyrone Downie appeared on keyboards, percussion, and backing vocals alongside Alvin "Seeco" Patterson on percussion. Junior Marvin took over on lead guitar, and the whole group was supported by the I-Threes on female backing vocals. The Zap Pow horns, Vin Gordon, Glen Da Costa, and David Madden, again appeared as the Wailers' horn line. *Exodus* garnered worldwide praise upon its release. The album also proved to have exceptional staying power; in 1999, *Time* magazine named it the most important album of the twentieth century. Some view the potency of the album as a testament to Bob's strength of resolve in the wake of his shooting.

Although Bob was still under a royalties contract with Cayman Music, he took writing credits for all of the songs on *Exodus*. The only exception was a shared credit for "One Love/People Get Ready." Here Bob credited Curtis Mayfield as the original composer of "People Get Ready." The 10 tracks on the album began with "Natural Mystic." In addition to "Gong," "Tuff Gong," and "Skip," Bob was sometimes nicknamed "Natural Mystic." The track opened with the rhythm section in its typical role. However, instead of simply beginning, the song faded in, with the beat at a steady walking-pace speed. Bob then entered with lyrics that came in three sections. The song contained three chorus-and-verse alternations. The first and the third were the same, and the middle echoed the same general sentiment. The song began with the evocation of a "natural mystic" who asked probing questions and carried with it the power of the biblical trumpets discussed in Exodus. While Bob did not quote the Bible directly, this song was an excellent setup for the tone that the vocals took in the song "Exodus." It also started the album off with the dire feeling that permeated the first four songs. Track two was "So Much Things To Say." The general sensibility of this song was not as dire or foreboding as that of "Natural Mystic," but it still contained a serious message. The form of the song was straightforward chorus-and-verse alternations. The I-Threes helped Bob usher in the opening chorus, after which he began the first verse. The chorus material testified to the important content of the verses by repeatedly chanting the song's title. The sentiment of the first verse's lyrics was serious, regardless of the upbeat and cheerful-sounding music. Verse one talked of the crucifixion of Jesus Christ. Bob went on to remind the listener of the sad ends of Marcus Garvey and Paul Bogle. He then braced the youth to continue the struggle begun by these historic figures.

Verse two implored the youth to continue fighting against oppression. Bob used the "I and I" language to strengthen his resolve. He also noted that his actions might follow the law of the land, but the only law he concerned himself with was God's (Jah's) law. Bob also made certain that the price for guilt would not be levied against just one person but would fall on all associated with the guilty party. "When the rain falls, it don't fall on one man's house" is Bob's warning that all guilty people would be held accountable for their actions.

Payment by the guilty remained the central message of the third song on *Exodus*. "Guiltiness" had a serious and dire tone. Here Bob was directly addressing his Hope Road attackers and telling them that they would reap the negative consequences of their evil deeds. The song unfolded in two large sections, the second of which repeated material from the first in a slightly altered form. The message of the song was direct and pointed. Bob again evoked a biblical story to add force to his convictions. He said that those who "lived a life of false pretense" shall "eat the bread of sorrow." Through this paraphrase of Psalm 127, Bob was damning the guilty to an unhappy fate.

"The Heathen" was the third of the tracks on this album that was written in response to the attempted assassination at Hope Road. The tone was again somber and serious. The song began with the chorus chanted in full male and female harmony. The message of the chorus was direct and was stated in the first line: "Jah put the heathen back deh 'pon the wall" (loosely "Jah put the heathen's back against the wall"). With this, Bob was pointing the firing squad at the gunmen who had sought to take his life. Gravity was added to the lyrics of these messages through biblical language from Job 4:8: "As a man sows, shall he reap." The first and third verses are the same and bookend the song with the sentiment that Bob and the Wailers would rise from their wounded positions and live to fight another day.

"Exodus," the title track of the album, tied Bob's circumstances to the biblical account of Moses and the Israelites as they were led out of exile. Here Bob allied the Rastas and himself with the biblical exodus out of Egypt. The similarities between the biblical story and this point in Bob's life were striking. Bob was currently in exile fearing that his life was in danger in Jamaica. Further, he was increasingly interested in African repatriation. The song itself was a major hit for Bob and the Wailers. Because of the accelerated drumming style and guitar playing, it became the group's first international hit. The single of this song was carried on white and black radio stations in both the United States and the United Kingdom and went on to become a worldwide top 10 hit.

The song itself began with the chanting of "Exodus, movement of Jah people." In the introduction, the guitar and drums started pushing the tempo, and the horns acted as punctuation at the ends of phrases. There followed a series of verse-and-chorus alternations that continued the comparison of Jamaican Rasta (such as Bob and the Wailers) and the Israelites in the Exodus section of the Bible. As Bob discussed leaving Babylon, he did so with the aid of specific lines from several chapters of Exodus. For example, the lyric "send us another Brother Moses gonna cross the Red Sea" replicates part of Exodus 23:31.

The direct and powerful messages of deliverance from oppression gave way to lighter-hearted fare on the second half of the album. "Jamming" was as relaxed as Bob could get at this stage in his life. The song was essentially a call for the sufferers to forget their cares, unite, and dance. The drumbeat was again a faster, rock-oriented groove, and the guitar was often heavily distorted. The four-beat "rocker" rhythm was an excellent choice for this call to dance. However, there were still some more serious undertones in this song. Bob stated that "'I and I' will see you through" as a means of again linking himself with Jah. Also, the line "no bullets can stop us now, we neither beg nor bow" needed no explanation.

"Waiting in Vain" was made up of seven sections and alternated verse and chorus in the typical popular-song style. The song described Bob's lengthy wait for a love interest who might never come. The song began with an eight-measure introduction that established the tempo, which was a return to the slower one-drop groove of earlier Wailers songs. This introduction led into the first verse statement, which detailed Bob's long suffering while waiting for this particular love interest, most likely Cindy Breakspeare. While Marley plaintively sang the lyrics of the phrase, which detailed the changing of the seasons, the harmony repeated the same four chords throughout. Through several verse-and-chorus alternations, Bob left the listener not knowing if he and the object of his desire would be united. Although Bob's heartfelt pining did not get resolved in the course of the song, it was still a significant success for the band. In 1977, "Waiting in Vain" climbed into the top 30 on the U.K. charts.

"Turn Your Lights Down Low" was another love song from the second half of the *Exodus* release. This song was Bob's most potent bedroom ode. The chorus minced no words: "I want to give you some love, so good good loving." Kwame Dawes called the song "full throttle seduction." He also posited that Bob's love in this song was a love "sanctioned by faith" through the "association of the glowing moon with Jah."[15] Again, Bob likely was singing this song to Cindy Breakspeare.

The perennial favorite "Three Little Birds" has long been a steadfast crowd-pleaser for lovers of the music of Bob and the Wailers. The lore of this song was that Bob often sat on the back steps of the house at Hope Road and rolled large spliffs, casting the seeds onto the ground. The birds in question were said to be the ground doves that frequented the house and ate up the seeds. The song itself was a moderate-speed reggae tune with a lighthearted message. The lyric "Don't worry about a thing cause every little thing gonna be alright" made up the majority of the lyrics (other than the mention of the birds themselves).

The final cut on *Exodus* was the artful blending of American rhythm and blues and Jamaican reggae. "One Love/People Get Ready" mixed Bob Marley and Curtis Mayfield (the legendary leader of the Impressions). Here Bob did a masterful job of combining the two songs' lyrics and meanings. In fact, the Mayfield song must have supplied Bob with the song's chorus. Mayfield wrote "U don't need no ticket, U just thank the Lord." Bob transformed the second half of this line into "Give thanks and praise to the Lord and I will feel alright." These words were the chorus.

The song's verses were likewise mixed. Mayfield wrote "there ain't no room for the hopeless sinner, who would hurt all mankind just to has his own." Bob took that line and converted it into a question to end his first verse. Bob's second verse used the second half of Mayfield's first. Here both lyrics started the same but diverged at the end. Bob's version unfolded, "Have pity on those whose chances grow thinner, there ain't no hiding place from the father of creation." Mayfield's lyric ended, "there ain't no hiding place against the kingdom's throne." In this case, Bob maintained the same sentiment but altered the words to his purpose. The sound of the two songs was completely different, with Bob's lyrics presented over a mid-tempo one-drop reggae groove. With the popularity of *Exodus,* Bob and the Wailers again prepared to tour in support of the record.

At the same time that the Wailers were living and recording in England, the Ethiopian royal family was living in exile in London. The family head was Haile Selassie's grandson, Crown Prince Zere-Yakob Asfa-Wossen, the pretender to his grandfather's abolished throne. Prince Wossan knew of the Wailers' music and Bob's pioneering spirit, and the two men had occasion to meet. At the meeting, Prince Wossan gave Bob a ring that had previously belonged to Haile Selassie himself. The gold ring had on it a golden Lion of Judah set in black onyx and immediately became Bob's most prized possession (which was important because Bob prized few material things); he wore it every day for the rest of his life.

April 1977 was spent rehearsing for the impending tour of the United States and Europe to support the release of *Exodus.* One night, Bob and Aston "Family Man" Barrett were driving in Ladbroke Grove, in northwest London, when they were stopped by the police and searched. The search produced two large ganja spliffs, one found on each man, and the two men were arrested and ordered to appear before a judge. Also, the police asked for Bob's address in order to search for more contraband. Cleverly, Bob gave the police the address of his personal retreat at Earls Court so that the rest of the band, which was staying in Chelsea, could avoid the same fate. Unfortunately, the search of Bob's house produced approximately one pound of ganja. On April 6, 1977, Bob and Aston "Family Man" Barrett were seen at

Marylebone Magistrates Court and found guilty of possession of a controlled substance. The judge fined them each 50 pounds and released them with a warning against a second offense. Escaping with a slap on the wrist, Bob and Aston "Family Man" Barrett left the courthouse.

The *Exodus* tour began in May, with the first show, in Paris, coming just a month after the album had been released. The tour got off to a good start and continued to go well; however, while in Paris, Bob injured his right foot during a soccer game. Upon inspection, Bob realized that he had lost the majority of his toenail and needed to see a doctor. The doctor removed a jagged piece of the nail, cleaned and bandaged the toe, and informed Bob that he needed to stay off his feet to allow the wound to heal properly. With the tour already scheduled and in progress, the rest that Bob's foot required was not forthcoming. He hoped that his foot would heal before the tour got to England, and, in the meantime, he played several concerts and traveled around Europe in pain.

The Paris show was held in a venue called the Pavillion de Paris in front of approximately 12,000 fans. The opening act was the Jamaican-born trombonist Rico Rodriguez, and the show was a big success.[16] The addition of Junior Marvin to the band made the Wailers' live show even more impressive, as he added a degree of rock guitarist bravado to the group. The I-Threes also began the tour with a greater stage presence by incorporating beautiful African dresses and choreography, developed by Judy Mowatt, to enhance their singing. The product was a Wailers show that was mesmerizing, both musically and visually.

From Paris, the Wailers traveled by bus to the next show in Brussels, and from there the band progressed to the Hague, Holland, Germany, and Scandinavia. Each stop was marked by an outstanding Wailers show filled with old hits and new material. A month into the tour, on May 1, the Wailers opened a week of concerts at London's Rainbow Theatre. By this point in the tour, the Wailers were in peak form and played as though controlled by a single person. However, after the final show of the week, Bob limped off stage to find his right boot filling with blood; the wound on his toe had reopened while he danced on stage.

After the European leg of the tour, Bob had a little break that he spent by traveling to Delaware and resting in the comfort of his mother's house. The American tour did not begin until the New York Palladium show in July, and Bob was badly in need of some recuperative time. The wound to his right big toe had refused to heal and while traveling around Europe had begun to fester. The injured foot was causing Bob such pain that it began to threaten the impending American tour, which was certain to be a big moneymaker. Pressure was mounting on Bob. The Wailers' tour of Europe had sent *Exodus* to number one in England and Germany, and it was felt that similar success could come in the United States from the tour.

Bob knew that he needed help, so he flew back to England and consulted with a foot specialist. The specialist examined Bob's injury and took some smears to look at under the microscope. The following day, the specialist informed Bob that he had detected cancerous cells and that Bob was facing amputation of his toe and part of his foot. Bob asked the doctor if there was any alternative and was told that if "a small part of the toe was amputated and the area cleaned of infection, that the cancer might be localized and possibly contained with normal therapy . . . [adding] that this alternative was a long shot, and recommended amputation as soon as possible."[17] Extremely displeased with the news, and suspecting that the proposed treatment was a setup by his business associates to ensure that he could go back on tour soon, Bob returned to the United States for a second opinion.

Together with his personal physician, Dr. Carl Frazier (known as PeeWee by the Wailers), Bob visited Dr. William Bacon, in Miami. Dr. Bacon had performed the surgery on Don Taylor after the shooting in 1976 and had saved his life. Bob trusted Dr. Bacon but was again told that part of his foot would have to be removed before the cancer spread. On July 20, a statement was released that announced the postponement of the American leg of the *Exodus* tour, citing Bob's soccer injury as the reason for the delay. On August 14, 1977, the *New York Times* printed the cancellation notice announcing that the American tour was postponed indefinitely. All tickets were refunded, and plans were made to reschedule the tour for fall of 1977. After the announcement, Bob was operated on at Cedars of Lebanon Hospital, in Miami. Part of Bob's toenail was removed and sections of cancerous flesh were removed from the area so that it could be cleaned.

The deadly melanoma had been removed, and Bob recovered from the surgery very quickly. He did so at a large suburban house that he had purchased on Vista Lane in Miami. It was large enough to accommodate his considerable entourage, his family, and his mother. Part of his recovery plan required him to maintain a regimen of medication, in addition to a change in diet that emphasized protein. The doctor had informed him that he needed to begin eating meat after several years of being a strict Italist. Bob realigned his life to reflect these changes, and within two months he had been given a clean bill of health. He was further relieved when *Exodus* was a big hit in the United States, even without the support of a tour.

As he healed, Bob worked at Criteria Studios, supervising the mixing and overdubbing of the remaining tracks from the London sessions. These London tracks were being prepared for release as the next Wailers' album. At this time, Bob and Don Taylor were also in the final stages of arranging a Wailers summer world tour that would begin in the United States, continue to Europe, and finish in Asia. Thanks to the worldwide popularity of the band, it had no difficulty booking shows anywhere that it wanted to perform. Even as he healed and made plans, Bob was composing new songs and reworking older ones. "Exodus" had been released as a single by Island, with "Waiting in Vain" on the B-side. Island was also about to release "Punky Reggae Party" as an English single. In Jamaica, Tuff Gong released "Punky Reggae Party" as a single coupled with another Marley/Perry collaboration called "Rastaman Live Up" as the B-side.

As Bob convalesced in Miami, his island home was reaching a dangerous boiling point. Kingston was wracked with violence, and there was a serious lack of leadership. The crime that had begun just before the 1976 election had continued unabated, aided by the illegal importation of guns. Also, the majority of the lower class had been left without direction by the political situation, and its members were saddled with a socialist regime that would neither provide for them nor protect them. This desperate situation led the Rastafarian sect the Twelve Tribes of Israel, of which Bob was a member, to become active in the Jamaican peace movement in January 1978.

Michael Manley had attempted to control the violence in Jamaica by ordering the national army into the streets to arrest known gunmen on sight. As a result of this action, two of Bob's old friends from his days in Trench Town were incarcerated. Bucky Marshall and Claudie "Jack" Massop were both hired guns working for opposing political parties. They were on opposite sides but were put in the same cell and began a friendly relationship because they had a shared friend in Bob. Massop had an idea of how to quell the violence in Jamaica, and he discussed it with his cellmate, Marshall. The two men, Massop, of the JLP and Marshall, of the PNP, would get their warring factions to agree to a ceasefire and begin negotiating an accord. As an example of their dedication to the idea, they would sponsor a Peace Concert and invite Bob Marley and the Wailers to headline the show. The irony of asking Bob to play at a concert that was arranged in part by the people who had been suspected of attempting to assassinate him was not lost on the two men, and they collectively agreed to ensure his safety.

The general idea behind the peace accord was that its institution would in turn cause the government to remove the army from the streets and end a great deal of the violence. Although getting the JLP and the PNP to agree to a ceasefire was a daunting task, convincing Bob Marley to return to the island seemed even more difficult. To assist in this task, the two men enlisted the help of the Twelve Tribes. They asked Vernon "Gad the Prophet" Carrington, the head of the Twelve Tribes, to act as the intermediary and to enlist Bob's aide, in addition to officially sponsoring the concert. Carrington agreed and sent members of the Tribe to Miami to urge Bob to play the concert. Understandably, Bob committed to appear only after he had a personal promise from Claudie Massop that he and his family would be safe. To this end, a meeting between Bob and Massop was scheduled in London for early February.

Bob and Massop met in London in February and discussed the Jamaican civil war and the role of the peace movement. During the meeting, Bob expressed continued concern for his safety, noting that the JLP could not guarantee him anything if it had not tried to have him killed 14 months earlier. At that point, Massop admitted that the attempt on Bob's life had been politically motivated and that elements of the JLP had been the offenders.

The PNP had heard of the meeting taking place in London and wanted to ensure that its interests were also being represented properly. Anthony Spaulding, the PNP's primary enforcer, ordered one of the party's henchmen to join the talks. Tony Welsh was another old friend of Bob's, as well as a PNP ghetto captain, and he was immediately dispatched to join the talks already in progress. Bob, Massop, and Welsh lived together for a week to work out the details of the ghetto ceasefire and the Peace Concert.

On February 23, the announcement was made in London that the Jamaican Peace Concert would take place on April 22. With the treaty and other arrangements in place, Bob returned to his house at 56 Hope Road in March. Immediately, the Wailers reformed, and rehearsals were begun in preparation for the upcoming world tour and the Peace Concert, which had been scheduled to kick it off. The Wailers' lineup was altered again by the return of two old members. Al Anderson was brought back into the band to augment Junior Marvin's guitar playing. Also, Earl "Wya" Lindo returned and was welcomed back into the ranks by everyone, including his replacement, Tyrone Downie. It might seem strange to have more than one lead guitarist in the ranks, but everyone fulfilled a specific role as ordered by Bob.

# Top Rankin', 1978–1979

The other tracks that had been recorded in the London sessions that yielded *Exodus* were released in January 1978 as the album *Kaya* (one of the many Rastafarian terms for ganja). The basic tenor of the album reflected Bob's contemplative mood in the wake of his shooting and the violence in his home country, expressed through mellow dance and love songs. The album cover was a grainy black-and-white picture of Bob smiling and exhibiting shoulder-length dreadlocks. The back jacket displayed a color drawing of a large spliff growing out of a marijuana plant, in keeping with the album title. Bob described the album to Ian McCann in February 1976 this way: "Kaya means herb. It's a password some of the brethren use in JA [Jamaica]. So 'Kaya' is really dealing with togetherness and humanity and peace, [because] the things of peace travel through the earth now. Yes, 'Rastaman Vibrations' and 'Exodus' were 'arder. This time we dealing with something softer."[1] Bob went on to exclaim that the relative hardness or softness of his songs was nobody's business but his own. The album overall could be seen as an intimate portrait of the lifestyle that Bob both espoused and loved.

*Kaya* included the songs "Easy Skankin'," "Kaya," "Is This Love," "Sun Is Shining," "Satisfy My Soul," "Misty Morning," "Crisis," "Running Away," and "Time Will Tell." The final three tracks were prophetic: "Crisis" described the situation that precipitated the need for the Peace Concert; Bob dealt with personal demons concerning his shooting in "Running Away"; and the final song, "Time Will Tell," was a Rasta *akete* hand-drumming hymn in which Bob discussed political power and Jamaica in general, concluding that "it looks like heaven but is actually hell." After the release of the new album, Bob traveled to New York to stay at the Essex House Hotel and answer his critics and the media.

Musicians on the *Kaya* album were Bob Marley on lead vocal, rhythm and acoustic guitar, and percussion; Aston "Family Man" Barrett on Fender bass and percussion; Carlton Barrett on drums and percussion; Tyrone Downie on keyboards and percussion; and Alvin "Seeco" Patterson on percussion. Julian (Junior) Marvin also supplied lead guitar parts, and the I-Three supported the instruments with backing vocals. Vin Gordon, Glen Da Costa, and David Madden supplied horn parts for the album. *Kaya* was released by Island Records and produced by Bob Marley and the Wailers.

*Kaya* kicked off with the track "Easy Skankin'." "Skankin'" was Jamaican slang for the type of dancing done to reggae music. Here Bob was singing a relatively relaxed tune about dancing to reggae music. The lyrics began with Bob saying, "excuse me while I light my spliff," which played right into the laid-back sentiment of the song and the overall spirit of the album. The song rides an up-tempo reggae groove with an active organ part and horn punches. The drumming was again in the rockers rhythm and propelled the song forward. The lyrics were a series of repeated statements without true verse and chorus alternations. Bob's message here was to relax, enjoy a spliff, and dance to reggae music. Throughout the song, the I-Threes repeat the Amharic word "wadada," which means "love."

"Kaya" was another relaxed song with relatively little autobiographical meaning. Without strict verse and chorus alternations, Bob repeated several series of words. The opening "wake up and turn me loose" drove into "got to have kaya now" and alluded to liberal ganja smoking (which as a Rastafarian sacrament was a ritualized part of Bob's daily life). In the middle of the song, Bob inserted the lyric "feelin' irie," which in Jamaican patois meant feeling "powerful, excellent, or cool." The sound of this song was in the rockers vein. Especially active parts were the backing vocals and the electric guitar. Not strictly autobiographical, the meaning here related to the 1970s Jamaican Rastafarian drug culture. The song was about smoking ganja, relaxing, and treating each other with respect.

"Is This Love" began with a short drum roll-off followed by the establishment of the chugging one-drop reggae groove. The song alternated verse and chorus statements, with the second and third verse being virtually the same. The first verse was a testament to Bob's desire to care for this particular love interest. Also in the first verse statement was an example of word painting. When Marley sang the lyric "with a roof right over our heads," the melody leaped up almost an octave to paint the roof image. This particular lyric was stated twice and set in the same manner both times.

Following the verse was the first chorus statement, in which the vocal presentation was dramatically altered. Marley sang the opening lyric in a syncopated triplet manner that created tension with the accompanying harmonies.

The triplet vocals were a repetition of the question "Is this love?" The rest of the chorus was presented in a less aggressive manner; however, there were some interesting harmonic turns. The chorus ended with an eight-measure bridge that was static harmonically. The general sentiment of this song was that Bob was doing whatever he had to in pursuit of this love interest. He was in a loving mood and wanted to share it.

"Sun Is Shining" had a markedly different musical feel from the rest of the album. Bob began singing after only one note on the guitar. The echo of the vocals and the organ-heavy accompaniment gave the song an otherworldly feeling. This ominous sound could easily be credited to Lee "Scratch" Perry's influence, as he was the original producer on the track. Bob began singing with an extended chorus statement that implored the listener to dance. It continued with an interesting day-by-day counting of passing time. Kwame Dawes hypothesized that Bob was listing the days as prisoners count their days in captivity.[2] Dawes's claim seemed to have validity as Bob went on to say that a new day was dawning (on Thursday), which could signal release from captivity. The middle of the song contained the lyric "lift up our heads and give Jah praises," which could reasonably be the direction that the prisoner of the chorus was driving in. Oddly, when the chorus returned, the events of the counted days were replaced with wordless scat singing, which shed no greater light on Bob's meaning but could allude to the prisoner's having already been released. Another possible meaning here can be gleaned through the knowledge that the song was originally written while Bob was working in Delaware. Certainly, he felt that his working conditions there resembled those of a prison, and he would have counted the days until he could return to Jamaica.

A heavy horn-line part and a complete change of sound and feeling ushered in track five, "Satisfy My Soul." The alternation of verse and chorus in this song was relatively straightforward, and the rockers rhythm was easy to identify. Here, Bob's message was also easy to identify; he wanted his "darling" to keep him company and "satisfy his soul." The opening verse started things off with Bob warning that he did not want his boat rocked and that he wanted things to be relaxed and easy. The chorus then reiterated the "satisfy my soul" lyric and ended with Bob expressing his delight in what his love interest had done to him. The rest of the song followed in kind and culminated in Bob's profession of happiness. The second and third verses were not separated by a chorus and had many of the same words. The song ended with another chorus statement fading out, reminding the listener that Bob's love interest did not just satisfy him physically but also satisfied his soul.

In a standard one-drop mid-tempo reggae rhythm, "She's Gone" expressed a sentiment contrary to that expressed in most of Bob's love songs. Usually Bob was connecting, or reconnecting, with a woman after seeking her for a time. In "She's Gone," his love interest has left him crying and will not be back. The song was written in a clear verse chorus form, with two iterations of each section. The first verse blamed the lover's absence on the pressure around Bob and the fact that this pressure began to feel like a jail. This encapsulated the sentiment of the entire song. The identity of the woman about whom this song was written was not clear. By this point in Bob's life, his relationship with Rita was more like the love between siblings than romance. In fact, during an interview in 1979, Bob was asked if he was married and he simply replied, "No."[3] It was common knowledge that Bob had had children with several other woman and that he had had relationships with still other women that did not yield children.

"Misty Morning" was track seven on the *Kaya* album. Another of the album's love songs, this track contained direct and pleading language about Bob's future. Cast in a verse and chorus exchange, the song expressed Bob's pain of love lost. The horn line provided an ascending melodic introduction that drove the song forward into the first chorus. The first verse found Bob describing how he gave to this love interest and received little in return. He then warned the listener not to seek love without anticipating loss by offering the metaphor "don't jump in the water if you can't swim." The chorus continued this foreboding, echoing the verse's statement that it was a sunless morning (hidden in the mist). The most powerful lyric was repeated many times at the end of the song; "I want you to straighten out my tomorrow" was Bob imploring this love interest to help brighten his sunless romantic future.

"Crisis" began the prophecies expressed in the last three songs on the album. Over a relatively slow one-drop groove, Bob lamented the continued problems in his life and on the island of Jamaica. He began the first verse with a continuation of the "sun" metaphor from "Misty Morning." The sun became a symbol of hope and optimism. Thus, when Bob sang, "they say the sun shines for all, but in some people's world, it never shine at all," he was extending the hopelessness that he had expressed previously. However, after the despair of the opening verse, Bob reversed the sentiment in the chorus. Here Bob sang that, regardless of the crisis, thanks and praises to Jah could lift him up from his unhappy situation. "Crisis" not only spoke for Bob's sadness in the wake of the assassination attempt but also reflected the larger weight of the deplorable postelection violence in Jamaica. Ever vigilant, Bob put his faith in Jah to provide relief from both scenarios.

"Running Away" continued Bob's reflection on his and his home country's strife. The consciousness of the opening chorus drove that point home, with Bob chanting, "you're unning away, but you can't run away from yourself." This finger pointing continued with the statement "you must have done something wrong." Bob was directly assailing those who wished to do him or Jamaica harm and making them accountable for their evil deeds. The dark mood of the song reflected Bob's confusion and sadness in the wake of the attack on his life, his own personal "crisis." By extension, he was also commenting on the situation in Jamaica, which was still gripped by a period of postelection gun-fueled violence. While Bob did commiserate with those whom he attacked in the lyric "every man thinketh his burden is the heaviest," he quickly removed himself from the comparison. The final chorus statement attested to this when Bob declared that he was not running away, even though he had to protect his life. After a biblical reference that warned against living in a house of confusion, Bob ended the song in direct defiance of his assailants. "Running Away" ended with Bob declaring that he had made the decision to leave Jamaica and that ultimately he would decide to return.

"Time Will Tell" marked a decisive and prophetic end to the final three songs and the album overall. The song was cast as a Nyabinghi hand-drumming piece with guitar overdubs. As Bob spread his perspective out on the future, he gained strength from his faith. The lyric "Jah would never give the power to the baldhead [white, non-dread-wearing minions of Babylon]," illustrated Bob wresting control over his life from the powers that sought to control or kill him. The song ended with Bob warning that Jamaicans should recognize that they were not living in heaven and that the island had, in fact, become a hell on earth for them.

Bob and the Wailers returned to Jamaica from London and convened at the house on Hope Road. The Peace Concert was held at Kingston's National Stadium on Saturday, April 22, 1978. Preparations had been intense, and the air of tension was magnified by the presence of policemen in the yard at Hope Road wearing bulletproof vests and carrying shotguns. The night of the sold-out concert, the front rows had been reserved for Prime Minister Manley, the opposition leader Edward Seaga, other important political figures, and popular music stars such as Mick Jagger of the Rolling Stones. Also on conspicuous display were hundreds of armed guards making sure that the concert attendees did not turn the show into a riot. The show opened with sets by many of Jamaica's new reggae elite, including Dennis Brown, Culture, the Meditations, Dillinger, LeRoy Smart, Trinity, the Mighty Diamonds, Althea and Donna, Junior Tucker, and Bongo Herman, all backed by Lloyd Parks and the We the People band.[4]

After intermission, the second half of the show began and exhibited Jamaica's major talents, including Inner Circle, Big Youth, and Hugh Beresford Hammond. They were followed by Peter Tosh and the Word Sound & Power band and the *akete* drumming group Ras Michael and the Sons of Negus. Near midnight, Bob Marley and the Wailers took the stage, and the audience erupted in cheers for their ghetto hero. The Wailers' set included the songs "Trench Town Rock," "Natural Mystic," "War," and the showstopper "One Love." The song literally stopped the show because, during its performance, Bob called Michael Manley and Edward Seaga on stage with him. With the leaders of the two opposing parties on stage, Bob grabbed their right hands and held them aloft as a symbol of Jamaican unity. After the historic moment had passed, the Wailers finished their set with the Rastafarian faith affirmation "Jah Live."

The Wailers then embarked on the world tour that was called "Kaya 78." The tour had been scheduled to kick off in Florida on May 4, but Junior Marvin encountered some health problems that resulted in more show cancellations. With some dates rescheduled, the tour began on May 19, in Ohio. In the interim, Bob traveled to London to make promotional videos for the new *Kaya* singles "Is This Love" and "Satisfy My Soul." Upon returning to Florida, Bob recorded two versions of a song by the Jamaican producer King Sporty. The song was called "Buffalo Soldier" because it linked the struggling Rastafarians with the black soldiers in the United States cavalry during the Indian wars.

The Kaya World Tour officially started with the May 19, 1978, show at the Music Hall in Cleveland. The newest incarnation of the Wailers was a large, but very tight, group that could perform long improvisations in live performance. They also carried with them state-of-the-art equipment that allowed for a wonderful live mix in performance. That month they played soldout shows in Cleveland, Columbus, Madison, Chicago, Milwaukee, and Minneapolis. The June shows were in Pittsburgh, Rochester, Detroit, Philadelphia, Boston, Buffalo, Washington, Montreal, and Toronto. While in New York, on June 15, Bob received the Third World Peace Medal from an African delegation to the United Nations led by Senegal's Mohammadu Johnny Seka. The tribute recognized Bob's efforts on behalf of disenfranchised blacks around the world and was presented to him by their representative. Bob was visibly moved by the experience.

The Kaya 78 tour continued, and, after a concert in Lenox, Massachusetts, the Wailers left for London. On the European leg of the tour, the group played soldout concerts in Paris, Stockholm, Copenhagen, Oslo, Rotterdam, Amsterdam, and Brussels, on the island Ibiza, and at an outdoor music festival in Staffordshire, England. Finished with the western European leg of the tour, the Wailers flew to Vancouver and prepared for a 10-day tour of the American West Coast. They played Seattle and Portland. As a testament to the band's increasing international audience, as Bob was preparing to go on stage at the Greek Theater in Berkeley, California, Ron Wood (one of the guitarists for the Rolling Stones) came backstage and introduced himself. The next night, the Wailers played the Starlite Amphitheater in Burbank, a show that was attended by Peter Tosh and Mick Jagger. At the height of the show, Peter marched on stage, and together he and Bob sang "Get Up, Stand Up" which they had cowritten years earlier.

The West Coast tour ended with a show in Santa Barbara, on July 23. It was the anniversary of Haile Selassie's birthday, and Bob Marley and the Wailers gave a scorching performance. The following night, the Wailers attended a party in their honor at the Los Angeles disco the Daisy, where there were many black American luminaries in attendance. Next, the Wailers returned to the southeast coast of the United States to make up the shows that had been canceled at the beginning of the tour. Meanwhile, Chris Blackwell was in

London sifting through the tapes from the London, Paris, Copenhagen, and Amsterdam shows in preparation for making another live album.

## Babylon by Bus

Released in late 1978, the live album *Babylon by Bus* contains 13 tracks from the London, Paris, Copenhagen, and Amsterdam shows of the 78 tour. The tracks that were combined for this release illustrated the Wailers at another peak of live performance power. The band was large, with two keyboard players and two lead guitarists. However, the meticulous rehearsing that Bob demanded resulted in an extremely tight live experience. Also, the Wailers rhythm section tended to push the tempo of each song slightly during live performances, which added a subtle air of urgency. An example of this was the performance of "Exodus," which at its increased tempo really was the "movement of Jah people."

The album began with Bob warming up the crowd by evoking the name of Emperor Haile Selassie I. The band then launched into "Rastaman Vibration." The other songs collected on the album were "Punky Reggae Party," "Exodus," "Stir It Up," "Rat Race," "Concrete Jungle," "Kinky Reggae," "Lively Up Yourself," "Reel Music," "War/No More Trouble," "Is This Love," "Heathen," and "Jamming." Although the songs were culled from four different live shows, they presented the Wailers at scorching potency. The quality and power of this release far overshadowed those of the 1975 *Live!* album, and it has been described by many as "one of the most influential live albums ever."

Back in Jamaica, the Wailers prepared for the next part of the tour, through Australia, New Zealand, and Japan. During the hiatus, Bob wanted to return to the studio, since the Wailers had not been in the studio for nearly two years and he had a large quantity of new material that he wanted to record while the group was in top form from being on the road. The new Tuff Gong Studio at 56 Hope Road was not quite ready for use, so Bob recorded five new songs on a four-track recorder. The new songs were "Jungle Fever," "Give Thanks and Praises," "I Know a Place (Where We Can Carry On)," "Who Colt the Game," and "Burn Down Babylon."

The Wailers then embarked on a Japanese tour that was successful, even though this was a part of the world in which a reggae band had never played. Next, the Wailers traveled to New Zealand, where Bob was greeted by a dozen female Maoris, whom he greatly enjoyed meeting.[5] The Wailers' Kaya 78 tour finally ended after covering the majority of the world. The band was exhausted, and Bob planned on resting in Miami for a month before returning to Jamaica. He had several albums worth of new material in his head and was eager to put them on tape.

Another thing that was on his mind constantly was planning a trip to Ethiopia. He had been pursuing this goal since 1976, but the war between

Ethiopia and Somalia over Eritrea had caused visa problems. In late 1978, Bob finally procured a visa and, with his old friend Alan "Skill" Cole, planned a trip to Africa. Cole had surfaced in Addis Ababa after the shooting at 56 Hope Road, where he had been coaching the Ethiopian airline soccer team. Bob flew to London, then to Nairobi, and finally to Ethiopia, where he visited historic sites connected with the life of Haile Selassie. He lived on a religious communal farm called *Shashamani,* attended a rally given by the Ethiopian Marxist government in support of the liberation movement in Rhodesia, and frequented local nightclubs to witness the popular music scene. At the rally, Bob learned that many Africans had been referring to Rhodesia by its African name, Zimbabwe. His experiences at the rally caused him to start working on a new song titled "Zimbabwe" while he was still in Africa.[6] Even while Bob was in Rhodesia, the country's fight for independence from apartheid rule continued, and this struggle served to fuel Bob's creativity.

## SURVIVAL

In Bob's absence, Tuff Gong Limited and the house at 56 Hope Road were run by his lawyer. Diane Jobson. She was in charge of the only multimillion-dollar record company in the third world and was overseeing the studio prep-arations and readying for Bob's return. Bob returned to Jamaica ready to go into the studio and begin the next chapter in the Wailers anthology. He had two years of new material to record and was no longer interested in recycling older Wailers songs for the new sessions. The time that Bob had spent in Africa had revitalized his faith in black unity and had given him a militant edge. The first single, called "Ambush (in the Night)," was produced in this new climate and released by Tuff Gong in early 1979. The song dealt with the assassination attempt on Bob and discussed the consequences of resisting a corrupt political system. That a song about the attempt on his life surfaced three years after the episode demonstrated that Bob was still highly disturbed and saddened by the events of late 1976.

It was clear that the Peace Concert had failed, as the truce had been broken and the violence in west Kingston was as bad as it had ever been. In February 1979, Claudie Massop was killed by the police (his autopsy revealed 42 bullets in his body) at a roadblock after rumors spread that he had sto-len the money made at the Peace Concert. In addition, Bob's old friend Lee "Scratch" Perry had suffered a breakdown and was institutionalized in Kingston's Belleview Hospital. All of these factors weighed heavily on Bob during the recording sessions of 1979. He was trying to finish the recordings for the new album in time for the projected U.S. tour in the fall. His life did have a degree of balance, though; he both worked and played hard during this period. He was constantly involved in games of soccer (regardless of the doctor's protests), and at this time he fathered his tenth child, this time with

Yvette Morris. His child with Morris was another daughter, who was named Makeba Janesta.

While recording and mixing the tracks for the new album, Chris Black-well brought a new producer in to assist in giving the record international appeal; his name was Alex Sadkin. With Sadkin's assistance, the new record was released in the summer of 1979, under the title *Survival* (the working title had been *Black Survival*). With the album completed, the Wailers again focused their energy on live performance. They played Reggae Sunsplash II, a huge Jamaican music festival held at Jarrett Park in Montego Bay in early July.[7] The Wailers would have headlined the first Sunsplash Concert, but they were already off the island in support of *Kaya*. Sunsplash II was the first show that the Wailers had played in Jamaica since the Peace Concert, and Bob was joined on stage by his sons Ziggy and Stevie, who danced around their father as he sang.

After the Sunsplash concert, Bob rehearsed the band for a benefit concert that it was scheduled to play in July, at Harvard Stadium, in Boston. The concert was to benefit a group called Amandla, which supported African lib-eration and freedom fighters.[8] Bob had been approached by Chester English, one of the group's representatives, and he had agreed to play for the cause. Also scheduled were the comedian Dick Gregory, the American R&B singer Patti LaBelle, the Latin jazz artist Eddie Palmieri, and the Nigerian drum-mer Babatunde Olatunji.[9] The 25 members of the Wailers' touring unit left Jamaica for the show in Boston on July 19, 1979. The entourage included musicians, technicians, a cook, and some family members. The show was called the "Festival of Unity," and Bob was excited to play a benefit for one of his favorite causes. The Wailers performed a superb reggae set before the 25,000 people who filled Harvard University's football stadium.

The show started with "Exodus," which featured Olatunji sitting in with the band on bongo drums. It ended with an encore that included the first public performances of the songs "Zimbabwe" and "Wake Up and Live." This last song contained an element that Bob rarely, if ever, did live on stage. Partway through the song, Bob began to scat a speech to the audience that he held to the melody and rhythm of the song. He spoke about unity, broth-erhood, Rastafarianism, and the plight of Africans in the mother country and abroad. The Wailers set ended to deafening applause, and the entire show was a success, collecting almost a quarter of a million dollars on behalf of African liberation. Interestingly, according to Steven Davis, 20,000 people left the show after the Wailers' set in midafternoon, apparently uninterested in the other bands that had yet to perform.[10]

Shortly after the Amandla concert, Bob Marley and the Wailers' ninth Island record was released. The return to militant lyrics was welcomed by many Wailers fans, but the new breed of militancy now involved the whole African diaspora (Pan-Africanism), not just Jamaica. This change was visually apparent in the cover album of *Survival,* which was a montage of flags from all the African nations on a black background, with a banner displaying the album title over a depiction of African slaves packed into the hold of a slave ship. The back of the album was stark in comparison; the song titles and a continuation of the slave banner from the cover were set on a black background.

The tracks contained on the new album discussed a mixture of topics, including rebellion, African liberation, Rastafarianism, assassination, and global suffering. The record comprised 10 new songs, including "So Much Trouble in the World," "Zimbabwe," "Top Rankin'," Babylon System," "Survival," "Africa Unite," "One-Drop," "Ride Natty Ride," "Ambush in the Night," and "Wake Up and Live." Although the album was arguably one of Bob's most militant, the messages were frequently couched in biblical language, if not direct quotations. The band lineup for the sessions that produced the album included the standard Wailers core (Bob, the Barrett Brothers, the I-Threes, Downie, Lindo, Marvin, Anderson, and Patterson), with the now-familiar addition of the Zap Pow horns (Madden, Da Costa, and Gordon). Also appearing on selected tracks were Anthony "Santa" Davis on percussion, Headley "Deadly Headley" Bennett on saxophone, Val Douglas on bass, and Mikey "Boo" Richards on drums. The album was produced by Bob, the Wailers, and Alex Sadkin.

Bob considered the *Survival* album the first third of a trilogy of releases that also included *Uprising* and *Confrontation*. The programmatic plan for the three albums was meant to be a repatriation plan for the African diaspora. The content of the three albums laid the groundwork for the ultimate confrontation between the followers of Rastafari and Babylon. Although Bob did not live to see the release of the *Confrontation* album, he still guided its creation and naming.

"So Much Trouble in the World" was the first track on the album, which was itself the first to be recorded at Marley's Tuff Gong studio. The content of the *Survival* album consisted completely of politically oriented songs, with no love songs that might dilute the serious nature of the message. Musically, "So Much Trouble in the World" was written in a style like that of Marley's early material. It was characterized by "the influence of James Brown particularly the ninth chords played [on guitar] by Al Anderson."[11] Typically, the song began with a four-measure introduction during which the drum and the rhythm guitar established the tempo while the keyboard (synthesizer) established the ominous tone of the album with its high and winding glissandos.

Formally, this song follows the plan of many popular songs. It unfolded in an alternation of chorus and verse statements, with the verses carrying the principal message. The message delivered in the three verse statements amplified the main lyric of the chorus sung by Bob, "so much trouble in the world." In the verses, Bob chastised those on "ego trips" and those whose heads were concerned with spaceships instead of the world situation as it continued to get worse. The second verse used one of Bob's favorite biblical images, the "corner stone." Bob commanded to not "leave another corner stone standing there behind," evoking Psalm 118 and the message that blessed are those who come in the name of the Lord. Fatalism crept into the third verse, in which Bob sang about "sitting on a time bomb." This idea of retribution and "what goes around" made Bob's militant point.

Another aspect of the presentation of the lyrics that added to the mood of the song was the tension created by Bob's performing the lyrics off the beat. In the middle of the chorus, Bob's syncopated singing style persisted for eight measures. This type of performance created an air of tension that intensified the dire message of the lyrics. The effect of the syncopated presentation was compounded by its delivery over a ninth chord played by Al Anderson on the guitar.

"Zimbabwe" began with another ominous opening, which led directly into the verse, in which Bob made the heady statement that "every man gotta right to decide his own destiny." The rest of the first verse played on the word "arm," conveying a message of both unity and military conflict. The chorus rhymed "right" and "fight" and expressed the position that Bob's African brothers had a right to overturn their oppressors. The second half of the verse allied Rastas and Zimbabwe with the lyric "natty dread it in Zimbabwe." This alliance was to lead to African liberation. Verse two focused on unity without internal struggle. Here Bob pushed the point that only a unified black populace could overcome Babylonian oppression. Verse three echoed that sentiment, warning against allowing division to make Africans easy to rule. While this material was not strictly autobiographical, Bob was certainly expressing his own thoughts on the African condition and the way things could be changed.

The third track on *Survival* was "Top Rankin'," which in Jamaican patois meant the highest and most respected person. The song was Bob's account-ing of how upper-class Jamaican whites treated lower-class blacks. In his own way, Bob used patois to deliver a twofold message through the song. The opening horn-line material led into the first verse, in which Bob reasserted his warning about oppression through division. His position gained gravity with the verse concluding ". . . want us to do is keep on killing one another." The first chorus statement delivered Bob's double message. When he asked "top rankin', are you skanking," he could have been asking whether the most powerful whites were dancing to reggae music (skankin') or, more likely, were they acting in cunning and dishonest ways and with ulterior motives, another meaning of the patois term "skankin'." This dual meaning delivered through patois became a favorite means by which Bob delivered his lyrical messages.

The middle of "Top Rankin'" did not contain the traditional instrumental solo that was common in verse and chorus songs. Instead, Bob inserted a new stanza of words that was part of neither the chorus nor the verse. In it, Bob described the beauty of brotherly and sisterly love, which came as a stark contrast to the division described in the surrounding verses.

"Babylon System" was an overt message of defiance delivered by Bob in opposition to the Babylonian captures. The opening verse lyric, "we refuse to be what you want us to be," immediately illustrated the song's theme. Bob went on to evoke a biblical context in the chorus, in which he described "trodding on the winepress." Thus, drawing on Job, chapter 24, Bob echoed the biblical sentiment that wicked people and those who murdered and mistreated the poor often went unpunished. The second verse saw him use one of Peter Tosh's favorite comparisons, describing the Babylon system as a vampire that sucked the blood of the poor. The song ended with Bob lamenting that "from the very day that we left the . . . fatherland, we've been trampled on," thus reinforcing his call for rebellion and repatriation.

The album's title track was an expert biblical lesson about worshipping false gods. The choruses of the song were short and repeated the claim that Rastas were the black survivors of 400 years of slavery and oppression in Jamaica. However, the verses compared episodes in the Bible and what Rastas had survived and how. The first verse cast the Rastas as long suffering, and the second compared their situation to that of Daniel, cast into the lion's den for worshiping the Lord in defiance of a decree issued by the king, Darius, as told in the Old Testament in Daniel, chapter 6. Just as Daniel's faith saved him, so has the faith of the Rastas saved them.

The third verse contained additional biblical associations, this time with the lyrics about Shadrach, Meshack, and Abednego. Daniel 3 recounts that these three were thrown into a fiery furnace by Nebuchadnezzar for their failure to worship his false god's golden image. However, in the furnace, a fourth figure, the Son of God, was seen; this figure keeps them from harm. This second Story of Daniel reference again allied the followers of Rastafari with the true-faith survivors of the Old Testament.

The first five songs of *Survival* together created a larger picture. In "So Much Trouble," Bob was identifying the problem. In "Zimbabwe," he gave a locale and a focus to the struggle. "Top Rankin'" identified how the righteous were fooled, and "Babylon System" completed the story by naming who was responsible for the suffering. "Survival" ended the story by illustrating that, through divine providence, upright and faithful people could persevere and overcome.

Once the righteous overcome their Babylonian captures, the next step is unity among all Africans. Bob sang of this in "Africa Unite," which began with a call to action: "we're moving right out of Babylon and going to our father's land." A relatively short and unassuming song, it delivered the message in two short verses and three chorus repetitions: Africa must unite to pave the way for successful repatriation and the successful coexistence of all black people. The song echoed the meaning of Psalm 133: that it was good and pleasant for brethren to unite. Bob extended to the "unification of all Africans (and all Rastaman)."

The sentiment of the second half of the *Survival* album was almost as dire as that of the first side. However, "One-Drop" was a lighthearted description of the now-characteristic Wailers drumming style. In fact, it extended beyond what Carlie was playing to include the actions of Aston and the guitarist. The one-drop reggae style ran counter to both standard Western music accents and the rock and roll back beat rhythm. In Western music, the accents in a four-beat measure were on the first and third beat. In rock and roll, the "back beat" was applied, and the accents shifted to beats two and four. One-drop rhythm was achieved when the first beat of a four-beat measure was left unaccented, the bass entered on the second beat, the bass drum (and a rim click) was played on the third beat, and the guitar provided off-beat chocked chords.

The song did not just illustrate how the one-drop rhythm worked; it was also a reiteration of the sentiment expressed on the first side of the album. When Bob sang, "I know Jah never let us down," he encapsulated the persistence and rebellious spirit of the Rastas. He amplified this sentiment with the call to "give us the teaching of His Majesty" because Rastas had no use for "devil philosophy." This song was at once catchy and compelling.

"Ride Natty Ride" was Bob's testament to the struggle of the Rastaman. The song praised not just the struggle but also the faithful who were persisting despite the struggle. The song was a verse-and-chorus ode to the perseverance of the faithful. The opening verse described overcoming this struggle as the job of "dready" (the Rastas). The second verse again evoked one of Bob's favorite biblical images with the lyric "the stone that he builder refuse shall be the head corner stone." With this messianic reference, Bob was again promising salvation to the suffering.

"Ambush in the Night" was another of Bob's damnations of his would-be assassins. In two verse and chorus alternations, Bob compared his own situation with that of all the followers of Rastafari. Verse one described how the Babylonian captors continue to keep the faithful weak through bribery, violence, hunger, and lack of education. Verse two repeated most of verse one with an alteration at the end of the stanza. The change to the lyrics allowed Bob to end the second verse with the more uplifting message of survival. The sound of the song was trademark Wailers. The one-drop groove was overlaid with Bob's lyrics and periodic distorted guitar lines, horn-line punctuations, and harmonica overdubs.

The final track on *Survival* was the call to action titled "Wake Up and Live." Bob put a fine point on the end of the album with this incendiary call for all black people to "wake up and live" and "rise you mighty people." The core of the song was the meaning of the chorus material, but Bob also injected biblical gravity into the verses. For example, verse two evoked Psalm 139 with mentions of "sand on the seashore" and "numbers." The message of the Psalm that Bob was superimposing on this song was that the Lord (Jah) knew all of one's thoughts and deeds and that there was no place that for one to hide. Just as the Lord knew the bad that people did, he also numbered the good and rewarded the righteous.

The composition of all of the songs on *Survival* was credited to Bob. However, "Wake Up and Live" was cowritten by Anthony "Santa" Davis. The mighty message and the call to action of this album paved the way for the second and third installments of the trilogy. *Uprising* came next, and the fulfillment of Bob's vision came in *Confrontation*.

After the release of *Survival,* the song "Zimbabwe" became an African nationalist anthem. Several musicians on the African continent covered it, and it sold well around the country. Bob had been adopted several years earlier by the guerrilla fighters of Zimbabwe's Patriotic Front, and the group was uplifted and fortified by the song. It codified the reasons why many of the soldiers were fighting the war at all and united them in a solidarity that would eventually lead to victory. With the release of the new album, Bob Marley was not just gaining notoriety around the world; he was identifying himself with black people worldwide.

The tour in support of *Survival* began in North America in October 1979, when the Wailers played at Harlem's Apollo Theater. The group played seven shows in four days at the Apollo, despite the fact that Bob had contracted a bad cold upon arriving in the cold weather of New York. They were playing an updated Wailers set that included material from the new album and ended with the encores "Get Up, Stand Up," "War," and "Exodus." Bob had orchestrated this stand of shows in Harlem as a means of crossing over to the long-distant black American audience. The gambit worked, and Bob quickly became the topic of much among American black music listeners.

After the Apollo shows, the seven-week North America tour began in earnest. At the show in Philadelphia, in front of the Black Musicians Association, Stevie Wonder joined the Wailers on stage, which attested to the increasing success of the Wailers' crossover attempts. The American tour was exhausting: 47 shows in 49 days, and Bob's cold stayed with him throughout. By mid-November, the group was on the West Coast for a show in Vancouver; it then returned to the United States. Throughout the tour, even in bad health, Bob was working on more new lyrics and experimenting with new chords to use on the next Wailers album.

The band spent the rest of November working in the Los Angeles area. It played a benefit show for the Sugar Ray Robinson Foundation at the Roxy Theatre on the Sunset Strip. In preparation for the show, the Wailers rehearsed for three hours, but Bob did not sing many of the lyrics of the songs being worked out. Instead, he dubbed certain phrases into the songs that the band was playing. They rehearsed all of the songs from *Survival* and Bob's newest creation, "Redemption Song," although they did not play it that night.

As he spent time on the West Coast, Bob's health gradually improved. The band was living in a hotel in West Hollywood, while Bob stayed in a rental house off the Sunset Strip, on Alta Vista. As part of the promotional aspect of the tour, Bob signed albums at the Tower Records in Hollywood, but he increasingly deflected interviewers to other members of the band or entourage. He was regaining his strength and needed time to recuperate without the constant disturbance of the media. Despite his tendency to avoid the media, Bob was one of the few popular-music stars of the time to enjoy a mutually beneficial relationship with reporters throughout the course of his mature career.

Once the Wailers' commitments in California were filled, the group traveled to Trinidad to play a concert. A large crowd assembled outside the sol-dout venue, and thousands of fans without tickets were driven away by tear gas fired by the police. The marathon *Survival* tour ended with a concert in Nassau, which was a benefit for the United Nations International Year of the Child. That night, Bob donated his performance and the royalties from the song "Children Playing in the Streets," which he had written for his own children four years earlier, to the cause.

Bob and his management spent the rest of 1979 planning the Wailers' schedule for the new year. The band had already planned a short visit to Africa early in the year, then a return to London to record the tenth album on Island Records, to be called *Uprising*. It would then launch another extensive tour that would keep Bob away from Jamaica during the next general election. The tour was to include every European nation, the United States, and Latin America and would culminate with the first substantial reggae tour of Africa, which would last through the beginning of 1981. This was a huge undertaking, and Bob changed the name of his company from Tuff Gong Limited to Tuff Gong International to reflect his now global endeavors and mindset.

# Blackman Redemption, 1980–1983

### UPRISING

The Wailers left Kingston on January 1, 1980, traveling first to London and then on to Gabon, in West Africa. They had been scheduled to play for President El Hadj Omar Bongo Ondimba's birthday, and the band was extremely excited about its first show in Africa.[1] However, the African trip proved to be both joyous and disappointing to Bob and the Wailers. Upon their arrival, they learned that they, and their opening act, the soul singer Betty Wright (also managed by Don Taylor), were not to perform for the public at all. Instead, they had been scheduled to play two shows, in a small tennis area, that would be attended by 2,000 of the Gabonese elite. Bob was disturbed by this but gratified when many young Gabonese citizens visited him to talk about Rastafarianism at the beachfront hotel where the group lived for two weeks.

The most disastrous part of the African trip took place when it was time to be paid after the second show. Bob had initially told Don Taylor that he would play the show for free and pay the travel costs out of his own pocket. Taylor responded that it would cost approximately $40,000 to make the trip and that the oil-rich Bongo family would gladly pay the Wailers' expenses. Bob instructed Taylor to take care of the negotiations, assuming that the Bongo family would be paying only the $40,000.

After the second show, there was some dispute about the fee that was to be paid, and it quickly became clear that there was a misunderstanding between Taylor and an employee of the Bongo family named Bobbitt. "Before the Wailers left Gabon, Bobbitt (Bobette) heard he was being blamed for an internal dispute among the Wailers and went directly to Bob, asking if there was some problem with the sixty-thousand-dollar fee that had been paid to Don Taylor."[2] Bobbitt also took the story to President Bongo, who delayed the Wailers' departure in order to meet with them and resolve the matter. Bob immediately realized that Taylor had planned to net $20,000 for himself from the shows, in addition to embarrassing Bob in front of an African ruler whom he respected. The Wailers returned to their hotel, and Bob and Don Taylor had a three-hour fight that was witnessed by the whole entourage. Interestingly, in his book *Marley and Me*, Don Taylor blamed the whole situation on Bobbitt, calling him unreliable and a "typical New York hustler."[3]

The events that transpired during the altercation between Bob and Don Taylor that night in Gabon were clouded in allegations and rumor. What was known was that Taylor spent much of the meeting confessing to Bob about his mishandling of Bob's money. For several years, at the height of the Wailers' popularity, Taylor was receiving $15,000 advances on many of Bob's shows. However, he would give Bob and the band only $5,000 of the advance and keep the remainder.

Another aspect of Taylor's double-dealing came in the transfer of money. Bob would give Taylor money, as much as $50,000 at a time, which he was supposed to give to Aston "Family Man" Barrett back in Jamaica. Taylor allegedly took this money and exchanged it at inflated rates on the currency black market, often receiving three times its value. He would then give Barrett only the legal rate of exchange and keep the illegally gained extra money. Once Bob coerced this information out of Taylor, allegedly by beating it out of him, he informed Taylor that he expected to be reimbursed for the stolen money. Taylor reportedly responded that he had lost all of the stolen money gambling and had no money to pay back the debt. On January 14, 1980, Bob Marley fired Don Taylor, and the Wailers left Gabon.

They returned to Jamaica and set about the business of recording material for the new album. In these sessions, the Wailers produced enough material for two full-length albums. The new record, titled *Uprising*, was released in May 1980 and displayed a strong Africanism instead of the heavier rock and horn sounds of the previous release. On *Uprising*, Junior Marvin and Tyrone Downie sang male harmony behind Bob's lead vocals. Also, Bob drew even more heavily on biblical quotations and paraphrases, taking his greatest inspiration from the Psalms. "Redemption Song," the last track on the album, was completely different from anything that Bob had previously recorded. Accompanying himself on acoustic guitar in true singer-songwriter style, Bob presented an autobiographical account of his life, told through the lens of the biblical story of Joseph. Bob said of the song, "it feel nice. (It was the first one we've done like that) for a long time. We used to do things like that one time, things I call lyrical sprinkle, just guitar, drums and singing, some kind of folk song spiritual. 'Redemption Song' strong. It's a real situation natural to I and I [referring to Bob and his God]."[4] About music, Bob said, "music is the biggest gun, because it save. It nuh kill, right?"[5] The album dealt with Bob's personal life more than any other previous release had, and the last track was his most poignant and intimate. Although he was not aware of it (some speculate that he was), "Redemption Song" was the final track on the last Bob Marley and the Wailers album that would be released during his lifetime.

The musicians who appeared on *Uprising* were Bob, the Barrett Brothers, and the I-Threes in their traditional roles. To this was added the following: Tyrone Downie on keyboard, percussion, and backing vocals; Alvin "Seeco" Patterson on percussion (hand drums); Junior Marvin on lead guitar and backing vocals; Earl "Wya" Lindo on keyboards; and Al Anderson on lead guitar. All tracks were recorded and mixed at Tuff Gong Studios in Kingston, Jamaica. Bob and the Wailers were credited as the producers for the release, and Blackwell was listed as executive producer. All songs on the album were credited as being written solely by Bob.

The album began with the track "Coming in from the Cold." This song was constructed in a series of repeating sections that do not really function in standard verse/chorus form. The tune began with a guitar and keyboard

Bob on stage in 1980. Courtesy of Photofest.

introduction that led into a moderately fast reggae groove in which the drums, bass, and guitar were more active than in the standard one-drop groove. Also, the keyboard and lead guitar lines occupied more musical space than on previously released tracks.

The general message of the lyrics of the song was that the sufferers were finally escaping from their negative circumstances. For Bob, the lyrics suggested that he was coming into his own to the fullest extent. The second stanza continued that message with the statement "when one door is closed . . . another (many more) is opened." Although Bob's relationship with Don Taylor had ended, he was embarking on a phase of his career in which he would have even greater control. Issues of morality were also addressed in the material of the third stanza, thus illustrating that this concern must have continued to weigh on Bob. It was common knowledge that Bob was not keeping up with his medical checkups as prescribed after his initial foot surgery. At issue was the vulnerability that Bob now felt. He addressed this feeling in the lyric "don't you let them kill your brotherman," a lyric that was repeated throughout the song.

"Real Situation" attested to Bob's banishment of all illusions from his personal life and his worldview. Over a brisk and steady drum beat, Bob compelled the listener to "check out the real situation" and concluded that the situation was so far gone that "it seemed like total destruction [was] the only solution." This apocalyptic message was also delivered in a song form that simply stated two large sections of words twice, with the repetition modified slightly to end the song.

Track three on the album, "Bad Card," was Bob's message of condemnation to Don Taylor. The song began and ended with lyrics describing "the way you draw bad card." This described Bob's feeling that Taylor had worked him too long. Eventually, Taylor had to show his cards (his true self) and in so doing identified himself as a con man holding too many aces. The cheating described in the song was a metaphor for the repeated skimming of money Taylor allegedly perpetrated over several years. Bob made his point more specifically with the verse words "propaganda spreading" and "bring another life to shame." Here Bob described Taylor's smoke screen, referring back to the problems with the Africa concert, which had threatened to bring down Bob's good name.

"We and Dem (Them)" was another of Bob's finger pointing odes. He declared in the song's opening that there was no way things could be worked out between the oppressed and the oppressor. The first verse quoted the Bible with the line "someone will have to pay for the innocent blood." The evocation of language from Psalm 106 told of the punishment of those who worshipped false gods. Bob knew that there would not be a meeting in the middle between the faithful and the followers of Babylon. In this song he continued his alliance with Rastafari and drove the wedge deeper between himself and the wicked in "high society."

The Wailers provided an active instrumental accompaniment to Bob's words on "Work." The drumming was more in the rockers style, with active accents; the guitar provided fills instead of off-beat chocked chords, and the bass repeated an ascending walking pattern. Through the alternation of two chorus and verse statements, Bob called Jah's people to work and then counted them into the verses. Both the first and the second verses contained largely the same words, which constitute a reverse counting song from five down to two. "Work" described Bob's hardworking attitude in the delivery of Jah's words. Bob enlisted his male backing singers for the reverse counting echoes, which made the song sound like a real work song. While the work was hard, Bob maintained that "Jah people can make it work."

The second half of *Uprising* began with "Zion Train." Introduced by an extended distorted guitar riff, the song was Bob's call for the righteous to expect passage to Zion. In the chorus material of the song, Bob was herald-ing the arrival of the train that will take the faithful to Zion. The verses were Bob's directions for who will ride. He included the man who could save his brother's soul, those who chose wisdom over wealth, and those with self-control. He also included the long-suffering with the lyric "two thousand years of history could not be wiped away so easily."

"Pimper's Paradise" was a short verse/chorus song about one of Bob's love interests. Some, like Kwame Dawes, speculate that it could have been about Bob's failing relationship with Cindy Breakspeare. However, this can-not be substantiated, and Dawes does note that Bob romanced several mod-els at the peak of his career. The song unfolded with the description of a girl who has cultivated a drug habit, who models for a living and was part of the jet set, and whose ego is causing her undoing. The chorus referred to this woman as a pimper's paradise, which Dawes describes as an "unsubtle way of calling her a whore."[6] The general tone of the song was not flattering, and Bob was clearly at his end with this woman.

"Could You Be Loved" was among Bob's least "reggae-sounding," songs with its obvious nod in the direction of black American popular music. The Wailers provided a bouncy, danceable harmonic background to Bob's only love song on the album. In no way characteristic of the content of *Uprising,* "Could You Be Loved" was an overt attempt by Bob to create crossover mar-ket success in the United States. The fast tempo, easy rhythms, and danceable feel helped the song become an American success. The lyrical content seemed to be a direct rebuttal of "Pimper's Paradise." Here Bob talked of everyone's ability to find love even though there would be rocky spots. He also talked of the poverty, oppression, and lack of education he saw in Jamaica.

"Forever Loving Jah" amplified the steadfast faith that Bob had expressed in "Jah Live." The Wailers again provided Bob with active and propulsive accompaniment for another of his heavily spiritual odes. Here Bob returned to his biblical imagery with evocations of Psalms. The first and second verses separated the good people from the bad. Then Bob followed with two more verses of biblical prophecy. The third verse evoked Psalm 8, with the language "revealed to the babe and the suckling." The biblical sentiment was that only the "youth" truly understood the words of God. Verse four advanced this message with a direct quotation from Psalm 1:3. With this, Bob highlighted the meaning of the song and its significance for his own life. Blessed are the righteous—the ungodly shall perish.

The final track on the album was a radical departure from the standard Wailers style. Here Bob sang a poignant song of protest, with only vocals and acoustic guitar in a sparse texture. The song is powerful because of its message and personal because it is the only track Marley released on which he sang alone, with only his acoustic guitar for accompaniment. The lyrics discussed religious matters and the relationship of slaves and masters on the colonial-era slave ships. Ian McCann said of the track, "as for the message, casting aside fears of man's vain and warlike science for a belief in a greater power, no more eloquent appeal on behalf of any religious belief was ever constructed."[7] This track was considered by many to be Marley's most intimate composition, with reference to the scoring. It was the last song that Marley played live in concert, and it was ultimately released in a full-band version. It was also the final song on the last Bob Marley and the Wailers album that Bob would live to see released.

The song began with an eight-measure guitar introduction that was presented in a horizontal melody, not in vertical harmonies. There followed three verse and chorus alternations with a short guitar bridge two-thirds of the way through the song. Every repetition of the chorus used the same words and music.

This song was another in which Marley employed biblical quotations or paraphrases to strengthen the meaning of the lyrics. The song opened with a slave reference likening Bob to a captive on the colonial-era slave ships; however, here he was a victim of mental, not physical, slavery. This was immediately followed by a reference to being rescued from a bottomless pit; this reflected language from Psalm 88, which offers God's love to those who feel forsaken. The first verse ended with a reflection of the language of Genesis 49:24. Bob quoted it thus: "my hand was made strong, by the hand of the almighty," which again allied him with Joseph and his biblical image as a fruitful bough. The third verse also included a biblical reference. Bob sang, "how long shall they kill our prophets while we stand aside and look," a paraphrase of Matthew 24:34, which discusses the damnation of such evildoers.

With another prolific recording session completed, Bob returned to Miami for a short break. He met with Danny Sims to discuss his lack of management, which was compounded by the fact that the recording of *Uprising* fulfilled his contract with Island Records. Sims informed Bob that he could get the Wailers a better contract and international distribution from Polygram. Armed with this new information, Bob went back to Jamaica and his house at 56 Hope Road. On February 6, 1980, Bob threw himself a big thirty-fifth birthday party. He surrounded himself with all his children and those of the Wailers band and entourage.

Jamaican musical style was changing again, and Bob took careful notice of this when he was at home for his birthday. In 1980, the biggest sound on the island was being made by Papa Michigan and General Smiley, two deejays who were on the cutting edge of "rub-a-dub."[8] The rub-a-dub style had a faster tempo than reggae, more like that of rock steady, and it was characterized by the use of the bass drum after beats two and four. Over this driving beat, the deejays would toast new lyrics (this refers to a deejay rapping or chanting over a song). A single by Michigan and Smiley was released on Hope Road Records, a Tuff Gong International subsidiary, and was played constantly at the house on Hope Road. The persistent noise, along with the presence of the Twelve Tribes Rastas and Bob's old friends from the ghetto, was a constant annoyance to Bob's neighbors.

When he returned from his birthday visit, Bob quickly noticed that the political and social situation was getting hot again in Jamaica as another national election loomed on the horizon. While he was on the island, he kept a low profile, and he soon returned to Miami to avoid conflict in Jamaica. In Miami, he was informed that his friend Bucky Marshall, who had worked to set up the One Love Peace concert, had been shot and killed at a dance in Brooklyn, New York. Before he could despair, Bob was also told that he had received a formal invitation to attend the independence ceremonies for the newly established nation of Zimbabwe, on April 17, 1980. In the wake of the popularity of his song "Zimbabwe," Bob was honored and amazed that his sung prophecy had been realized. The reigning Smith and Muzorewa government had finally realized that it could not maintain control and had begun talks with the Patriotic Front forces. In London, the opposing forces agreed to hold an open election that would permit the guerrillas to vote. The election was held, and Robert Mugabe's Marxist ZANU party won in a landslide. Because Bob's music had played a large role in the revolutionary process, Mugabe's General Secretary, Edgar Tekere, personally invited Bob to be one of the dignitaries at the independence celebration.

Two weeks before Bob was scheduled to attend the celebration in Zimbabwe, two African businessmen visited him at his home in Miami. The men had come to invite Bob Marley and the Wailers to perform as part of the official Independence Day program. Bob was honored by the invitation and replied that he would pay the Wailers' travel expenses himself.

The invitation had arrived on very short notice, but all the arrangements were made, and three days later the Wailers arrived at Salisbury (Harare) airport. The ZAPU leader Joshua Nkomo, Mugabe's minister of home affairs, along with his cabinet, met them. Also at Salisbury to meet Bob was Mugabe himself, accompanied by Britain's Prince Charles, who was in the country for the final lowering of the British flag. Shortly after Bob and the Wailers arrived in Salisbury, a chartered Boeing 707 followed, carrying 21 tons of

Wailers equipment. The Wailers had brought their own stage, a 25,000-watt public-address system, and a 12-man road crew. It is speculated that it cost Bob Marley a quarter of a million dollars to perform at the Zimbabwe Independence Day celebration.

At 8:30 P.M. on the night of the celebration, Bob and the Wailers left for Rufaro Stadium on the outskirts of Salisbury. At the venue, Bob talked briefly with Prince Charles before the ceremony began. Zimbabwe was the final African nation to shed colonial rule, making it the fiftieth independent African state. The British flag was lowered, and as the red, gold, black, and green flag of Zimbabwe was raised, the assembled troops fired a 21-gun salute. Immediately after the declaration of Zimbabwean independence, the Wailers were announced and hurried onto the stage.

The Wailers came on-stage and immediately launched into Bob's song "Zimbabwe." Ten minutes into their set, the Wailers stopped playing because the Rhodesian riot police had fired tear gas outside the gates of the stadium to disperse a horde of gatecrashers; the venue held 35,000 people, and many who had come to the show did not have tickets and could not get inside. The gas had infiltrated the stadium, and in a panic the I-Threes were rushed off the stage. A few minutes later, a relative state of calm was restored, and the Wailers played the song "War." They had been scheduled to play for only 10 minutes but performed for half an hour. The following evening, Bob Marley and the Wailers played a full-length concert to 40,000 excited Zimbabweans. After the shows, the Wailers departed Africa, and it was noticed on the plane back to London that Bob was looking ill and ashen.

In May 1980, the Wailers launched the Tuff Gong *Uprising* tour in Zurich, Switzerland. On this tour, the Wailers played to more than a million fans, in 12 European countries, in the span of six weeks. This schedule required them to perform six shows a week, with each show in a different city. They appeared in England, Scandinavia, Germany, Italy, Dublin, Ireland, and France and then returned to England. While touring, Bob was working on a song about the terrible political situation in Jamaica. Called "Slogans," the song was not released until November 8, 2005, on the greatest hits compilation *Africa Unite: The Singles Collection*.

Through the course of the European Tuff Gong *Uprising* tour, Bob Marley and the Wailers had no manager. Thus, when the European leg ended and Bob returned to Miami, his financial affairs were in complete disarray. After his firing, Don Taylor had sued Bob for a million dollars, and in turn Bob was countersuing Taylor. Compounding his monetary, legal, and management problems, Bob learned that there was civil war raging in Kingston. Marley wanted to return home to see his children, but he was warned by Danny Sims that if he went to Jamaica his life would be in danger. Preparing for the next election, Edward Seaga and his JLP party were being supported by the American CIA, and if Bob returned to the island his presence would be interpreted as a tacit endorsement of Manley's PNP party and would result in violence. Sims also delivered some good news to Bob: he mentioned a potential multi-million-dollar offer from Polygram to switch labels when the Wailers were no longer under contract to Island.

The American leg of the tour was scheduled to begin in September 1980. However, by August, members of the Wailers had noticed a visible deterioration in Bob's health. He was thin and pale and had been increasingly quiet and withdrawn. His friends and bandmates attributed this to the extreme rigor of the European tour that had just ended. Everyone in the Wailers' touring party was exhibiting some sign of fatigue or exhaustion. No one thought that Bob's health was in serious danger, since his cancer had been held in check by the operation on his toe.

The American tour was set to begin September 16 in Boston; it would then move on to New York for two shows with the Commodores at Madison Square Garden. Bob's health was frail, but he refused to talk about it with anyone other than a comment to the guitarist Al Anderson that he had a pain in his throat and head. In Boston, Bob Marley and the Wailers kicked off the American tour, playing a set that spanned the Wailers' songbook and culminated in songs from *Uprising*. The next day, the Wailers traveled to Providence by bus, and Bob did several radio interviews in support of the concert at the Providence Civic Center. Both the Boston and the Providence shows were not up to the standard established on the European tour. Bob's voice sounded tired and hoarse, and rumors began flying that Bob was "free-basing" cocaine (smoking cocaine, free of alkaloids).

## FLY AWAY HOME

After Rhode Island, the Wailers went to New York, where Bob was scheduled for two days of interviews before the Madison Square Garden shows. In New York, on September 18, the Wailers took up residence at the Gramercy Hotel, but Bob isolated himself by staying at the Essex House on Central Park. With this physical separation, the Wailers knew that something was wrong. In the past, Bob always stayed in the same hotel as the rest of the band so that he could supervise concert preparations. The next day, Bob did radio interviews and made an appearance at the Jamaican Progressive League before departing for Madison Square Garden for the Wailers' sound check. When he and the band arrived, the stage crew was still building the Commodores' set, and the Wailers' sounds check was postponed and then canceled. That night Bob Marley and the Wailers took the stage, and, after Errol Brown engineered a decent live mix during the first few songs, Bob gave an amazing performance in front of 20,000 fans.

Bob spent the day after the second Madison Square Garden show lying in bed totally exhausted. Tour events continued on around him, but Bob could not pay attention to them. The next morning, Rita called Bob to see if he wanted to accompany her to an Ethiopian Orthodox Church service.

He deflected her invitation, saying that he was too tired from the New York concerts to go out. In the late morning, Bob, Alan "Skill" Cole, and a few friends went for a jog in Central Park. While jogging, Bob called out to Cole, and, as he turned around, Bob fell into his arms, unable to move his neck. Cole and his friends carried Bob back to the hotel, and in a few hours he had regained his mobility.

Rita learned of Bob's seizure and rushed to his hotel to ascertain the seriousness of the situation. Bob comforted Rita, saying that he was feeling better and that he would meet her that night at a reggae club called Negril, in Greenwich Village. When Rita and the other I-Threes arrived, they were informed that Bob had felt sick again and had just left with Cole. That Monday, the Wailers were scheduled to fly to Pittsburgh for the next show on the tour. Rita contacted Bob about riding together to the airport, and he lied, saying that he was not making the flight since he had another interview to do in New York and that he would meet them in Pittsburgh the next day.

With his wife and bandmates on the way to Pittsburgh, Bob and his personal physician, Dr. Frazier, went to a neurologist who examined Bob, taking X-rays and a brain scan. The neurologist discovered a large cancerous brain tumor and informed Bob that the collapse in Central Park had been a stroke. Further, he was told that the rest of the tour would have to be canceled immediately, because the neurologist predicted that he only had two or three weeks left to live. Bob responded to the horrifying news by saying that he wanted another opinion and that he was going to Pittsburgh. That night, Bob made the trip to Pittsburgh and, upon checking into the hotel, was met by Rita, who tried to stop the tour as soon as she saw her husband. Bob was still in charge, and he refused to cancel the Pittsburgh show scheduled for the next evening.

Bob Marley and the Wailers played their final show on September 23, 1980, at Pittsburgh's Stanley Theater. Bob came out on stage without introduction and launched into a 90-minute show in which the Barrett Brothers rushed the beat so that Bob would not get too tired. The set included "Natural Mystic," "Positive Vibration," "Burnin' and Lootin'," "Then Belly Full," "Heathen," and a mixture of "Running Away" and "Crazy Baldhead." It was difficult to tell that Bob was suffering, given the energy that he expended during the show. The next set comprised "War/No More Trouble," "Zimbabwe," "Zion Train," "No Woman, No Cry," "Jamming," and "Exodus." The first encore was "Redemption Song," performed by Bob acoustically and alone on stage. The Wailers then returned to the stage for "Coming in from the Cold" and "Could You Be Loved." This was to be the end of the concert, but Bob wanted to play more, and no one in the band would refuse him. Bob Marley and the Wailers returned to the stage and played "Is This Love" and "Work." "As Bob sang the backward numerical verses—'Five days to go working for the next day / Four days to go. . .'—the rest of the band realized the show was over at last and that Bob was literally counting the Wailers down to the end."[9]

After the Pittsburgh concert, the American tour was canceled, and the main concern of the Wailers entourage turned to Bob's worsening health. Rita took Bob to his mother's in Miami and set about getting him the best doctors that she could find. Bob underwent more testing at Cedars of Lebanon Hospital, after which he was referred to the Memorial Sloan-Kettering Cancer Center, in New York. At Sloan-Kettering, on October 7, Bob learned that he had cancer in his lungs and stomach, as well as a malignant brain tumor. The doctors gave him a new appraisal of his situation and informed him that he had four to five weeks left to live. They also started him on radiation, trying to reduce the size of the tumor on his brain. Bob's presence at Sloan-Kettering was leaked to the media, and on October 8, news of Bob's cancer was announced on the New York radio station WLIB.

After his failing health was made public, Bob checked into the Wellington Hotel and continued to take radiation therapy as an outpatient. He initially reacted well to the radiation and began to feel stronger. He felt well enough to watch his friend Muhammad Ali's last fight against Larry Holmes, and he attended a concert given by the British rock group Queen. He even tried to play soccer with Alan "Skill" Cole, but he was unable to run effectively and soon sat on the sidelines and watched.

Still in New York, Bob suffered a setback when he had a smaller stroke that incapacitated him to the point that standing was difficult. The doctors now began chemotherapy on Bob that caused him to lose 25 pounds. His hair also began to fall out, and the chemotherapy made his scalp burn. He requested some scissors and cut off his remaining dreadlocks, trying to get some relief from the side effects of his treatments. Bob continued to lose weight and began to look as though he would not last much longer.

At this point, his mother began pressuring him to be baptized into the Ethiopian Baptist Church. She had been so baptized, while Bob was in utero, but he always refused her requests. Further, the Twelve Tribes, of which Bob was already a member, considered the Ethiopian Baptist Church to be a rival. Bob agreed to the baptism out of mortal fear and as a favor to his mother. On November 4, 1980, Robert Nesta Marley was baptized into the Ethiopian Orthodox Church and christened Berhane Selassie, "Light of the Holy Trinity." Bob was beginning to die; he continued to lose weight and was now paralyzed from the waist down.

At this point, Bob's personal physician learned of a holistic cancer treatment that was being used in Bad Wiessee, Germany, by a Dr. Josef Issels.[10] His treatment was unorthodox, and he had been blacklisted by the American Cancer Society. However, his record did reflect some success with cancer sufferers. Bob's condition was worsening quickly, and it began to seem that the chemotherapy itself was killing him. Alan "Skill" Cole and Dr. Frazier contacted Dr. Issels and made plans for Bob to become his patient.

On November 9, Bob and a small circle of friends arrived at Dr. Issels's clinic, called Sunshine House, located in the Bavarian Alps. When Bob arrived,

Bob in a contemplative mood. Courtesy of Photofest.

he was in such poor condition that he was expected to die within days. Issels immediately began treating Bob, and within the day he had gained the ailing Rasta's trust and stabilized some of his symptoms. Issels confirmed the cancer in Bob's head, lungs, and stomach and began treatments, consisting of hyperthermia (artificially raising one's body temperature), blood transfusions, and injections of THX, an anticancer drug that was illegal in the United States. Amazingly, Bob began to respond to Dr. Issels's treatments, and he regained a little of his strength.

After being with Dr. Issels for a month, Bob found that his condition continued to improve. He stayed on the Sunshine House estate, living in a ground-floor apartment in an adjacent building with his mother. Twice a day, Bob walked with assistance to his treatment sessions, which involved shooting 180-degree beams of ultraviolet heat at his tumors. The hope was that the heat would weaken the cancer cells and allow the drugs to work. Bob silently endured the painful treatments.

For his thirty-sixth birthday, on February 6, 1981, many of the Wailers visited Bob in Bad Wiessee. The whole Wailers band was there except for the Barrett Brothers. The revelers found Bob in reasonably good condition and high spirits. He was involved in Tuff Gong International business again, talking to his lawyer, Diane Jobson, via overseas telephone calls and was even able to do some exercising. His hair had begun to grow back, but he was still losing weight (Jobson estimated that Bob weighed less than 100 pounds at his birthday party).

By the end of March, Cedella noticed that her son was again losing his strength. He could not endure the walks to take his treatment and lay in bed for days at a time. Bob then refused to eat or drink anything, leaving Cedella helpless. She sang to him, and together they spent hours reading the Bible. Soon, he was too weak to read and had friends read to him while he lay in bed. To everyone's amazement, Dr. Issels went on vacation in early April, leaving Bob to be cared for by his staff. Bob weighed a mere 70 pounds, and Diane Jobson protested the doctor's decision to leave. To make matters worse, the other Wailers began calling Bob to get money that they felt he owed them. It was known that Bob had no written will, and it was believed that he was on his deathbed. Without a will, Rita would inherit everything when Bob died.

Bob underwent surgery, in late April, to reduce the intense abdominal pain that he had been suffering. On May 3, 1981, Dr. Issels admitted to Diane Jobson and Cedella Booker that he had given up hope for Bob. He told the two women that Bob had less than two weeks to live and that if they wanted to take him home they must leave soon or Bob would not survive the trip. Jobson chartered a plane, and they returned to Miami. Upon his arrival, on May 9, Bob entered Cedars of Lebanon Hospital. There the staff said all they could do was to keep him comfortable.

On May 11, Bob's vital signs started to fade, and the doctors told Rita that he would not last more than a few hours. Rita began singing a hymn to Bob, and, as his breathing became shallow, she called his mother and told her to come to the hospital. However, by the time Cedella arrived, Bob had made a slight recovery, and together his wife and mother began to pray. He said that he was feeling better, but he took the opportunity to say goodbye to his sons Ziggy and Stephen. Bob asked his mother for a glass of water, at about 11:30, that he drank completely. Then some nurses had Cedella help them roll Bob onto his side for an x-ray. After the x-ray, Bob fell asleep, and a little while later he awoke and asked his mother to come close to him. When she did, he lost consciousness, and within a few minutes he was gone. Robert Nesta Marley, the first international third-world superstar, died at approximately 11:45 A.M., on Monday, May 11, 1981.

A memorial service was held the following Thursday at Bob's house on Vista Lane, in Miami. Chris Blackwell, Don Taylor, Danny Sims, most of the Wailers, and a daylong procession of friends attended the service. In the main hall of the house, Bob's body lay in a bronze casket opened to reveal his body from the waist up. In his right hand was a copy of the Bible, opened to the Twenty-third Psalm, and his left hand rested on his guitar.[11] On Tuesday, May 19, Bob's body was brought back to Jamaica for a two-day state funeral arranged by the office of the Prime Minister. Edward Seaga, who had been elected the previous year, bestowed the Jamaican Order of Merit on Bob. Ziggy accepted the award on his father's behalf, and with it Bob's title became the Honorable Robert Nesta Marley, O.M. On May 20, a national day of mourning was declared to allow Bob's body to lay in state.[12]

The next day, Bob's body was displayed at the National Arena for all Jamaicans to view. Forty thousand Jamaicans came to the Arena, and the police were forced to use tear gas on the crowd as it became uncontrollable. Members of the Twelve Tribes, in addition to Jamaican police, guarded Bob's body during the viewing. The following morning, Bob's coffin was brought to the Jamaican headquarters of the Ethiopian Orthodox Church on Maxfield Avenue for his funeral. After the service, a motorcade transported Bob's body past his house at 56 Hope Road and back to the National Arena. A public service was held that included a performance by the Wailers without Tyrone Downie, who was too grief stricken to attend. Bob's mother, his half-sister Pearl Livingston, and a friend named Ora sang a song written by Cedella called "Hail." Then the I-Threes, supported by the Wailers, sang "Rastaman Chant" and "Natural Mystic."

The actual service began at 11:00 A.M. and was led by Archbishop Yesuhaq. He had baptized Bob the previous year and now supervised his funeral service. Bob's immediate family, seated in the second row, watched as Governor-General Florizel Augustus Glasspole, the Jamaican Governor General, Michael Manley, and Alan "Skill" Cole read the lessons assigned to them by the Archbishop. Cole felt that the Twelve Tribes were being overlooked in the service, and when it was his turn to ascend the stage he deviated from the plan and shouted out to the members of the Rastafarian sect in the audience. After Cole finished his passage from Isaiah, the Archbishop read from Matthew 5 (Jesus' Sermon on the Mount). The entire arena rose to its feet for the Lord's Prayer, and the service closed with an elegant eulogy by Edward Seaga. Although Seaga was in power in Jamaica, he and Bob were complete opposites in ideology; nonetheless, he paid respect to the fallen reggae star and duly noted Bob's contribution to Jamaica.

After the public funeral service, members of the Twelve Tribes carried Bob's body out of the National Arena. A long motorcade had assembled to shepherd Bob's body back to his birthplace at Nine Miles. On the 55-mile trip, the procession passed thousands of Jamaicans who had gathered on the sides of the road to bid farewell to Bob. In Bog Walk, on the Ewarton Road, the hearse broke down, and the coffin had to be transferred to a truck, which carried it the rest of the way to St. Ann parish. Arriving at Bob's birthplace five hours later, the coffin was placed in a white mausoleum that had been erected behind the house that Bob's grandfather had built for him and his mother when Bob was a newborn. Edward Seaga, Archbishop Yesuhaq, and countless Jamaicans were there to witness Bob's burial. He was entombed in the mausoleum, which was then sealed three times amid talk that someone would try to steal the gold ring that had been given to Bob by Haile Selassie. A red metal plate with a gold Star of David marked the first seal; the second was a metal grate that was bolted on, and the third was a layer of concrete. With the mausoleum securely sealed, the ceremony ended, and the crowd began to thin. Robert Nesta Marley, the third world's biggest star, had been born on the same hill 36 years earlier.

# Posthumous Releases

### CHANCES ARE

When Bob died, he left behind a prodigious library of recordings; however, there were also many unreleased songs that have continued to surface. In the intervening years, countless releases have appeared on the market. Some of these releases were sanctioned by the family, but many were not. The recording quality was often poor, and the release was a means for making some fast money. Several of the more important posthumous recordings included *Chances Are, Confrontation, Legend,* and *Africa Unite: The Singles Collection,* among others.

In 1981, Danny Sims released a nine-song album of previously unreleased or remixed versions of songs recorded between 1968 and 1972. Included on the album *Chances Are* were the tracks "Reggae on Broadway," "Gonna Get You," "Chances Are," "Soul Rebel," "Dance Do the Reggae," "Mellow Mood," "Stay with Me," and "I'm Hurting Inside." The front of the LP was a black-and-white picture of Bob smiling underneath a full head of dreadlocks. The back included smaller pictures of Bob on tour, performing live, on the tour bus, relaxing in his soccer gear, and singing and playing his guitar. The album was panned by critics because it was seen as an exploitation of the memory of the recently fallen artist.

The songs on the album reflected a formative part of Bob's early career. They varied widely in style, sound, and tone. The recordings were the product of Bob's brief association with Cayman Music. During that period, Bob was simultaneously trying to build a new style that was not the standard Jamaican rock steady sound and to create something that had American crossover potential. The result was a series of songs that sounded like approximations of American rhythm and blues with some early reggae components. Further complicating the styles of the songs on this release was the fact that "Gonna Get You" and "Stay with Me" were written by the African American songwriting team Norman and Pyfrom. "Reggae on Broadway" was as close as Bob's songwriting got to straight forward rhythm and blues, while "Soul Rebel" was an early example of what roots reggae would become. It represented a marked departure for the Wailers early vocal trio, abandoning as it did the attempt at doo-wop harmonizing. It was replaced by the true Wailers sound.

Because this release was a compilation over which Bob had no control, there was no unified message to hold the songs together. There were some telling autobiographical stories, but nothing as cohesive as would be found in his mature works. The stories of the love songs, "Mellow Mood," "Stay with Me," "Hurting Inside," and "I'm Gonna Get You," ran the gamut from the pain of lost love to direct invitations into the bedroom. For example, in "Mellow Mood" Bob attempted to seduce his love interest with the come-on "I'll play your favorite song." However, this was immediately followed by his suggesting that they could "rock it all night long," which purposely left the listening wondering what Bob intended "rock it" to mean.

"Reggae on Broadway" reflected Bob's desire to find a means by which his music could make an impact in the American market. The songs had strong undertones of early 1970s black American popular music in the vein of Sly and the Family Stone. The American sound of the song did not reflect just Bob's crossover dreams; it also was indicative of a musical trend that had influenced Bob. Numerous times, Bob detailed the influence of black American popular music on his own songs. In 1968, Bob traveled to the Bronx, in New York City, to meet and jam with the legendary African American singer-songwriter Jimmy Norman. During the meeting, Norman showed Bob how to make several of his songs sound more like American R&B. He also supplied Bob with several songs that he and his writing partner, Al Pyfrom, had written. Present at this meeting and jam session were Bob, Norman, Pyfrom, Rita, and Norman's wife, Dorothy. Much of the resulted material went on to appear on *Chances Are*.[1] Bob's association with Norman extended past this meeting, and Norman even visited with Bob in Jamaica, where he met Prince Buster and important figures in the Rastafarian culture.

"Soul Rebel" talked of Bob's early life in Jamaica and his disassociation from mainstream Jamaican culture. Here Bob ignored those who gossiped or tried to do him wrong and advised that travel (moving out of Babylon) was the best way to escape an undesirable situation. "Dance Do the Reggae" was one of Bob's lesser-known songs. The lyrics presented a clever approach to wooing a potential partner. Here Bob opined that he wanted to be the music of his lover's soul. The chorus was a suggestive play on words in which Bob evoked the words of the song's title; they could literally dance together or, taking the words metaphorically, go to bed together. Although the songs on *Chances Are* were a testament to Bob's early songwriting capabilities, its release immediately after Bob's death was seen as the desperate actions of vultures, not as an attempt to further his legacy through the exposure of early material.

## CONFRONTATION

In 1983, Tuff Gong International and Island Records released *Confrontation,* the last of the trilogy of albums that represented Bob's concept for the redemption of all black people. Although he did not live to see the release of this album, he had approved the album's title in advance. He did not, however, live long enough to choose the songs on the album, so what might have been will never be known. The song list was compiled by Rita and included an interesting variety of tracks: "Chant Down Babylon," "Buffalo Soldier," "Jump Nyabinghi," "Mix Up, Mix Up," "Give Thanks and Praises," "Blackman Redemption," "Trench Town," "Stiff Necked Fools," "I Know," and "Rastaman Live Up!" Bob was pictured on the front of the album riding a white horse slaying a dragon with a lance, imagery from the story of St. George, in a painting by the Wailers' art director, Neville Garrick.[2] The back jacket contains an adaptation of a traditional Ethiopian painting of the battle of Adowa, which took place in 1896. The original painting depicts the first battle between the Ethiopians and the Italians, one that would be revisited during the reign of Haile Selassie I.

All of the songs on *Confrontation* were recorded at Tuff Gong Studios during the same sessions that produced the tracks for *Survival* and *Uprising.* Bob was no longer alive to act as the producer, so the Wailers and Errol Brown filled in. Rita Marley was credited as executive producer. Musicians present on the release were Bob on lead vocals and rhythm guitar, the Barrett Brothers on rhythm, Junior Marvin on guitar and backing vocals, Tyrone Downie and Earl "Wya" Lindo on keyboards, Alvin "Seeco" Patterson on hand drums, and the I-Threes on female backing vocals. Also credited was the horn line of Glen Da Costa, David Madden, and Nambo. Additional percussion was supplied by Devon Evans and Earl "Santa" Davis.

Bob's unending call to cast off oppression was heard at the start of the album with the song "Chant Down Babylon." Through continued use of biblical imagery of Babylon, Bob's message here was that the strength of reggae music could crumble the weakness of the oppressor, just as the Walls of Jericho had been brought down. The song was written while Bob and the Wailers were in Brussels during the *Survival* tour. It was recorded during the *Uprising* sessions and pointedly reasserted Bob's belief that Babylon could be conquered.

Track two was co-authored by N. G. Williams (aka King Sporty). "Buffalo Soldier" allied struggling Rastafarians with the black soldiers in the U.S. cavalry during the Indian wars. Here Bob functioned at once as teacher and preacher. He admonished the listener to "know your history" or be damned to repeat it. He wrote the song after having read about the African slaves brought to the United States to fight against the Native Americans. The material in the first verse directly equated the American buffalo soldier with the Rastas. Both groups were taken from Africa, one fighting for American freedom, the other for freedom in Jamaica. Although not strictly autobiographical, songs such as this are a window into Bob's soul. He wrote about what he believed, and he lived his beliefs.

"Jump Nyabinghi" was pure exhilaration in musical form. Bob composed this song in 1979 and injected it with a variety of Rastafarian sentiments. The chorus of this song was a chanted sendup of a type of dancing that accompanied traditional Nyabinghi drumming sessions. The verses, which contained biblical allusions, talked of moving and dancing to the Nyabinghi rhythms. Continuing his assault on Babylon, Bob evoked the story of the fall of Jericho's walls (Hebrews 11) when men were able to subdue kingdoms, live in righteousness, and work miracles through their faith. Anther Rastafarian element of the lyrics of this song was Bob's mention of herb and the suru board.[3] Bob was a notorious marijuana smoker; however, Rastas believe that smoking marijuana is part of their religious sacraments. They cite biblical passages that support this assertion.

Track four was "Mix Up, Mix Up," which was constructed after Bob's death from a two-track recording that Rita discovered. With the assistance of Neville Garrick and Errol Brown, the original vocals were converted into the version that appeared on *Confrontation*. Through the course of the lengthy verse words, Bob was trying to work through his feelings in the wake of his problems with Don Taylor. The first verse ended with the core sentiment of the song: "he who hide the wrong . . . did the wrong still." The distrust and confusion caused by this deception had infected Bob's whole existence, and he went on to mention constant stumbling blocks and then listed the days of the week, implying that there was no rest from these problems.

The middle of the song continued with Bob's ruminations over having been lied to. Bob did not swear in his lyrics, but the middle of the third verse there was a bit of a slip. The lyric unfolded "but through your fu . . . respect, and through your false pride," with no complete word supplied before "respect." The omitted word could have been "fuckery," which was Jamaican patois for wrong or unfair actions. He finished the verse with added vitriol, describing how he had been taken for a ride. However, he did reach a sort of resolution toward the end of the song. When he repeated that he wanted to "clear his wheels" and that he did not care who suffered as a result, Bob was attempting to put the Taylor fiasco in the past.

The delicate and tranquil quality of "Give Thanks and Praises" has caused some to consider this song linked to "Redemption Song." Regardless, here Bob made a half-spoken and half-sung testament to the divinity of Jah. He opened the song with praises to Jah, followed by a verse that compared Jah to the biblical figure Ham. He chose Noah's son Ham because he was described in the Old Testament as a prophet, thereby allying Jah with Ham and furthering Jah's position as a prophet.[4] The rest of the song contained lyrics in which Bob associated himself with Jah and heaped praise on him.

"Blackman Redemption" was cowritten by Bob and Lee "Scratch" Perry and was recorded in 1978 just prior to the One Love Peace Concert. A straightforward message presented in Jamaican slang, this song talked of the spread of Rastafari and Bob's belief that the world would eventually recognize Haile Selassie's divinity. Bob evoked the Jamaican patois "cool runnings" repeatedly in this song. Meaning "peaceful journey," during the 1970s the phrase came to mean "peace and/or assurance" and was used as a greeting or parting phrase. Here, Bob used it to mean that the youth agreed to peace and that that message was being spread. Beyond that, Bob advised that there was no need to be "jumpy" or "bumpy," which here meant nervous. The themes of redemption and peace filled the song. The central verse of the song described Haile Selassie I as having descended from King David through the line of Solomon.

"Trench Town" was Bob's testament to his boyhood and his teenage home. The song began with his lamenting his submersion in a sea of oppression, which became a prison. However, he added that, although he came from Trench Town, he was still able to free himself and his people from bondage. He achieved this through music and in so doing answered his own question, "can anything good come from Trench Town?" With this song Bob was paying homage to the place that made him into the success that he became.

Like "Crazy Baldheads," "Stiff Necked Fools" was another of Bob's attempts at separating himself from the wicked minions of Babylon. Here he painted the oppressors as vain and wrong and as living in a fantasy world. Bob then sang of the uplift of the righteous through wisdom. The center of the song was a biblical paraphrase from Proverbs 10:15: "destruction of the poor is in poverty." Bob used this to reveal the sentiment of the entire proverb, which was that one who lies is a fool, but the mouth of the righteous man is a well of life. Bob saw himself as that righteous man.

One of the older songs that made the album, "I Know" was originally recorded in the 1976 *Rastaman Vibration* sessions. This was immediately apparent upon hearing the song. Again, Bob had usurped the lighter American popular-music style. It had a distinct disco sound that ultimately won it praise in Jamaica and in the United Kingdom. The song's lyrics contained the singular message that no matter how bad the circumstances, Jah will be there for support. Bob compared himself to a ship battered by the sea but noted that no matter what the season, Jah would protect and care for the faithful.

The final song on *Confrontation* was also cowritten with Lee "Scratch" Perry. In a straightforward mid-tempo one-drop reggae groove, Bob gave respect to the Rastafarian faithful. He again evoked biblical images to ally the Rasta with those who beat insurmountable odds. The examples that Bob chose were David slaying Goliath and Samson slaying the Philistines. In each case, an underdog overcame oppression because he was righteous and God was on his side. Here Bob was allying the Rastafarian faithful with these biblical success stories to prepare them for just such a battle. This was the confrontation for which the album was named.

## LEGEND: THE BEST OF BOB MARLEY AND THE WAILERS

Island Records released one of Bob's most famous albums, titled *Legend,* in 1984 with the subtitle *The Best of Bob Marley and the Wailers.* Made available in different versions in England and the United States, the album contained 14 tracks that encapsulated the second half of Bob's career. In the Wailers tradition, a tour was launched in support of the album, with Junior Marvin and Tyrone Downie taking turns singing the lead vocals. Bob's eldest son, Ziggy, joined the tour on the American West Coast and sang the lead vocals for the concert in Los Angeles.

Because it was a greatest-hits collection, the album listed all of the musicians that Bob recorded with during the Island/Tuff Gong portion of his career (including Peter, Bunny, and Touter). The tracks were culled from recordings made between 1972 and 1981. As Bob was regarded as a legendary singer-songwriter, the idea that a single-disc collection could represent his output was a stretch. However, *Legend* did a respectable job of encapsulating Bob's mature career.

Upon its release, *Legend* lived on the American Top 200 album ranks for more than two years. It spent 129 weeks on the U.K. top charts. The album logged 584 weeks (just over 11 years) on Billboard's Top Pop Catalogue Album chart. It sold in excess of 10 million copies in America alone and has gone on to be certified 10 times platinum. To this day, the album remains the best-selling album by a Jamaican and the best-selling reggae album in history. The chart positions and awards were a testament to the strength of the songs chosen for the album, which included "Is This Love," "No Woman, No Cry," "Could You Be Loved," "Three Little Birds," "Buffalo Soldier," "Get Up, Stand Up," "Stir It Up," "One Love/People Get Ready," "I Shot the Sheriff," "Waiting in Vain," "Exodus," and "Jamming."

## TALKIN' BLUES

The album *Talkin' Blues* was released in February 1991, and was a conglomeration of several different recordings made between 1973 and 1975. The majority of the material came from an interview and live-in-the-studio performance that Bob and the Wailers did in 1973 at the Record Plant studio; the rest was from a show at the Lyceum, in London, in 1975. This recording was broadcast by the San Francisco radio station KSAN-FM. The occasion was inauspicious as the Wailers had just been kicked off the Sly and the Family Stone tour; however, the band made the best of an otherwise disappointing tour attempt. This particular Wailers incarnation did not include Bunny, whose place was taken by Joe Higgs. Of particular interest, the album contained snippets of an interview that Bob gave in September 1975. Prior to the release of *Talkin' Blues,* none of these particular song versions had been available.

Song on the album were "Talkin' Blues," "Burnin' and Lootin'," "Kinky Reggae," "Get Up, Stand Up," "Slave Driver," "Walk the Proud Land," "Lively Up Yourself," "You Can't Blame the Youth," "Stop That Train," "Rastaman Chant," "Am-A-Do," "Bend Down Low," and "I Shot the Sheriff." "You Can't Blame the Youth" and "Stop That Train" were written and sung by Peter. "Walk the Proud Land" was written by Bunny and released on several of his later albums. "Am-A-Do," written and sung by Bob, had not been released on any prior Island/Tuff Gong release. In the interview material, in which Bob spoke with Dermott Hussey, that separated the songs, Bob discussed the breakup of the original Wailers and his belief in Haile Selassie I. The discussion of Selassie was especially poignant because the interview took place just a month after Selassie died.

"Am-A-Do" was a true Wailers rarity. It was originally recorded in 1974 but was never released. It came from the same sessions that generated the singles "Talkin' Blues" and "Bend Down Low." The song was a mildly off-kilter love ode. Here Bob professed his love for a woman, and it was reciprocated. Now the two had to contend with the realities of physical love. The language in the song was direct and urgent. Bob commanded the woman to "do it with your badself" and told her that he had to "do it with you (again)." The language was not subtle, and the song was unique in Bob's output.

## Bob Marley: Songs of Freedom

A massive collection of Bob Marley and the Wailers material was released in 1992. Brought out by Tuff Gong and Island Records in 1999, *Songs of Freedom* was a four-CD set originally distributed in a numbered million-copy limited edition. *Songs of Freedom* was a highly regarded and sought-after collection because of its quality and because it included material from throughout Bob's career, from early singles to his final performance. The set began with early singles like "Judge Not," "One Cup of Coffee," and "Simmer Down." Also on the first disc were "Bus Tem Shut (Pyaka)" and the original recordings of "Mellow Mood," "Stir It Up," and "Thank You Lord."

Disc two contained several previously unreleased tracks, including an alternate version of "Trench Town Rock" and an acoustic medley of "Guava Jelly," "This Train," "Corner Stone," "Comma Comma," "Dewdrops," "Stir It Up," and "I'm Hurting Inside." A major unreleased track in this compilation was "Iron, Lion, Zion." Here Bob strengthened his resolve in a discussion about his Rastafarian faith on the "rock" (Jamaica).

Disc three began with "No Woman, No Cry" live at the Roxy, which had not been released but which is now available on the freestanding *Live at the Roxy, Hollywood, California, May 26, 1976—The Complete Concert,* which was released in 2003. The rest of disc three was filled with different versions of many of Bob's mature favorites. Disc four continued the alternative mixes of favorite songs. The gem was the final track, "Redemption Song," performed live at the Stanley Theater, in Pittsburgh. Recorded on September 23, 1980, this was Bob's last performance.

The box set contained many seminal Bob and the Wailers recordings and was collectable for the range and variety of songs. Accompanying the four CDs was a 63-page book with meticulous recording information, color photographs that spanned Bob's career, a brief biography, and descriptions of each song. Equally interesting to amateurs and experts both, this set was a must-have for reggae fans around the world. Collectively, the songs on this release exemplified Bob's concept of freedom as he became an international symbol of freedom.

## NATURAL MYSTIC THE LEGEND LIVES ON: BOB MARLEY AND THE WAILERS

In 1995, Tuff Gong and Island Records released a follow-up to the single-disc greatest-hits album *Legend. Natural Mystic: The Legend Lives On* was a compilation of a series of previously released songs that were popular but that did not make the *Legend* album. In addition, several more obscure songs were included, such as "Iron, Lion, Zion," "Keep On Moving," and "Time Will Tell." The material on this release was culled from various recordings made between 1976 and 1995. Producers of the material on the album included Bob, Blackwell, the Wailers, Errol Brown, Steve Smith, Lee "Scratch" Perry, Ingmar Kiang, and Trevor Wyatt.

The album was compiled by Chris Blackwell and Trevor Wyatt and included the following tracks: "Natural Mystic," "Easy Skankin'," "Iron, Lion, Zion," "Crazy Baldheads," "So Much Trouble in the World," "War," "Africa Unite," "Trench Town Rock (Live)," "Keep On Moving," "Sun Is Shining," "Who the Cap Fit," "One Drop," "Roots, Rock Reggae," "Pimper's Paradise," and "Time Will Tell." Overall, the album was an excellent edition to the Tuff Gong/Island catalogue and included two selections remixed by Ingmar Kaing and Trevor Wyatt, "Iron, Lion, Zion" and "Keep On Moving."

## ONE LOVE: THE VERY BEST OF BOB MARLEY AND THE WAILERS

Another interesting album from the Tuff Gong/Island library was *One Love: The Very Best of Bob Marley and the Wailers.* Released in 2001, this set of 20 songs represented a fresh approach to the continued reissuing of Bob's material. Here, Bill Levenson and Maxine Stowe included the truly stand-out songs from each previously released album, including the posthumous releases. Thus, the *Very Best* contained songs that were originally released between 1973 and 1992.

The collection enhanced the libraries of collectors and included the songs "Stir It Up" (from *Catch A Fire*); "Get Up, Stand Up" and "I Shot the Sheriff" (from *Burnin'*); "Lively Up Yourself" (from *Natty Dread*); "No Woman, No Cry" (from *Live!*); "Roots, Rock, Reggae" (from *Rastaman Vibration*); "Exodus," "Jamming," "Waiting in Vain," "Three Little Birds," "Turn Your Lights Down Low," and "One Love/People Get Ready" (from *Exodus*); "Is This Love" and "Sun Is Shining" (from *Kaya*); "So Much Trouble in the World" (from *Survival*); "Could You Be Loved" and "Redemption Song" (from *Uprising*); "Buffalo Soldier" (from *Confrontation*);" "Iron, Lion, Zion" (from *Legend*); and "I Know a Place." Of note, "I Know a Place" had never been previously released on an officially licensed Bob Marley and the Wailers album.

## AFRICA UNITE: THE SINGLES COLLECTION

Released in November 2005, *Africa Unite: The Singles Collection* was a unique posthumous offering. The album was conceived of as a commemoration of Bob's sixtieth birthday and was a celebration of his career. The release contained early songs, mature works, one previously unreleased track ("Slogans"), and remixes of a couple of Bob's seminal hits.

The album included the following tracks: "Soul Rebel," "Lively Up Yourself," "Concrete Jungle," "I Shot the Sheriff," "Get Up, Stand Up," "No Woman, No Cry (Live)," "Roots, Rock, Reggae," "Exodus," "Waiting in Vain," "Jamming," "Is This Love," "Sun Is Shining," "Could You Be Loved," "Three Little Birds," "Buffalo Soldier," "One Love/People Get Ready," "Africa Unite (Will.i.am remix), "Slogans," and "Stand Up Jamrock" (Ashley Beedle remix). The final three songs were the most compelling because they were not available before this release.

Will.i.am, a member of the American hip-hop collective the Black Eyed Peas, created the remix of "Africa Unite." The remix of Bob's most direct affirmation of African freedom and unification was done on December 15, 2004. The song originally appeared on the1979 *Survival* album, but, in Will.i.am's new version, the message was brought alive again. Will.i.am added a more active and propulsive beat and doubled the length of the track. The hip-hop update refreshed the song and cast it in a more contemporary mold, thus inviting a fresh listen.

"Slogans" was recorded in 1979 in a Miami bedroom. The original tape of the song was discovered in Bob's mother's house, and two of his sons, Stephen and Ziggy, constructed the instrumental tracks around the vocal skeleton that Bob had left behind. According to Blackwell, the tape contained seven or eight songs, with Bob's vocals over drum-machine beats. The product was an excellent approximation of what Bob might have done himself. An interesting note was that rock-guitar god Eric Clapton supplied the lead guitar tracks for the song. Bob's message in the song was as fresh on its reappearance as it was in the late 1970s. Here Bob was berating both church and state for their decades of deception and propaganda. Lyrics such as "no more sweet talk from a pulpit" were along the lines of other of Bob's direct condemnations of the Catholic Church. Those who sought to confuse the people were described as hypocrites whose words confused and weakened the sufferers. Rita said of the song, "he's still protesting, still speaking for the people who have been downtrodden on."

The final track on this release was "Stand Up Jamrock," an inventive mashup of "Get Up, Stand Up" and "Welcome to Jamrock."[5] This mashup was created by the English DJ Ashley Beedle, who combined two enormously successful songs. Of special importance, this song represented the union of Bob's work and the music of his son Damian, a union that Bob did not live long enough to realize. Mixing the old and the new put an interesting spin on both songs, and the combined message was compelling. "Get Up, Stand Up" was Bob's call to action to the Jamaican people, as well as to black people around the world. Damian's song was released as the title track to his album of September 2005. "Welcome to Jamrock" was a reggae hip-hop hybrid with mainstream American crossover appeal that had not been realized since Bob's mature releases. While Bob called for movement, Damian bemoaned the poor conditions of the Jamaican underclass and updated Bob's message about their being prisoners on the "rock."

## THE DELUXE EDITIONS

In 2001, Island and Tuff Gong began re-releasing the Wailers' main material in digitally remastered two-CD sets. Each release included the original recording from the previously released album plus previously unreleased versions of each song recorded during the same time period. The reproduction of this material was supervised by Bill Levenson, and the plan was to create deluxe editions of all of the Bob Marley and the Wailers' Island Records releases.[6] Thus far, five two-disc sets have been issued: *Catch a Fire* (2001), *Exodus* (2001), *Legend* (2002), *Rastaman Vibration* (2002), and *Burnin'* (2004).

The remastered versions of the original albums were made from the original analog tapes and represented a cleaner version of the songs. The gems were found in the additional discs of obscure or previously unreleased material. The additional disc on the *Catch a Fire* release contained the unreleased Jamaican versions of the songs that appeared on the original album. In addition, versions of the songs "High Tide or Low Tide" and "All Day, All Night" were added. The tracks were originally recorded at Dynamic, Harry J's, and Randy's Studios, in Kingston, Jamaica.

Also released in 2001 was the deluxe edition of *Exodus*. Disc one contained the original 10 songs digitally remastered from the original tapes. However, to these were added five alternate songs and versions of "Roots," "Waiting in Vain," "Jamming" (long version), "Jamming," and "Exodus." Disc two was a collection of five live songs and five studio recordings made by Lee "Scratch" Perry. The live songs included "The Heathen," "Crazy Baldheads," "War/No More Trouble," "Jamming," and "Exodus," all recorded during the *Exodus* tour live at the Rainbow Theater in London on June 4, 1977. The studio recordings were made in July and August 1977 and included "Punky Reggae Party" in two versions, "Keep On Moving," the Curtis Mayfield song, in two versions, and an advertisement for *Exodus*.

The deluxe-edition re-release of *Rastaman Vibration* came in 2002. The first disc was again a digital remastering of the original album, but with bonus tracks. Here Levenson added eight songs recorded in Kingston or London at the same time that the original album was being made. "Want More," "Crazy Baldhead," "War," and "Johnny Was" were all unreleased alternate mixes of the songs that actually appeared on the original record. Disc two was the May 26, 1976, live performance from the *Rastaman Vibration* tour at the Roxy. Added to this were two versions of "Smile Jamaica" from the late 1976 sessions that yielded that single. The deluxe edition of *Legend* was also released in 2002. The first disc contained the original 16 tracks digitally remastered, and the second contained alternate versions of the same 16 songs. The alternate recordings range from remixes made between 1980 and 1984 that presented the *Legend* material in a different order from the original.

The most recent of the deluxe-edition releases was the 2004 version of *Burnin'*. Disc one was again the original album in digitally remastered versions, but with the addition of five songs that were recorded during the *Burnin'* sessions but not used on the album. "Reincarnated Souls," "No Sympathy," "The Oppressed Song," and two versions of "Get Up, Stand Up" now round out the album. "Reincarnated Souls," written by Bunny, was meant to be the original album title. Bunny also wrote "The Oppressed Song," and Peter penned "No Sympathy." All of these tracks were originally recorded at Harry J's Studio in Kingston.

Disc two was a 12-song live set from the November 23, 1973, show Live at Leeds. All of the tracks here were previously unreleased and were recorded for Island Records using its mobile studio. The Wailers band was a tight and stripped-down unit for this show, with only Bob, Peter, the Barrett Brothers, and Earl "Wya" Lindo performing.

# Life after Death:
# The Legend Lives On

Bob died without a will, leaving the control of his multimillion-dollar estate to his wife, Rita Marley. This resulted in years of legal battles for royalties, property, and ownership of Bob's music. After Bob's death, Rita moved Tuff Gong Recording studios and production offices to Marcus Garvey Drive. She then converted the house at 56 Hope Road into a museum and library where international guests are welcome to take guided tours of the property and house.

Unfortunately, Rita struggled with the management of the majority of Bob's financial interests and business relationships, including the treatment of the members of the Wailers band. By 1986, the majority of the band was forced to sign contracts that bought out their future royalties for small but immediate sums. Then, in 1987, it was announced that Rita and her advisers—her lawyer, David Steinberg, and her accountant, Marvin Zolt—were under investigation for alleged acts of fraud. It was rumored that the three had agreed to withhold several of Bob's offshore assets and keep them separate from the rest of his Jamaican estate. During the investigation, Rita was removed as manager of the estate, and the court appointed a Jamaican bank to administer it. Subsequently, the bank froze all the estate holdings, including the house in Miami that Bob had purchased for his mother.

Lawsuits, deceit, and general chaos threatened to overshadow the musical legacy of Bob Marley. The entirety of Bob's estate was put up for sale by the Jamaican government for the relatively paltry sum of $8 million. Chris Blackwell's Island Logic Inc. was the highest bidder, and, against the objections of the family, the estate was sold. In March 1989, Blackwell bought the rights to all of Bob's recordings, his song catalogue, and all future royalties and real estate for $8.6 million. He then sold Island Records in the summer of 1989 to the German record conglomerate Polygram. In 1998, Polygram was sold to Seagrams.

Despite this constant transfer of ownership, Bob's music continues to stand the test of time. This is attested to in a number of ways, one of which is the awards that are heaped on Bob even in death. Marley was inducted into the Rock and Roll Hall of Fame in 1994, received the forty-third Grammy Lifetime Achievement Award, and has a star on the Hollywood Walk of Fame. In February 1981, Bob was awarded Jamaica's third highest honor, the Jamaican Order of Merit. In 1999, *Time* magazine voted *Exodus* the album of the century. Also, the song "One Love" was named the song of the millennium by the BBC. Each February, the Jamaican government presents a Bob Marley Award for Culture. Among other awards, the Caribbean Music Expo annually presents the Bob Marley Lifetime Achievement Award. His continued recognition as a highly talented and respected artist is reflected in his transcendent popularity decades after his death.

The sheer number of Bob's recordings that have sold is staggering. Since 1991 (when SoundScan became reliable), more than 21.3 million recordings by Bob Marley and the Wailers have been sold.[1]

February 6, 2005, was an important date for the Marley family. If Bob were still alive, this date would have marked his sixtieth birthday. International concerts were staged as part of the celebration, and Bob Marley festivals were held around the world. Rita "mounted a month long celebration in Ethiopia, the spiritual homeland of the Rastafarian religion . . . [said Rita] being his 60th birthday, I thought it was an appropriate time to do this."[2]

Bob's legacy lives on through his 11 children, only 4 of which were with Rita. Rita, Cedella, and the children created the Bob Marley Foundation in 1991 with the express purpose of supplying education, training, and food to underprivileged parts of Africa. The Marley Group of companies has now grown to 10 individual entities, which include Tuff Gong International and Rita Marley Music. In addition, on February 6, 2005, Bob's house at 56 Hope Road in St. Andrew Parish was officially declared a protected Heritage Site.

Although Bob Dylan refused to be tagged the spokesman for a generation, Bob Marley reveled in being accorded a similar title. Bob Marley wanted to lead people; specifically, he wanted to lead his people to Zion and out of their Babylonian captivity. Most important, he wanted to lead people through his music. The abundant and often autobiographical messages found in his lyrics demonstrate his acceptance of his roles as leader, guide, and prophet. The directions that he gave in his final three albums were meant to provide a plan for the changes that he believed that members of the African diaspora had to make. Bob himself said it best: "reggae is a vehicle that is used to transmit a message of redemption to people on earth today. We use it fe dat . . . because I don't see no other music can carry the message as good as it. [Reggae] is like a heavy duty machine."[3]

# Selected Discography

Unknown information in the lists below is noted with a question mark.

**SINGLES**

| Year/Title (A- and B-sides) | Producer/Studio/Label Number |
|---|---|
| *1962* | |
| Judge Not/Do You Still Love Me | Leslie Kong/Beverley's/WI 088 |
| *1963* | |
| One Cup of Coffee/Exodus | Kong/Beverley's/WI 128 |
| *1965* | |
| Simmer Down/I Don't Need Your Love | Dodd/World Disc/JB186 |
| Lonesome Feelings/There She Goes | Dodd/World Disc/JB 211 |
| Train to Skaville (Soul Brothers)/ I Made a Mistake (Wailers) | Dodd/Ska Beat/JB 226 |
| It Hurts to Be Alone/Mr. Talkative | Dodd/World Disc/WI 188 |
| Playboy/Your Love | Dodd/World Disc/WI 206 |
| Hoot Nanny Hoot (Peter Tosh)/ Do You Remember (Bob Marley) | Dodd/Island/WI 211 |
| Hooligan/Maga Dog (Peter Tosh) | Dodd/Island/WI 212 |
| Shame and Scandal (Peter Tosh)/ The Jerk | Dodd/Island/WI 215 |
| Don't Ever Leave Me/Donna | Dodd/Island/WI 216 |
| *1966* | |
| What's New Pussycat/Where Will I Find | Dodd/Island/WI 254 |
| And I Love Her/Do the Right | Dodd/Ska Beat/JB 230 |
| Independent Anniversary Ska (Skatalites)/ Jumbie Jamboree (Wailers) | Dodd/Island /WI 260 |

| | |
|---|---|
| Put It On/Love Won't Be Mine | Dodd/Island/WI 268 |
| He Who Feels It Knows It/Sunday Morning | Dodd/Island/WI 3001 |
| Let Him Go (Rude Boy Get Bail)/ Sinner Man | Dodd/Island/WI 3009 |
| Dancing Shoes/Don't Look Back | Dodd/Rio/R 116 |
| Rude Boy (Wailers)/Ringo's Theme (Rolando Alphonso and the Soul Brothers) | Dodd/Doctor Bird/DB 1013 |
| Good Good Rudie (Wailers)/ Oceans 11 (City Slickers) | Dodd/Doctor Bird/DB 1021 |
| Rasta Put It On (Peter Tosh)/ Ska with Ringo (Rolando Alphonso and the Soul Brothers) | Dodd/Doctor Bird/DB1039 |
| Pussy Galore (Lee Perry and Wailers)/ Provocation (Rolando Alphonso) | Dodd/Studio One (U.K.)/? |
| Who Feels It Knows It/Sunday Morning | Dodd/Island/WI 3001 |
| Love and Affection/Teenager in Love | Dodd/Skabeat/JB 228 |

*1967*

| | |
|---|---|
| Bend Down Low/Mellow Mood | Wailers/Wail'n'Soul/? |
| I Am the Toughest (Peter Tosh)/ No Faith (Marsha Griffiths) | Dodd/Island/WI 3042 |
| Bend Down Low/Freedom Time | Dodd/Island/WI 3043 |
| Nice Time/Hypocrite | Clancy Eccles/Doctor Bird/ DB 1091 |
| Come by Here (Norma Frazier)/ I Stand Predominant | Dodd/Studio One (U.K.)/SO 2024 |

*1968*

| | |
|---|---|
| Stir It Up/This Train | Wailers/Trojan/TR 617 |
| Nice Time/Hypocrite | Wailers/Tuff Gong/? |

*1969*

| | |
|---|---|
| Soon Come/version | Leslie Kong/Beverley's/S.R. 133 |

*1970*

| | |
|---|---|
| Stranger in Love (John Holt)/Jailhouse | Dodd/Bamboo/BAM 55 |
| Soul Shake Down Party/version (Beverley's All-Stars) | Kong/Trojan/TR 7759 |
| My Cup/Son of Thunder (Upsetters) | Lee Perry/Upsetter/US 340 |
| Dreamland/My Cup version (Upsetters) | Lee Perry/Upsetter/US 342 |
| Mr. Brown/Dracula (version of Mr. Brown, Upsetters) | Perry/Upsetter/US 354 |
| Duppy Conqueror (Wailers)/Zig Zag | Perry/Upsetter/US 348 |
| Duppy Conqueror/version | Perry/Upsetter/US 348 |
| Duppy Conqueror (Wailers)/ Justice (Upsetters) | Perry/Upsetter/US 348 |

| | |
|---|---|
| Cross the Nation (Wailers)/ version (Upsetters) | Perry/Upsetter (NYC)/LP 007 |
| Cross the Nation/All in One (medley) | Perry/Upsetter (NYC)/LP 007 |
| Mr. Chatterbox/Walk through the World (unknown artist) | Bunny Lee/Jackpot/JP 730 |
| To the Rescue/Run for Cover (maybe a version of To the Rescue) | Wailers/Escort/ERT 842 |
| Upsetting Station/Dig Your Grave | Perry/Upsetter/US 349 |
| Duppy Conqueror/Justice (Upsetters) | Perry/Unity/UN 562 |
| Run for Cover/Sun Is Shining | Wailers/Tuff Gong/? |

### 1971

| | |
|---|---|
| Mr. Brown/Dracula | Perry/Upsetter/US 354 |
| Stop the Train/Caution | Kong/Summit/SUM 8526 |
| Freedom Train/version | Kong/Summit/SUM 8530 |
| Kaya/version (Upsetters) | Perry/Upsetter/US 356 |
| Small Axe/All in One | Perry/Upsetter/US 357 |
| More Axe/The Axe Man (both Small Axe versions) | Perry/Upsetter/US 369 |
| Dreamland (Wailers)/version (Upsetters) | Perry/Upsetter/US 371 |
| Small Axe/What a Confusion (David Barker) | Perry/Punch/PH 69 |
| Down Presser/Got the Tip (Junior Byles) | Perry/Punch/PH 77 |
| Small Axe (Wailers)/version (Upsetters) | Perry/Upsetter (NYC)/LP 009 |
| Secondhand/Secondhand, part 2 | Perry/Upsetter (NYC)/LP 9001 |
| More Axe/Axe Man | Perry/Upsetter (NYC)/? |
| Duppy Conquer (Wailers)/ Justice (Upsetters) | Perry/Shelter-Capital/7309 |
| Duppy Conquer/Duppy Conquer (A-side stereo/B-side mono) | Perry/Shelter-Capital/7309 |
| Duppy Conqueror/version | Perry/Clocktower/CT 505 |
| Let the Lord Be Seen in You/ White Christmas | Wailers/Supreme/? |
| I Like It Like This/I Am Sorry | Wailers/Supreme/SUP 216 |
| Soultown/Let the Sun Shine on Me | Wailers/Bullet/BU 464 |
| Lick Samba/version | Wailers/Bullet/BU 493 |
| Trench Town Rock/Grooving Kingston. (12-inch) (version) | Wailers/Green Door/GD 4005 |
| Lively Up Yourself/ Live (Tommy McCook) | Wailers/Green Door/GD 4002 |
| Picture on the Wall (Rass Dawkins & Wailers/version (Upsetters) | Perry/Upsetter/US 368 |

### 1972

| | |
|---|---|
| Keep on Moving/African Herbsman | Perry/Upsetter/US 392 |
| Mellow Mood/Bend Down Low | Sims, Nash, Perkins/Wirl/? |
| Reggae on Broadway/Oh Lord I Got to Get There | Sims, Nash, Perkins/CBS (UK)/ CBS 8114 |

| | |
|---|---|
| Guava Jelly/Redder Than Red | Wailers/Green Door/GD 4025 |
| Screwface/Face Man | Wailers/Punch/PH 101 |
|   (version of Screwface) | |
| You Should Have Known Better/ | Wailers/Punch/PH 114 |
|   Instrumental version | |

*1973*

| | |
|---|---|
| Baby Baby We've Got a Date/ | Marley/Blue Mountain/BM 1021 |
|   Stop That Train | |
| Concrete Jungle/Reincarnated Soul | Marley/Island/WI 6164 |
| Concrete Jungle/No More Trouble | Marley & Blackwell/Island/1215 |
| Rock It Baby/Stop That Train | Marley & Blackwell/Island/1211 |
| Get Up, Stand Up/Slave Driver | Marley & Blackwell/Island/ WI 6167 |
| I Shot the Sheriff/Pass It On/ | Marley/Island/IDJ ? |
|   Duppy Conqueror (3-song EP/ | |
|   12-inch) | |

*1974*

| | |
|---|---|
| Soul Shake Down Party/Caution | Kong/Trojan/TR 7911 reissue |
| African Herbsman/Stand Alone | Perry/Black Heart/45 8042 |
| Mr. Brown/version | Kong/Trojan/TR 7926 |
| So Jah Seh/Natty Dread | Marley/Island/WIP 6262 |
| Lively Up Yourself/So Jah Seh | Marley/Island/IS 027 |
| No Woman, No Cry/Kinky Reggae | Steve Smith & Chris Blackwell/ |
|   (both live at Lyceum) | Island/16398 AT (WIP 6244) |

*1975*

| | |
|---|---|
| Trench Town Rock/I Shot the Sheriff | Marley/Island/IDJ 7 |
| No Woman, No Cry/Kinky Reggae | Marley/Island/WIP 6244 |

*1976*

| | |
|---|---|
| Mr. Brown/Trench Town Rock | Perry/Trojan/TR 7979 |
| Jah Live/Concrete Jungle | Marley/Island/WIP 6265 |
| Johnny Was/Cry to Me | Marley/Island/WIP 6296 |
| Roots, Rock, Reggae/Stir It Up | Marley/Island/WIP 6309 |
| Roots, Rock, Reggae/Cry to Me | Marley/Island/IS 060 |
| Positive Vibration/Roots, Rock, Reggae | Marley/Island/WIP 26348 |
| Who the Cap Fit/Roots, Rock, Reggae | Marley/Island/IS 072 |

*1977*

| | |
|---|---|
| Three Little Birds/Three Little Birds dub | Wailers/Island/IS 236 |
| Reggae on Broadway/Oh Lord | Sims, Nash, Perkins/CBS/CBS 4902 |
| Exodus/Stir It Up | Marley/Island/IS 089 |
| Exodus/Instrumental version | Marley/Island/WIP 6390 |
| Exodus/Instrumental version | Marley/Island/IXP-7 |
| Waiting in Vain/Roots | Marley/Island/IS 092 |
| Waiting in Vain/Roots | Marley/Island/WIP 6402 |
| Jamming/Punky Reggae Party | Marley & Perry/Island/WIP 6410 |

| | |
|---|---|
| Jamming/No Woman, No Cry (live) (3-song EP/12-inch) | Marley/Island/IS 49755 |

*1978*

| | |
|---|---|
| Is This Love/Crisis (version) | Marley/Island/IS 099 |
| Is This Love/Crisis | Marley/Island/WIP 6420 |
| Satisfy My Soul/Smile Jamaica | Marley/Island/WIP 6440 |
| War/No More Trouble/Exodus (live) | Blackwell & Jack Nuber/Island/ IPR 2026 |

*1979*

| | |
|---|---|
| Stir It Up/Rat Race (live) (both taken from *Babylon by Bus* album) | Blackwell & Nuber/Island/ WIP 6478 |
| So Much Trouble in the World/ Instrumental version | Wailers & Alex Sadkin/Island/ WIP 6501 |
| Survival/Wake Up and Live | Marley/Island/WIP 6553 |
| Survival/Wake Up and Live | Marley/Island/IS 49080 |
| One Drop/Kaya | Marley/Island/IS 49156 |
| Could You Be Loved/One Drop/ Ride Natty Ride (3-song EP/12-inch) | Marley/Island/WIP 6610 |
| Wake Up and Live, pt. 1/Wake Up and Live, pt. 2 | Wailers & Sadkin/Island/IS 49080 |
| Zimbabwe/Survival | Wailers & Sadkin/Island/WIP 6597 |

*1980*

| | |
|---|---|
| Zimbabwe/Africa Unite/Wake Up and Live (3-song EP/12-inch) | Marley/Island/12-inch WIP 6597 |
| Could You be Loved/One Drop | Marley/Island/WIP 6610 |
| Could You be Loved/One Drop/ Ride Natty Ride (3-song EP/12-inch) | Marley/Island/12-inch WIP 6610 |
| Three Little Birds/Every Need Got an Ego to Feed (version of Pimper's Paradise) | Marley/Island/WIP 6641 |
| Redemption Song/band version | Wailers & Blackwell/Island/ WIP 6653 |
| Redemption Song/version/I Shot the Sheriff (3-song EP/12-inch) | Marley/Island/12-inch WIP 6653 |
| Coming In From the Cold/ Redemption Song | Marley/Island/IS 49636 |

*1981*

| | |
|---|---|
| Thank You Lord/Wisdom | Sims, Nash, Perkins (JAD)/Trojan/ TRO 9065 |
| Reggae on Broadway/Gonna Get You (12-inch) | Sims, Nash, Perkins/Cotillion/ 79250 |
| Reggae on Broadway/Reggae on Broadway (long and short versions; 12-inch) | Sims, Nash, Perkins/Cotillion/ DMD 291 |
| Reggae on Broadway/Gonna Get You | Sims, Nash, Perkins/ Cotillion/46023 |

| | |
|---|---|
| Reggae on Broadway/Gonna Get You | ?/Warner/K79250 |
| Jammin'/No Woman, No Cry | Marley/Island/IS 49755 |
| Chances Are/Dance Do the Reggae | ?/?/WEA 79275 |

*1982*

| | |
|---|---|
| Natural Mystic/Carry Us Along | ?/Island/WIP 6774 |
| Buffalo Soldier/Buffalo dub | Wailers & Errol Brown/Island/ IS 108 |
| Soul Shakedown Party/Caution | ?/Trojan/TROT 9074 |
| Waiting in Vain/Blackman Redemption | Wailers & Brown/Island/ 106637–100 |

*1983*

| | |
|---|---|
| Buffalo Soldier/Buffalo dub (12-inch) | Marley/Island/DMD 628 |

*1984*

| | |
|---|---|
| One Love/So Much Trouble/ People Get Ready/Keep On Moving (both are remakes from the *Legend* album on 12-inch EP) | Marley/Island/12-inch IS 169 |
| One Love (extended version)/ So Much Trouble/Keep On Moving (12-inch) | ?/Island/12-inchIS169 |
| Waiting in Vain/Black Man Redemption | ?/Island/IS 180 |
| Waiting in Vain/Black Man Redemption Marley Mix Up (12-inch) (a. Exodus, b. Positive Vibration, c. Pimpers Paradise, d. Punky Reggae Party medley) | ?/Island/12-inch IS 180 |
| Could You be Loved/Jamming/ No Woman, No Cry/Coming in from the Cold (12-inch) | ?/Island/12-inch IS 210 |

*1990*

| | |
|---|---|
| Could You Be Loved/Africa Unite | Marley/Island/422–875 676–4 |

*1991*

| | |
|---|---|
| Get Up, Stand Up (live 12-inch from *Talkin' Blues*) | Marley/Island/PR12-inch 6651–1 |

*1992*

| | |
|---|---|
| Iron, Lion, Zion/Smile Jamaica/ Three Little Birds/Iron, Lion, Zion (12-inch mix) | Marley/Island/864405–2 |

## ALBUMS

| **Title** | **Year/Producer/Studio/ Label Number** |
|---|---|
| *The Wailers (Jamaica's Top Rated Singing Sensation, Accompanied by the Soul Brothers)* | *mid-1960s/Dodd/Studio One* |

Put It On; I Need You; Lonesome Feeling; What's Up Pussycat; One Love; When the Well Runs Dry; Ten Commandments of Love; Rude Boy; It Hurts to Be Alone; Love and Affection; I'm Still Waiting Simmer Down.

*The Best of the Wailers*                    ?/Kong/Beverley's/BLP 001
Soul Shake Down Party; Stop That Train; Caution; Soul Captives; Go Tell It on the Mountain; Can't You See; Soon Come; Cheer Up; Back Out; Do It Twice.

*Shakedown*                                  ?/Kong/ALA/ALA 1982
Soul Shake Down Party; Stop That Train; Caution; Soul Captives; Go Tell It on the Mountain; Can't You See; Soon Come; Cheer Up; Back Out; Do It Twice.

*Soul Captives*                              circa 1970/Kong/ALA/
                                             ALA 1986
(Also released under the titles *Shakedown, Soul Shakedown, Best Sellers,* and *The Best of the Wailers*)
Soul Shake Down Party; Stop That Train; Caution; Soul Captives; Go Tell It on the Mountain; Can't You See; Soon Come; Cheer Up; Back Out; Do It Twice.

*Bob Marley and the Wailers*                 ?/Kong/Hammer/HMR 9006
(Same tracks as above, but in a different sequence)

*Reggae Revolution Vol. 2*                   ?/Perry/Pressure Disc/50028
Keep On Moving; Don't Rock My Boat; Put It On; Fussing and Fighting; Duppy Conqueror; Memphis; Riding High; Kaya; African Herbsman; Stand Alone; Sun Is Shining; Brain Washing.

*The Wailing Wailers*                        1965/Dodd/Studio One/S1001
(A compilation of singles from Studio One)
Put It In; I Need You; What's New Pussycat; One Love; When the Well Runs Dry; Ten Commandments of Love; Rude Boy; It Hurts to Be Alone; Love and Affection; I'm Still Waiting; Simmer Down.

*Soul Rebels*                                1970/Perry/Upsetter/TBL 126
(Also Trojan TBL 126 and a reissue in 1989)
Soul Rebel; Try Me; It's Alright; No Sympathy; My Cup; Soul Almighty; Rebels Hop; Corner Stone; 400 Years; No Water; Reaction; My Sympathy.

*Soul Revolution*                            1971/Perry/Upsetter/
                                             TTL65ATTL65B
(Also Maroon LOPTTL65B/TI65A and issued in the U.S. on Black Heart)
Keep On Moving; Don't Rock My Boat; Put It On; Fussing and Fighting; Duppy Conqueror; Memphis; Riding High; Kaya; African Herbsman; Stand Alone; Sun Is Shining; Brain Washing.

*Soul Revolution II*                         1971/Perry/Upsetter/TTL65/
                                             66A/B
(Reissue of this album without words; also released in the U.K. on Trojan TTL65A/B; 66A/B)

*African Herbsman*                                    1973/Perry/Trojan/TRLS 62
(This album was reissued in 1988, CDTRL 62, and formed part of the Trojan
*Early Years 1969–73* box set)
  Lively Up Yourself; Small Axe; Duppy Conqueror; Trench Town Rock;
  African Herbsman; Keep On Moving; Fussing and Fighting; Stand Alone;
  All in One; Don't Rock the Boat; Put It On; Sun is Shining; Kaya; Riding
  High; Brain Washing; 400 Years.

*Catch a Fire*                                        1973 (April)/Marley &
                                                      Blackwell/Island/ILPS 9241
(Reissued by Mango ILPM 9241, 1987; Tuff Gong TGLLP 1/CD & TGLCD,
1990)
  Concrete Jungle; Slave Driver; 400 Years; Stop That Train; Baby We've Got a
  Date; Stir It Up; Kinky Reggae; No More Trouble; Midnight Ravers.

*Burnin'*                                             1973 (November)/Wailers &
                                                      Blackwell/Island/ILPS 9256
(Reissued as Mango ILPM 9256, 1987; Tuff Gong TGLLP 2, CD TGLCD 2,
1990)
  Get Up, Stand Up; Hallelujah Time; I Shot the Sheriff; Burnin' and Lootin';
  Put It On; Small Axe; Pass It On; Duppy Conqueror; One Foundation; Rasta
  Man Chant.

*Natty Dread*                                         1974 (October)/Blackwell and
                                                      the Wailers/Island/ILPS 9281
(Reissued: Mango ILPM 9281, CD CID 9281, 1987; Tuff Gong TGLLP 3, CD
TGLCD 3, 1990)
  Lively Up Yourself; No Woman, No Cry; Them Belly Full (But We Hungry);
  Rebel Music (Three O'clock Road Block); So Jah Seh; Natty Dread; Bend
  Down Low; Talkin' Blues; Revolution.

*The Best of Bob Marley and the Wailers*              1974/Coxsone/Studio One/
                                                      GW 0002
(A compilation of Studio One recordings)
  I Am Going Home; Bend Down Low; Mr. Talkative; Ruddie; Cry to Me;
  Wings of a Dove; Small Axe; Love Won't Be Mine; Dancing Shoes; Sunday
  Morning; He Who Feels It Knows It; Straight and Narrow Way.

*Rasta Revolution*                                    1974(July)/Perry/Trojan/
                                                      TRLS 89
(Reissued in 1988, CDTRL 89; forms part of the Trojan *Early Years 1969–73*
box set)
  Mr. Brown; Soul Rebel; Try Me; It's Alright; No Sympathy; My Cup; Duppy
  Conqueror; Rebel's Hop; Corner Stone; 400 Years; No Water; Reaction; Soul
  Almighty.

*Live! Bob Marley and the Wailers*                    1975 (May)/Steve Smith and
                                                      Blackwell/Island/ILPS 9376

(Reissued by Mango ILPM 9376, 1987; CD CID 9376, 1987; Tuff Gong TGLLP 4, CD TGLCD 4, 1990 (a/k/a *Live at the Lyceum*)
   Trench Town Rock; Burnin' and Lootin'; Them Belly Full; Lively Up Your-self; No Woman, No Cry; I Shot the Sheriff; Get Up, Stand up.

*A Taste of the Wailers*                    1975 (May)/Marley, Blackwell, &
                                            Wailers/Island/ISS 3
(Released only in the U.K. as a promotion for the tour that produced the *Live!* album)
   Lively Up Yourself; Kinky Reggae; No Woman, No Cry; Get Up, Stand Up; I Shot the Sheriff; Stir It Up; Natty Dread.

*The Best of Bob Marley and the Wailers*    1976/Dodd/Studio
                                            One-Buddah/SO 1106
   Destiny; Ruddie Boy; Cry to Me; Love Won't Be Mine; Play Boy; Sunday Morn-ing; Put It On; I Need You; What's New Pussycat; Where Is My Mother; Wages of Love; Ruddie Boy (appears twice, second time is mislabeled "Jailhouse").

*The Birth of a Legend*                     1976/Dodd/Calla/CAS 1240
(Two-record compilation of Studio One oldies, rereleased on Epic ZGT 46769)
   I Made a Mistake; One Love; Let Him Go; Love and Affection; Simmer Down; Maga Dog; I am Going Home; Donna; Nobody Knows; Lonesome Feeling; Wings of a Dove; It Hurts to Be Alone; I'm Still Waiting; Who Feels It Knows It; Do You Remember; Dancing Shoes; I Don't Need Your Love; Lonesome Track; Do You Feel the Same Way; The Ten Commandments of Love.

*Rastaman Vibrations*                       1976 (April)/Marley & Wailers/
                                            Tuff Gong/ILPS 9383
(Reissued as Mango ILPM 9383, CD CID 9383, 1987; Tuff Gong TGLLP/CD 5, 1990)
   Positive Vibration; Roots, Rock, Reggae; Johnny Was; Cry to Me; Want More; Crazy Baldhead; Who the Cap Fit; Night Shift; War; Rat Race.

*The Birth of a Legend*                     1977/Dodd/CBS/XZ 34859
   I Made a Mistake; One Love; Let Him Go; Love and Affection; Simmer Down; Maga Dog; I Am Going Home; Donna; Nobody Knows; Lonesome Feeling.

*Birth of a Legend 1963–1966*               1977/Dodd/Epic/ZGT 46769
(Originally released on two Calla LPs; reissued by Legacy Records in 1990)
   Simmer Down; It Hurts to Be Alone; Lonesome Feelings; Love and Affec-tion; I'm Still Waiting; One Love; I Am Going Home; Wings of a Dove; Let Him Go; Who Feels It Knows It; Maga Dog; I Made a Mistake; Lone-some Tracks; Nobody Knows; Ten Commandments of Love; Donna; Do You Remember; Dancing Shoes; I Don't Need Your Love; Do You Feel the Same Way.

*Early Music*                                    1977/Dodd/CBS/XZ ZX 34760
Wings of a Dove; It Hurts to Be Alone; I'm Still Waiting; Do You Remember;
Dancing Shoes; I Don't Need Your Love; Lonesome Track; Do You Feel the
Same Way; The Ten Commandments of Love.

*Exodus*                                         1977 (May)/Marley & Wailers/
                                                 Island/ILPS 9498
(Reissued as Mango ILPM 9498, 1987; CD CID 9498, 1987; Tuff Gong:
TGLLP/CD 1990)
Natural Mystic; So Much Things to Say; Guiltiness; The Heathen; Exodus;
Jamming; Waiting in Vain; Turn Your Lights Down Low; Tree Little Birds;
One Love/People Get Ready.

*Kaya*                                           1978 (March)/Marley &
                                                 Wailers/Island/ILPS 9517
(Reissued as Mango ILPM/CID 9517, 1987; Tuff Gong TGLLP/CD, 1990)
Easy Skankin'; Kaya; Is This Love; Sun Is Shining; Satisfy My Soul; She's
Gone; Misty Morning; Crisis; Running Away; Time Will Tell.

*Babylon by Bus*                                 1978 (December)/Marley &
                                                 Wailers/Island/ISLD 1298
(Double live album recorded at the Pavilion in Paris; reissues: Tuff Gong
TGDLP/CD 1, 1990)
Positive Vibrations; Punky Reggae Party; Exodus; Stir It Up; Rat Race; Con-
crete Jungle; Kinky Reggae; Lively Up Yourself; Rebel Music; War/No More
Trouble; Is This Love; Heathen; Jamming.

*Survival*                                       1979 (October)/Marley, Wailers,
                                                 & Alex Sadkin/Island/ILPS 9542
(Reissued as Mango ILPM/CID 9542, 1987; Tuff Gong TGLLP/CD 8, 1990)
So Much Trouble in the World; Zimbabwe; Top Rankin'; Babylon System;
Survival; Africa Unite; One Drop; Ride Natty Ride; Ambush in the Night;
Wake Up and Live.

*Uprising*                                       1980 (June)/Marley &
                                                 Wailers/Island/ILPS 9596
(Reissued as CD CID 9596, 1987; Tuff Gong TGLLP/CD 9, 1990)
Coming in from the Cold; Real Situation; Bad Card; We and Dem; Work;
Zion Train; Pimper's Paradise; Could You Be Loved; Forever Loving Jah;
Redemption Song.

*Soul Revolution Part II*                        1981/Perry/Pressure Disc/LPS 507
Keep On Moving; Don't Rock My Boat; Put It On; Fussing and Fighting;
Duppy Conqueror; Memphis; Riding High; Kaya; African Herbsman; Stand
Alone; Sun Is Shining; Brain Washing.

*Reggae*                                         1981/Perry/Pressure Disc/50028
Keep On Moving; Don't Rock My Boat; Put It On; Fussing and Fighting;
Duppy Conqueror; Memphis; Riding High; Kaya; African Herbsman; Stand
Alone; Sun Is Shining; Brain Washing.

*Reggae Revolution Volume 3*                    1981/Perry/Pressure Disc/50029
Mr. Brown
Duppy Conqueror; Rebel's Hop; 400 Years; Soul Almighty; Lively Up Your-
self; Small Axe; Trench Town Rock; All in One; Keep On Moving.

*Chances Are*                                    1981/Sims, Nash, Perkins/
                                                 Cotillion/SD 5228
Reggae on Broadway; Gonna Get You; Chances Are; Soul Rebel; Dance Do
the Reggae; Mellow Mood; Stay with Me; (I'm) Hurting Inside.

*Soul Rebel*                                     1982/Sims, Nash, Perkins/
                                                 New Cross/NC 001
(Compilation issued in the U.K. on New Cross and in Germany on
Bellaphon)
There She Goes; Put It On; How Many Times; Mellow Mood; Changes *(sic)*
Are; Hammer; Tell Me;  Touch Me; Treat You Right; Soul Rebel.

*Marley, Tosh, Livingston, and Associates*      1982/Dodd/Studio One/
                                                 FCD 40471
Another Dance; Lonesome Track; Rolling Stone; Can't You See; Let Him
Go; Dance with Me; Maga Dog; I Want Somewhere; Hoot Nanny Hoot;
Dreamland.

*Marley*                                         1982/Perry/Phoenix/Phoenix 10
Kaya; Mr. Brown; Rebel's Hop; 400 Years; Soul Almighty; My Cup; Corner
Stone; No Water; Reaction; Try Me.

*Jamaican Storm*                                 1982/Sims, Nash, Perkins/Accord/
                                                 SN 7211
(Same album as *Soul Rebel* on Holy Cross)
There She Goes; Put It On; How Many Times; Mellow Mood; Chances Are;
Hammer; Tell Me; Touch Me; Treat You Right; Soul Rebel.

*Bob Marley Interviews*                          1982/various producers/
                                                 Tuff Gong/RM007
Natural Mystic; Trench Town Rock; Redemption Song; Babylon System;
Time Will Tell; Natural Mystic (appears twice); Revolution; Survival; One
Drop; Roots, Rock, Reggae; Guava Jelly; Rat Race.

*Bob Marley and the Wailers (Box Set)*           1982/various producers/Mango/
                                                 BMSP 100
(Nine Island LP collection)
Catch a Fire; Burnin'; Natty Dread; Live!; Rastaman Vibration; Exodus; Kaya;
Survival; Uprising.
(release limited to 10,000 copies aimed at the U.S. market)

*Confrontation*                                  1983/Blackwell & Wailers/
                                                 Island/7 90085–1
(Also released in the U.K. as a picture disc; reissues: Mango ILPM/CID 9760,
1987; Tuff Gong TGLLP/CD 10, 1990)

Chant Down Babylon; Buffalo Soldier; Jump Nyabinghi; Mix Up, Mix Up; Give Thanks and Praises; Blackman Redemption; Trench Town; Stiff Necked Fools; I Know; Rastaman Live Up.

*Bob Marley and the Wailers: In the*          1983/various producers/
*Beginning*                                   Trojan/TRLS 221
(This album also forms part of the Trojan box set *The Early Years 1969–1973*)
  Soul Shakedown Party; Adam and Eve; Brand New Second Hand; Cheer Up; This Train; Jah Is Mighty; Caution; Thank You Lord; Keep On Skankin'; Wisdom; Stop the Train; Mr. Chatterbox; Turn Me Loose.

*Legend: The Best of Bob Marley*          1984/Island/7 90169-1
  (Greatest hits collection; producers include Steve Smith, Bob Marley and the Wailers, Chris Blackwell, and Errol Brown, with five dance remixes by Eric Thorngren noted with an *)
(Island BMW 1, 1984; Picture Disc PBMW 1, 1984; CD/CID 103, 1985; Tuff Gong TGDCD 1, 1990)
  Is This Love; No Woman, No Cry*; Could You Be Loved; Three Little Birds; Buffalo Soldier*; Get Up, Stand Up; Stir It Up; One Love/People Get Ready; I Shot the Sheriff; Waiting in Vain*; Redemption Song; Satisfy My Soul; Exodus*; Jamming*.

*The Wailers: Reggae Greats*          1984/various producers/Mango/
                                      MLPS 9575
(Forms part of Island's "Greats" series of reggae reissues)
  Concrete Jungle; No More Trouble; Get Up, Stand Up; Rock It Baby; Burnin' and Lootin'; Small Axe; Pass It On; Midnight Ravers; Stop That Train; Rastaman Chant.

*Bob Marley and the Wailers: Bob, Peter,*          1985/Sims, Nash, Perkins/
*Bunny, and Rita*                                  Jamaica/JR 10002
(JAD sides with new music tracks added)
  Oh Lord; It Hurts to Be Alone; Lonesome Feeling; Milkshake and Potato Chips; Touch Me; Lonely Girl; The World Is Changing; Treat You Right; Soul Shake Down Party.

*Bob Marley and the Wailers: Rebel Music*          1986/various producers/Island/
                                                   ILPS 9843
(Reissued as Tuff Gong TGGLP/CD 11, 1990)
  Rebel Music; So Much Trouble in the World; Them Belly Full; Rat Race; War; Roots; Slave Driver; Ride Natty Ride; Crazy Baldhead; Get Up, Stand Up.

*Bob Marley Roots: Early Recordings*          1987/Lee Perry/TKO Magnum/
*from Reggae's Greatest Superstar*            MM008
  Soul Shakedown Party; Caution; Do It Twice; Back Out; Try Me; Corner Stone; No Water; Soul Almighty; I Made a Mistake; Ley *(sic)* Him Go; I'm Going Home; Nobody Knows; The Wings of a Dove; Soul Captives; Don't Rock the Boat; Stand Alone.

*Soul Revolution I and II*                    1988/Perry/Trojan/TRLD 406
(Double LP; contains the original *Soul Revolution* album and its instrumental
versions from 1971)

*Reggae Roots*                                1988/?/Garland/?
No More Trouble; Baby We've Got a Date; Rainbow Country; Slave Driver;
Duppy Conqueror; Natural Mystic; Keep On Movin'; Stir It Up; Kinky Reg-
gae; Stand Alone; Concrete Jungle.

*Bob Marley: His 24 Greatest Hits*            1990/various producers/SAAR/
                                              CD 0282
(Compilation CD released by SAAR as part of "The Entertainers" series)
Stir It Up; One Love; Rebel's Hop; 400 Years; Riding High; Slave Driver; Soul
Almighty; Duppy Conqueror; Small Axe; Baby We've Got a Datel;Kinky Reg-
gae; Concrete Jungle; No More Trouble; Mr. Brown; Soul Rebel; Trench Town
Rock; Lord I'm Comin'; Back Out; Soul Shakedown Party; Do It Twice; Soul
Captive; Stop the Train.

*Bob Marley and the Wailers:*                 1990/various producers/Epic/
*The Birth of a Legend*                       ZGK 46769
(Digitally remastered collection of early Wailers tracks released by CBS and Epic
Records)
Simmer Down; I Hurts to Be Alone; Lonesome Feelings; Love and Affec-
tion; I'm Still Waiting; One Love; I Am Going Home; Wings of a Dove; Let
Him Go; Who Feels It Knows It; Maga Dog; I Made a Mistake; Lonesome
Track; Nobody Knows; The Ten Commandments of Love; Donna; Do You
Remember; Dancing Shoes; I Don't Need Your Love; Do You Feel the
Same Way.

*Bob Marley*                                  1990/?/JCI Associated Labels/?
400 Years; Corner Store; Kaya; Mr. Brown; My Cup; No Water; Reaction;
Rebel's Hop; Soul Almighty; Try Me.

*Talkin' Blues*                               1991/Island-Tuff Gong/
                                              422–848 243
(Live and studio recordings with interview clips of Marley with Dermont
Hussey)
Talkin' Blues; Burnin' and Lootin'; Kinky Reggae; Get Up, Stand Up; Slave
Driver; Walk the Proud Land; Lively Up Yourself; You Can't Blame the Youth;
Stop That Train; Rastaman Chant; Am-A-Do (previously unreleased).

*All the Hits*                                1991/various producers/Rohit/
                                              RRLP 7757
(U.S. release only; each track is accompanied by an instrumental version)
Redder Than Red; Nice Time; Hypocrites; Mellow Mood; Thank You Lord;
Mr. Chatterbox; I've Got to Cry; Hey Happy People; Power & More Power;
I've Got the Action.

*Nice Time*                                   1991/various producers/
                                              Esoldun-Lagoon/REG 1–115

(*All the Hits* repackaged as a double LP)
Redder Than Red; Nice Time; Hypocrites; Mellow Mood; Thank You Lord;
Mr. Chatterbox; I've Got to Cry; Hey Happy People; Power & More Power;
I've Got the Action.

*One Love*                                  1991/Dodd/Heartbeat/
                                            HB111–112
(Two-CD compilation of Studio One material, reissued in 1992)
This Train; Simmer Down; I Am Going Home; Do You Remember; Mr. Talkative;
Habits; Amen; Go Jimmy Go; Teenager in Love; I Need You; It Hurts to Be Alone;
True Confession; Lonesome Feeling; There She Goes; Diamond Baby; Playboy;
Where's the Girl for Me; Hooligan; One Love; Love and Affection; And I Love Her;
Rude Boy; I'm Still Waiting; Ska Jerk; Somewhere to Lay My Head; Wages of Love;
I Am Gonna Put It On; Cry to Me; Jailhouse; Sinner Man; Who Feels It Knows It;
Let Him Go; When the Well Runs Dry; Can't You See; What Am I Supposed to Do;
Rolling Stone; Bend Down Low; Freedom Time; Rocking Steady.

*Bob Marley: Exodus*                        1991/live recording/On Stage
                                            CD/12002
(One of two Italian live releases made possible by differences in copyright laws.
This was not the same as the Tuff Gong *Exodus* release.)
Is This Love; Jamming; Easy Shanking *(sic)*; Get Up, Stand Up; Exodus; No
Woman, No Cry; Positive Vibration; Crisis; I Shot the Sheriff

*Bob Marley: Songs of Freedom*              1992/various producers/
                                            Island-Tuff Gong/TGCBX1
(Released as a four-CD box set; also as an eight-album vinyl set in Jamaica
TGLBX1, 1993.
Includes 64-page full-color booklet and track-by-track annotations by Rob Par-
tridge, Timothy White, Chris Salewicz, Rabbit, and Derrick Morgan)
CD 1: Judge Not; One Cup of Coffee; Simmer Down; I'm Still Waiting; One Love;
Put It On; Bus Dem Shut; Mellow Mood; Bend Down Low; Hypocrites; Stir It Up;
Nice Time; Thank You Lord; Hammer; Caution; Back Out; Soul Shakedown Party;
Do It Twice; Soul Rebel; Sun Is Shining; Don't Rock the Boat; Small Axe; Duppy
Conqueror; Mr. Brown; CD 2: Screwface; Lick Samba; Trench Town Rock; Craven
Choke Puppy; Guava Jelly; Acoustic Medley; I'm Hurting Inside; High Tide or Low
Tide; Slave Driver; No More Trouble; Concrete Jungle; Get Up, Stand Up; Rasta-
man Chant; Burnin' and Lootin'; Iron, Lion, Zion; Lively Up Yourself; Natty Dread;
I Shot the Sheriff; CD 3: No Woman, No Cry; Who the Cap Fit; Jah Live; Crazy
Baldheads; War; Johnny Was; Rat Race; Jammin'; Waiting in Vain; Exodus; Natural
Mystic; Three Little Birds; Running Away; Keep On Moving; Easy Skankin'; Is This
Love; Smile Jamaica; Time Will Tell; CD 4: Africa Unite; One Drop; Zimbabwe; So
Much Trouble; Ride Natty Ride Babylon System; Coming in from the Cold; Real
Situation; Bad Card; Could You Be Loved; Forever Loving Jah; Rastaman Live Up;
Give Thanks and Praise; One Love; Why Should I; Redemption Song.

*Songs of Freedom* (15-track sampler)       1992/various producers/Tuff
                                            Gong/TGCS 1

(Promotional CD teaser for the box set)
Simmer Down; Put It On; Nice Time; Soul Rebel; Trench Town Rock; Slave Driver; Burnin' and Lootin'; No Woman, No Cry; War; Jammin'; Time Will Tell; Africa Unite; Coming in from the Cold; Could You Be Loved; Redemption Song.

*The Upsetter Record Shop—Part 1: The Complete Soul Rebels* 1992/Perry/Esoldun-Lagoon/LG2 1040
(Each track is followed by an instrumental version); Soul Rebels (version); No Water Can Quench My Thirst (version); Rebel Hop (version); No Sympathy (version); It's Alright (version); Reaction (version); Corner Stone (version); 400 Years (version); Make Up *(sic)*, correct title, My Cup (version); Try Me (version); Soul Almighty (version).

*The Upsetter Record Shop—Part 2:*          1992/various producers/
*Rarities*                                  Esoldun-Lagoon/LG21044
(Each track on this album is followed by an instrumental version)
Concrete Jungle (version); Screw Faces *(sic)*, correct title, Screwface (version); Love Life (version); Satisfy My Soul (version); Rainbow Country (version); Long Long Winter (version); Put It On (version); Don't Rock My Boat (version); Keep On Moving (version).

*The Very Best of The Early Years 1968–74*    1992/various producers/Music
                                              Club/MCCD 033
(Tracks drawn from the Trojan Archives)
Trench Town Rock; Lively Up Yourself; Soul Almighty; Wisdom; Caution; Cheer Up; Thank You Lord; Stop the Train; This Train; Small Axe; More Axe; Don't Rock My Boat; Keep On Moving; Brand New Second Hand; Kaya; Turn Me Loose; Sun Is Shining; Keep On Skankin'.

*Bob Marley: I Shot the Sheriff*              1993/live performance/On Stage
                                              CD/12037
(An Italian live album recorded at the Quiet Knight Club, Chicago on June 10, 1975; available because of Italian copyright laws)
Trench Town Rock; Rebel Music; Natty Dread; Midnight Ravers; Slave Driver; Concrete Jungle; Talkin' Blues; I Shot the Sheriff.

*The Early Years 1969–1973*                   1993/various producers/Trojan/
                                              CDTAL 60
(Limited-edition 4-picture-CD set with 60-page booklet; includes the complete albums)

*Rastaman Vibration; African Herbsman; In the Beginning; Soul Revolution II.*
*Burning Reggae Soul*                         1993/?/Pair?
(Originally released as two LPs; contains 19 tracks)
Soon Come; There She Goes; Hammer; How Many Times; All in One; Don't Rock the Boat; Back Out; Go Tell It on the Mountain; Cheer Up; Mr. Brown; Chances Are; Touch Me; 400 Years; Can't You See; Sun Is Shining; Treat You Right; No Water; Corner Stone; You Can't Do That to Me.

*Songs of Bob Marley*                          1994/various producers/VP/?
Satisfy My Soul; Running Away; Three Little Birds; Time Will Tell; Talkin'
Blues; Love and Affection; So Much Trouble in the World; Waiting in Vain;
One Drop; Soul Rebel; Redemption Song.

*All the Hits*                                 1995/various producers/Jamaican
                                               Authentic Classics Music/?
Redder Than Red; Redder Than Red dub; Nice Time; Nice Time dub; Hypo-
crites; Hypocrites dub; Mellow Mood; Mellow Mood dub; Thank You Lord;
Thank You Lord dub; Mr. Chatterbox; Mr. Chatterbox dub; My Cup; My
Cup dub; Soul Almighty; Soul Almighty dub; Satisfy My Soul; Satisfy My Soul
dub; Try Me; Try Me dub.

*Bob Marley Interviews: So Much*               1995/various producers/
*Things to Say*                                RAS/RAS 3171
(Includes excerpts from an interview by Neville Willoughby; with 12 songs, this
collection was done in celebration of Marley's fiftieth birthday.)
Natural Mystic; Trench Town Rock; Redemption Song; Babylon System; Time
Will Tell; Natural Mystic; Revolution; Survival; One Drop; Roots, Rock, Reggae;
Guava Jelly; Rat Race.

*Natural Mystic: The Legend Lives On*          1995/various producers/
                                               Island-Tuff Gong/314524103–2
(An anthology of social commentary that was released as an addendum to *Legend*)
Natural Mystic; Easy Skankin'; Iron, Lion, Zion; Crazy Baldheads; So Much
Trouble in the World; War; Africa Unite; Trench Town Rock (live); Keep On
Moving (remix); Sun Is Shining; Who the Cap Fit; One Drop; Roots, Rock,
Reggae; Pimper's Paradise; Time Will Tell.

*Bob Marley's 50th Birthday:*                  *1995/various producers/*
*Commemorative Set of Five Limited*            *Trojan/?*
*Edition CD Singles*
(Each disc contains a specific single in multiple versions, some performed by
guest artists)
CD 1: Keep On Moving (Bob Marley and the Wailers); Keep On Moving (instrumental with the Upsetters); Keep On Moving (John Holt cover version); Moving
Version; Keep On Skankin' (Bob Marley and the Wailers); CD 2: Duppy Con-
queror (Bob Marley and the Wailers); Duppy Conqueror (instrumental with the
Upsetters); Mr. Brown (Bob Marley and the Wailers); Dracula (instrumental with
the Upsetters); Duppy Conqueror (2nd version with Bob Marley and the Wailers); CD 3: Small Axe (Bob Marley and the Wailers); Battle Axe (instrumental
with the Upsetters); Shocks 71 (DJ version with Dave Barker and the Upsetters);
Axe Man (bongo version with the Upsetters); More Axe (2nd version); CD 4:
Kaya (Bob Marley and the Wailers); Kaya (instrumental with the Upsetters); Turn
Me Loose (2nd version with Bob Marley and the Wailers); African Herbsman
(instrumental with the Upsetters); African Herbsman (Bob Marley and the Wailers); CD 5: Dreamland (Wailers); Dreamland (instrumental with the Upsetters);
Picture On the Wall (Ras Dawkin and the Wailers); Dreamland Version (DJ ver-
sion with the Upsetters); Dream Version (2nd version with the Wailers).

*Soul Almighty—the Formative Years, Vol. 1*  1996/?/Avid?
(Released as an enhanced CD; contains music and a video of "What Goes
Around Comes Around" playable on a CD-ROM drive)
  Splish for My Splash; Fallin' In and Out of Love; What Goes Around Comes
  Around; Stranger on the Shore; Selassie Is the Chapel.

*Bob Marley and the Wailers: The Rarities,*   1996/various producers/
*Volume 1*                                     Jamaican Gold/?
(Two-CD set)
  Shocks of Mighty; Shocks of Mighty (version); All in One; One in All; Copa-
  setic; More Axe; Axe Man; Duppy Conqueror; Zig Zag; Run for Cover; Pic-
  ture on the Wall; Man to Man; Nicoteen *(sic)*; Rock My Boat; Like It Like
  This.

*The Rarities, Volume II*                      1996/various producers/Jamaican
                                               Gold/?
(Two-CD set)
  Dreamland; Dreamland (version); Jah Is Mighty; Turn Me Loose; Second
  Hand; Second Hand (part 2); Brand New Second Hand; Love Life; Keep On
  Moving; Keep On Skankin'; Mr. Brown; Mr. Brown (version); Send Me That
  Love.

*Bob Marley: The Gold Collection*             1997/various producers/
                                               Proper-Retro/R2CD 40–48
(Two-CD compilation manufactured in the EU)
  CD 1: Trench Town Rock; Soul Rebel; Kaya; Go Tell It on the Mountain; Try
  Me; It's Alright; No Sympathy; No Water; Rainbow County; There She Goes;
  Mellow Mood; Treat You Right; Chances Are; Hammer; Touch Me; Caution;
  Soul Captives; Can't You See; Reaction; 400 Years; CD 2: Natural Mystic;
  Lively Up Yourself; Soul Shakedown Party; Soon Come; Cheer Up; Back Out;
  Do It Twice; Keep On Moving; Don't Rock My Boat; Put It On; Fussing and
  Fighting; Duppy Conqueror; Small Axe; Riding High; African Herbsman;
  Stand Alone; Sun Is Shining; Mr. Brown; Stir It Up; Stop That Train.

*Bob Marley and Friends:*                      1997/various producers/Trojan/
*Roots of a Legend*                            CDTAL 901
(Two-CD compilation of early material)
  CD 1: Sho cks of Mighty, part 1; Shocks of Mighty, part 2; Don't Let the Sun
  Catch You Crying; Upsetting Station; Zig Zag; Run for Cover; Long Long
  Winter; All in One; Copasetic; One in All; More Axe; Shocks 71; The Axe Man;
  Send Me That Love; Man to Man; Nicoteen *(sic)*; Don't Rock My Boat; Like
  It Like This; Love Light Shining; I Gotta Keep On Moving; Moving Version;
  Rainbow Country; CD 2: Dreamland; Dreamland (version); Dreamland Version
  2; The Crimson Pirate; Arise Blackman; Rightful Ruler; The Return of Alcapone;
  Maga Dog; Skanky Dog; Boney Dog; Downpresser; Moon Dust; Rudies Med-
  ley; Rude Boy (version); Dun Valley; Brand New Second Hand; Brand New
  Second Hand (version); Romper Room; Them a Fi Get a Beaten; Get a Beaten;
  Selassie Serenade; Leave My Business.

*Bob Marley*                                      1997/various producers/Rialto/
                                                  RMCD 206
(Twenty-track compilation by Rialto as part of their Archive Series)
  Mr. Brown; Soul Rebel; Duppy Conqueror; 400 Years; Try Me; African
  Herbsman; Keep On Moving; Fussing and Fighting; Stand Alone; My Cup; Put
  It On; Sun Is Shining; Rebel's Hop; Brand New Second Hand; Corner Stone;
  No Water; Jah Is Mighty; Riding High; Brainwashing; Dreamland.

*Bob Marley and the Wailers:*                     *1997/various producers/*
*The Collection, volume 1*                        Hallmark 390572
(Three-CD compilation manufactured in England)
  CD 1: African Herbsman; Mr. Brown; Soul Almighty; Stand Alone; Small
  Axe; Rebel's Hop; No Sympathy; Keep On Moving; Soul Rebel; Brand New
  Second Hand; Chances Are; Stop That Train; Hammer; Wisdom; This Train;
  Touch Me; Caution; Thank You Lord; CD 2: Rainbow Country; Lively Up
  Yourself; Natural Mystic; Kaya; My Cup; Put It On; Cheer Up; Can't You See;
  Treat You Right; Soul Shakedown Party; Tell Me; Duppy Conqueror; Mellow
  Mood; Trench Town Rock; Soon Come; How Many Times; Go Tell It on the
  Mountain; Don't Rock My Boat; CD 3: Sun Is Shining; Brainwashing; Try Me;
  Fussing and Fighting; It's Alright; All in One; There She Goes; Corner Stone;
  Riding High; 400 Years; More Axe; Put It On (version); No Water; Turn Me
  Loose; Soul Rebel (version); Reaction; Adam and Eve.

*The Complete Bob Marley and the Wailers,*    1997/Sims/JAD/JAD-CD-1002
*1967–1972, Part 1*
(Three-CD compilation by Bruno Blum and Roger Steffens for JAD Records)
CD 1: *Rock to the Rock, 1968*              Produced by J. Nash and
                                            A. Jenkins
  Rock to the Rock; Rocking Steady; How Many Times; Touch Me; Mel-
  low Mood; There She Goes; Soul Rebel; Put It On; Chances Are; Love;
  Bend Down Low; The World Is Changing; Nice Time; Treat You Right;
  What Goes Around Comes Around; What Goes Around Comes Around
  (version).

CD 2: *Selassie Is the Chapel, 1968–69–70*   Produced by J. Nash and
                                             A. Jenkins
  Don't Rock My Boat; The Lord Will Make a Way; Chances Are; Selassie Is
  the Chapel; Tread Oh; Feel Alright; Rhythm; Rocking Steady; Adam and
  Eve; Wisdom; This Train; Thank You Lord; Give Me a Ticket; Trouble
  on the Road Again; Black Progress; Black Progress (version); Tread Oh
  (version).

CD 3: *Best of the Wailers, 1969–70*       Produced by L. Kong, Wailers, B. Lee
  Sugar Sugar; Stop the Train; Cheer Up; Soon Come; Soul Captives; Go Tell
  It on the Mountain; Can't You See; Give Me a Ticket; Hold on to This Feel-
  ing; Mr. Chatterbox; Soul Shake Down (version); Soon Come (version); Mr.
  Chatterbox (version); Hold on to This Feeling (version).

*The Complete Bob Marley and the Wailers,*    1997/Sims/JAD/JAD-CD-1004
*1967–1972, Part II*

(Three-CD compilation by Bruno Blum and Roger Steffens for JAD Records)
CD 1: *Soul Rebels, 1970*                    Produced by Lee Perry
Try Me; It's Alright; No Sympathy; My Cup; Soul Almighty; Rebel's Hop
Corner Stone; 400 Years; No Water; Reaction; Dub tracks: My Sympathy;
Soul Rebel (version); Try Me (version); It's Alright (version); No Sympa-
thy (version); My Cup (version); Soul Almighty (version); Rebel's Hop
(version); Corner Stone (version); No Water (version); No Water (version);
Reaction (version); Rebel Version; CD 2: *Soul Revolution, 1970*; Keep On
Moving; Put It On; Fussing and Fighting; Memphis; Riding High; Kaya;
African Herbsman; Stand Alone; Dub tracks: Brain Washing (version); Keep
On Moving (version); Don't Rock My Boat (version); Fussing and Fight-
ing (version); Put It On (version); Duppy Version; Memphis (version);
Riding High (version); Kaya (version); African Herbsman (version); Stand
Alone (version); Dun Is Shining (version); Brain Washing (version); CD 3:
*More Axe, 1970–71*; Kaya; Love Light; Second Hand; Jah Is Mighty; Run
for Cover; Man to Man; Downpresser; Don't Rock My Boat; More Axe;
Long Long Winter; All in One; Turn Me Loose; Dub tracks: Kaya (version);
Battle Axe (version); Long Long Winter (version); Second Hand (version);
Downpresser (version); Shocks of Mighty (version); Axe Man (version;
Nicoteen (version).

*Bob Marley and the Wailers: Soul Rebel,*      1997/various producers/
*Birth of a Legend*                            Hallmark/306542
(Ten-track compilation by Hallmark for Carlton Home Entertainment)
Soul Rebel; There She Goes; Treat You Right; Put It On; Tell Me; How Many
Times; Mellow Mood; Chances Are; Hammer; Touch Me.

*Bustin' out of Trench Town*                   1998/various producers/?/?
Thank You Lord; Wisdom—The Lips of the Righteous; Mr. Chatterbox;
Soul Shake Down Party; Cheer Up; Caution; Stop the Train; Soul Rebel;
Mr. Brown; Try Me; It's Alright; My Cup; No Sympathy; Corner Stone; 400
Years; Reaction; Duppy Conqueror; Sun Is Shining; Kaya; African Herbsman;
Keep On Moving; Fussing and Fighting; Stand Alone; Bend Sown Low/Nice
Time/One Love/Simmer Down/It Hurts to Be Alone (Medley); Don't
Rock My Boat; Put It On; Small Axe; Dreamland; Brand New Second Hand;
Trench Town Rock; Lively Up Yourself; Jah Is Mighty; Keep On Skankin';
Turn Me Loose; More Axe.

*The Complete Bob Marley and the*              1999/Sims/JAD/JAD-CD-1005
*Wailers: 1967 to 1972, part III*
(Third in the series of three multi-CD rereleases of the sides of JAD music)
CD 1: All in One (medley of Bend Down Low/One Love/Simmer Down/
Love and Affection); All in One (part 2: medley of Love and Affection/Put It
On); Keep On Skankin'; Dreamland; Love Light; Brand New Second Hand
(false start); Brand New Second Hand; Shocks of Mighty; Keep On Moving
(also known as I'm Gonna Keep On Moving); Keep On Moving (extended
version); Keep On Moving (extended version 2); Concrete Jungle; Screwface;
Satisfy My Soul; Send Me That Love; Comma Comma; Jungle Dub (dub

version of Concrete Jungle); Dracula (dub version of Mr. Brown); Love Light (dub version); Dreamland (dub version); Face Man (dub version of Screwface); Satisfy My Soul (dub version); CD 2: Screwface; Redder Than Red; Lively Up Yourself; Trouble Dub; Dub Feeling; Satisfy My Soul; Kingston 12; Pour Down the Sunshine; Gonna Get You; Cry to Me; Reggae on Broadway; I'm Hurting Inside; Oh Lord, Got to Get There; Dance Do the Reggae; Stay with Me; Guava Jelly; Guava (dub version of Guava Jelly); Red (dub version of Redder Than Red); Live (dub version of Lively Up Yourself); Samba (dub version of Lick Samba); Screwface (dub version); Grooving Kingston (dub version of Trench Town Rock); Choke (dub version of Craven Chock Puppy); Satisfy My Soul (dub version).

*Bob Marley and the Wailers: The Complete*     *1999/Lee Perry/Culture Press/*
*Soul Rebels and the Upsetter Record Shop*     CP 017
(French release of material from 1969 and 1970; all tracks originally recorded at Harry J's and Wirl Studios in Kingston, Jamaica)
    CD 1: Soul Rebels; Soul Rebels (version); No Water; No Water (version); Rebel Hop; Rebel Hop (version); No Sympathy; No Sympathy (version); It's Alright; It's Alright (version); Reaction; Reaction (version); Corner Stone; Corner Stone (version); 400 Years; 400 Years (version); Make Up; Make Up (version); Try Me; Try Me (version); Soul Almighty; Soul Almighty (version); CD 2: Concrete Jungle; Concrete Jungle (version); Screwface; Screwface (version); Love Life; Love Life (version); Satisfy My Soul; Satisfy My Soul (version); Rainbow Country; Rainbow Country (version); Long Long Winter; Long Long Winter (version); Put It On; Put it On (version); Don't Rock My Boat; Don' Rock My Boat (version); Keep On Movin'; Keep On Movin' (version).

*Bob Marley and the Wailers Destiny:*     *1999/Clement Dodd/*
*Rare Ska Sides from Studio One*     Heartbeat/HB 191
(Collection of mostly previously unrecorded early songs from the Wailers' time at Clement Dodd's Studio One facility)
    Destiny; Wages of Love; Do You Feel the Same Way Too; Your Love; Don't Ever Leave Me; Don't Ever Leave Me (take 2); I Need You So; Rock Sweet Rock; Another Dance; I Stand Predominant; Where Is My Mother (acoustic version); Where Is My Mother (band version); Dance with Me; What's New Pussycat; Treat Me Good; Jerking Time (a/k/a Jerk in Time); Do It Right; Let the Lord Be Seen in Me; White Christmas.

*The Complete Upsetter Collection:*     *2000/Lee Perry/Trojan/*
*Bob Marley and the Wailers*     *TDOXCD 013*
(Six-CD collection of all known vocal, instrumental, and DJ versions of the Upsetter recordings)
    CD 1: Soul Rebel; Soul Rebel (version); Soul Rebel (alternate version); Soul Rebel (dub version); Run for Cover (Soul Rebel version); Try Me; Try Me (dub version); It's Alright; It's Alright (dub version); It's Alright (alternate version); No Sympathy; No Sympathy (dub version); My Cup; Version of Cup; Rebel's Hop; Rebel's Hop (dub version); Corner Stone; Corner Stone (dub version); Jah Is Mighty (Corner Stone version); CD 2: 400 Years; 400 Years (dub version); No Water;

No Water (dub version); Reaction; Reaction (dub version); Soul Almighty; Soul Almighty (dub version); Shocks of Mighty, part 1; Shocks of Mighty, part 2; Shocks of Mighty (dub version); True Love; Cloud Nine; Don't Let the Sun Catch You Crying; Don't Let the Sun Catch You Crying (dub version); Duppy Conqueror; Dubby Conqueror (version); Upsetting Station; Duppy Conqueror (alternate mix); CD 3: Mr. Brown; Mr. Brown (dub version); Small Axe; More Axe; Battle Axe; Shocks 71; More More Axe; The Axe Man; Picture on the Wall; Picture on the Wall (version); Dreamland; Dreamland (instrumental); Dreamland (version); Dreamland (version 2); All in One (medley of Bend Down Low/Nice Time/One Love/Simmer Down/It Hurts to Be Alone/Lonesome Feeling; All in One (part 2, medley of Love and Affection/Put It One/Duppy Conqueror); Copasetic (medley—dub version of Bend Down Low/Nice Time/One Love/Simmer Down/It Hurts to Be Alone/Lonesome Feeling); Downpresser; Downpresser (dub version); CD 4: Long Long Winter; Long Long Winter (dub version); Love Light; Love Light (dub); Love Light (alternate version); Send Me That Love; What a Confusion; Man to Man; Man to Man (dub version); Keep On Moving (dub version); Keep On Moving; Keep On Moving (dub version 2); Keep On Moving (moving version); Keep On Moving (alternate version); Don't Rock My Boat; Don't Rock My Boat (dub version); Don't Rock My Boat (alternate version); Like It Like This (Don't Rock My Boat version); Don't Rock My Boat (alternate mix); CD 5: Put It On; Put It On (dub version); Fussing and Fighting; Fussing and Fighting (dub version); Memphis; Memphis (dub version); Riding High; Riding High (dub version); Kaya; Kaya (dub version); Turn Me Loose; African Herbsman; African Herbsman (dub version); Stand Alone; Stand Alone (dub version); Sun Is Shining; Sun Is Shining (dub version); CD 6: Brain Washing; Brain Washing (dub version); Brand New Second Hand; Brand New Second Hand (dub version); Brand New Second Hand (alternate version); Concrete Jungle; Concrete Jungle (dub version); Rainbow Country; Rainbow Country (dub version); Satisfy My Soul; Keep On Skankin'; Natural Mystic; Natural Mystic (dub version); I Know a Place; I Know a Place; Who Colt the Game; Who Colt the Game (dub version).

| *Bob Marley and the Wailers:* | 2000/Dodd/Heartbeat/ |
| *Climb the Ladder* | 11661–7751–2 |

(Collection of songs from the Studio One recording days; some tracks were previously unreleased)

Dancing Shoes; Put It On; Lonesome Track; Climb the Ladder; Love Won't Be Mine This Way; Dreamland; Lemon Tree; Nobody Knows; Wings of a Dove; Sinner Man; Ten Commandments of Love; Sunday Morning; I Made a Mistake; I Don't Need Your Love; Donna; The Jerk; Just in Time.

| *Bob Marley and the Wailers: Catch a Fire* | 2001/Marley & Blackwell/ |
| | UMe/314548635–2 |

(One of the Deluxe Edition reissues; the second CD is the original release digitally remastered, and the first is outtakes and versions from sessions of the same period)

CD 1: Concrete Jungle; Stir It Up; High Tide or Low Tide; Stop That Train; 400 Years; Baby We've Got a Date; Midnight Ravers; All Day, All Night; Slave

Driver; Kinky Reggae; No More Trouble; CD 2: Concrete Jungle; Slave Driver; 400 Years; Stop That Train; Baby We've Got a Date; Stir It Up; Kinky Reggae; No More Trouble; Midnight Ravers.

*Bob Marley and the Wailers: Exodus*          2001/Marley & Blackwell/
                                              UMe/314586408–2
(The second of the Deluxe Edition re-releases. Disc one contains the original album in a digitally remastered version with additional tracks, and the second disc contains live material recorded at the Rainbow Theater during the *Exodus* tour, along with additional Lee Perry tracks)

   CD 1: Natural Mystic; So Much Things to Say; Guiltiness; The Heathen; Exodus; Jamming; Waiting in Vain; Turn Your Lights Down Low; Three Little Birds; One Love/People Get Ready; Additional tracks: Roots; Waiting in Vain (alternate version); Jamming (long version); Jamming (version); Exodus (version); CD 2 (live tracks from the Rainbow Theater show, June 4, 1977): The Heathen; Crazy Baldhead/Running Away; War/No More Trouble; Jamming; Exodus; Lee Perry Tracks: Punky Reggae Party; Punky Reggae Party; Keep On Moving; Keep On Moving; Exodus.

*One Love: The Very Best of Bob*          2001/various producers/
*Marley and the Wailers*                  UMᶜ/314542855–2
(A greatest-hits collection that culls material from the entire Island Records period; there are no new tracks here, but the album represents an interesting approach)

   Stir It Up; Set Up, Stand Up; I Shot the Sheriff; Lively Up Yourself; No Woman, No Cry; Roots, Rock, Reggae; Exodus; Jamming; Waiting in Vain; Three Little Birds; Turn Your Lights Down Low; One Love/People Get Ready; Is This Love; Sun Is Shining; So Much Trouble in the World; Could You Be Loved; Redemption Song (band version); Buffalo Soldier; Iron, Lion, Zion; I Know a Place.

*Legend: The Best of Bob Marley*          2002/Marley &
*and the Wailers*                         Blackwell/UMᶜ/314586714–2
(The third Deluxe Edition re-release., Disc one contains the original album in a digitally remastered version, and the second contains a series of remixes of the original material)

   CD 1: Is This Love; No Woman, No Cry; Could You Be Loved; Three Little Birds; Buffalo Soldier; Set Up Stand Up; Stir It Up; Easy Skankin' (bonus track); One Love/People Get Ready; I Shot the Sheriff; Waiting in Vain; Redemption Song; Satisfy My Soul; Exodus; Jamming; Punky Reggae Party (bonus track); CD 2: One Love/People Get Ready (extended version); Waiting in Vain; Jamming; Three Little Birds (dub version); Could You Be Loved; No Woman, No Cry; Coming in from the Cold; Buffalo Soldier; Jamming; Waiting in Vain; Exodus; Lively Up Yourself; One Love/People Get Ready.

*Bob Marley and the Wailers:*          2002/Marley & Blackwell/
*Rastaman Vibration*                   UMᶜ/440063446–2

(The fourth of the Deluxe Edition re-releases. Disc one contains the original album in a digitally remastered version with additional tracks, and disc two contains the May 26, 1976 Roxy Theater show and two additional tracks)

CD 1: Positive Vibration; Roots, Rock, Reggae; Johnny Was; Cry to Me; Want More; Crzy Baldhead; Who the Cap Fit; Night Shift; War; Rat Race; Additional tracks: Jah Live; Concrete; Rots, Rock, Reggae; Roots, Rock Dub; Want More; Crazy Baldhead; Johnny Was; CD2: Introduction; Trench Town Rock; Burnin' and Lootin'; Them Belly Full; Rebel Music; I Shot the Sheriff; Want More; Mo Woman, No Cry; Lively Up Yourself; Roots, Rock, Reggae; Rat Race; Smile Jamaica Sessions (late 1976): Smile Jamaica (part one); Smile Jamaica (part two).

*Bob Marley and the Wailers:*                    2003/Suha Gur/UM^c/
*Live at the Roxy*                               B0000516–02
(Recorded live at the Roxy, Hollywood, California, May 26, 1976—complete concert)

Introduction; Trench Town Rock; Burnin' and Lootin'; Them Belly Full; Rebel Music; Want More; No Woman, No Cry; Lively Up Yourself; Roots, Rock, Reggae; Rat Race; Encore: Positive Vibration; Get Up, Stand Up/No More Trouble/War.

*Bob Marley and the Wailers:*                    2004/various producers/UM^c/
*Grooving Kingston 12*                           B0002093–02
(Three-CD set includes work with Lee Perry, early Tuff Gong material, and JAD tracks recorded in London)

CD 1: Concrete Jungle; Screwface; Lively Up Yourself; Redder Than Red; Craven Choke Puppy; Do Good (Big Youth); Trench Town Rock; Kingston 12 Shuffle (U-Roy with Bob Marley and the Wailers); Lick Samba; Guava Jelly; Satisfy My Soul; Run for Cover; Pour Down the Sunshine; Send Me That Love; Lovelight; Ammunition (version); Face Man (version of Screwface); Live (Tommy McCook); Red (version of Redder Than Red); Grooving Kingston 12 (version of Concrete Jungle); Samba (version of Lick Samba); Jelly (version of Guava Jelly); Satisfy (version of Satisfy My Soul); CD 2: Black Progress; Kaya; African Herbsman; Who Is Mr. Brown; My Cup; Downpresser; Small Axe; Dreamland; Fussing and Fighting; Keep On Moving; Second Hand; All in One; Black Progress (version); Kaya (version); African Herbsman (version); Downpresser (version); Dracular *(sic)* (version of Mr. Brown); Downpresser (version); Battle Axe (version of Small Axe); Dreamland (version); My Cup (version); Keep On Moving (version); Second Hand (part 2 version); CD 3: (First eight songs are an acoustic medley); Guava Jelly; This Train; Cornerstone; Comma Comma; Dewdrops; Stir It Up; I'm Hurting Inside; Cry to Me; Sun Is Shining; Heathen's Rage (Johnny Love and Peter Tosh); Satisfy My Soul; Rock My Boat; I Like It Like This (Johnny Lover); Hold on to This Feeling; Rock to the Rock; Rocking Steady; I'm Hurting Inside; Music Gonna Teach (a/k/a Music Lesson); I'm Still Waiting; Babe (version of Satisfy My Soul); Sun Is Shining (version); Hold on to This Feeling (version); Music Gonna Teach (version).

*Bob Marley and the Wailers: Burnin'*            2004/Marley & Blackwell/UM^c/
                                                 B0003359–02

(The fifth Deluxe Edition re-release. Disc one contains the original album digitally remastered with bonus tracks, and disc two contains similar tracks from a previously unreleased live recording form the Leeds show of November 23, 1973)

CD 1: Get Up, Stand Up; Hallelujah Time; I Shot the Sheriff; Burnin' and Lootin'; Put It One; Small Axe; Pass It On; Duppy Conqueror; One Foundation; Rasta Man Chant; Bonus tracks: Reincarnated Souls; No Sympathy; The Oppressed Song; Get Up, Stand Up (unreleased alternate take); Get Up Stand Up (unreleased single version); CD 2: Duppy Conqueror; Slave Driver; Burnin' and Lootin'; Can't Blame the Youth; Stop That Train; Midnight Ravers; No More Trouble; Kinky Reggae; Get Up, Stand Up; Stir It Up; Put It On; Lively Up Yourself; Unreleased tracks: Back against the Wall; Call Me Dada; Don't Draft Me; Dutch Pot; Every Day Is Such a Lonely Day; Feel All Right; I Love Music; I'll Come Back in a Song; I'm Having a Real Good Time; I'm Like a Wounded Lion in the Jungle; Irie Riding; Jailbreaker (writing demo); Jingling Keys; Jump Them out of Babylon (writing demo); Place of Peace (writing demo); Pray for Me (writing demo); Record a New Song (writing demo); Rescue Me; Shakeup; Shoot up the Town; Sophisticated Psychodelocation; Sugar, Sugar (Archies' hit); Turn Over.

# Notes

## CHAPTER 1

1. Roger Stephens, "Bob Marley: Rasta Warrior," *The Rastafari Reader: Chanting Down Babylon* (Philadelphia: Temple University Press, 1998), 254.

2. Actually, Marley's first and middle names were originally reversed. He was born Nesta Robert Marley, but the names were switched when he applied for a passport at age 17.

3. Christopher Farley, *Before the Legend: The Rise of Bob Marley* (New York: HarperCollins, 2006), 4.

4. Timothy White, *Catch a Fire: The Life of Bob Marley*, revised edition (New York: Henry Holt), 53.

5. Farley, *Before the Legend: The Rise of Bob Marley*, 16. Farley's book does much to dispel early myths about Bob's childhood. He went back to the original sources of information, interviewing family members and those closely associated with Bob, and was able to peel back 25 years of false accounts.

6. White, *Catch a Fire: The Life of Bob Marley*, 62.

7. White, *Catch a Fire: The Life of Bob Marley*, 62.

8. Although Bob's father has been repeatedly described as white, Christopher Farley uncovered that when Bob's paternal grandparents wed, his grandfather was listed as white and his grandmother was listed as colored. This was a startling revelation, as it meant that Bob's own father was of mixed-race heritage. Farley, *Before the Legend: The Rise of Bob Marley*, 20.

9. Stephen Davis, *Bob Marley*, rev. ed. (Rochester, VT: Schenkman Books, 1990), 13.

10. White, *Catch a Fire: The Life of Bob Marley*, 14.

11. Ian McCann, *Bob Marley: In His Own Words* (New York: Omnibus Press, 1993), 10. This book was an invaluable source in the course of writing this book, as it contains pages of Bob Marley quotations divided by topic.

12. Davis, *Bob Marley*, 16.

13. Davis, *Bob Marley*, 18.

14. Davis, *Bob Marley*, 23.

15. For further reading on Bustamante and Manley see Horace Campbell, *Rasta and Resistance: From Marcus Garvey to Walter Rodney* (Trenton, NJ: African World Press, 1987), 81–87.

16. Rebekah Mulvaney, *Rastafari and Reggae: A Dictionary and Sourcebook* (Westport, CT: Greenwood Press, 1990), 75.

17. Bunny Wailer is the last surviving original member of the legendary singing trio The Wailers, which also included Bob Marley and Peter Tosh. Bob and Bunny grew up together and shared the dream of becoming musicians. Toward that goal, they joined with Peter Tosh and began studying music with the legendary musician Joe Higgs. During the early years of the Wailers, Livingston was the most shy of the three singers. He began to come into his own in 1970, while the group worked with the producer Lee "Scratch" Perry, when he took center stage for the recording of "Rebel's Hop," "Riding High," and "Brain Washing." In 1972, the connection between the Wailers and Perry yielded a record deal with the Island imprint, and Livingston also released material on his own Solomonic label. The following year, the Wailers released the album *Catch a Fire*, which marked the true beginning of their popularity. Next, they released *Burnin'*, which contained a pair of songs that showcase Livingston. The year 1973 was also a turning point for the Wailers, as Livingston refused to tour. Joe Higgs took his place, and the rest of the Wailers went on without him. After Tosh and Marley returned to Jamaica, the original three Wailers began to disband. Interestingly, it was at this time that Livingston began to refer to himself as Bunny Wailer. By 1974, neither Tosh nor Livingston was in the group. Livingston continued to work with his own label. In 1976, he released his first solo album, titled *Blackheart Man*, which was well received and led to a second album, *Protest*, the following year. In 1979, Livingston released his third album, *Struggle*, followed by a Marley tribute album in the wake of the lead Wailers' death, in 1981. Livingston remained successful throughout the 1980s but did not receive well-deserved exposure because he refused to tour outside Jamaica. In September 1987, Tosh was murdered in his own house, leaving Livingston as the last remaining member of the now-legendary trio. In the 1990s, Livingston was active creating a 50-song collection of Marley songs, which was released in 1995 as an album called *Hall of Fame*. He has won three Grammys and continues to be active in the Jamaican popular music scene. He currently lives on a farm outside Kingston.

18. Davis, *Bob Marley*, 29.

19. For further information on the development of reggae music in Jamaica see David Moskowitz, *Caribbean Popular Music: An Encyclopedia of Reggae, Mento, Ska, Rock Steady, and Dancehall* (Westport, CT: Greenwood, 2005).

20. Ska became the most important music in Jamaica in 1961–1962. It replaced the island tendency to remake American rhythm-and-blues standards and injected Jamaican music with its own spirit. The ska movement coincided with the island's independence and was fostered by an intense interest in asserting Jamaican national identity and pride. The general ska band lineup was a core of singer, guitar, bass, and

drums, supplemented by a horn line of varying size. At the barest minimum, the horn line included saxophone, trumpet, and trombone. The style itself was a mixture of influences, including Jamaican mento, American rhythm and blues, jazz, jump bands, calypso, and others. It took over the island and invaded the radio, dancehalls, and clubs. The ska beat was fast and appropriate for dancing and emphasized offbeat accents that propelled the music forward.

21. McCann, *Bob Marley: In His Own Words*, 11.

22. Desmond Dekker was born Desmond Dacres on July 16, 1941, and lived until May 25, 2006. He was a Jamaican ska and reggae singer and songwriter. Together with his band, the Aces, he had one of the first international Jamaican hits with "Israelites." Other hits included "007" and "It Mek." Before the ascent of Bob Marley, Dekker was the best-known Jamaican musician outside his country and one of the most popular within it.

## Chapter 2

1. Joe Higgs (1940–1999) first appeared on the Jamaican popular music scene in the late 1950s. He had several successful singles and ultimately worked with the famed Jamaican producer Clement "Coxsone" Dodd at his Studio One facility. Higgs was instrumental in the transformation of style from ska to rock steady and pushed forward into the early reggae sound. In addition to Bob, Peter, and Bunny, Higgs also worked with Lynn Taitt and Jimmy Cliff.

2. Stephen Davis, *Bob Marley*, rev. ed. (Rochester, VT: Schenkman Books, 1990), 31.

3. Peter Tosh (1944–1987) exhibited an early love of music and began singing and playing homemade instruments at an early age. He joined Bob and Bunny after meeting them in Joe Higgs's backyard but went solo after the release of *Burnin'*, in 1973. His solo career was critically acclaimed, and he released several successful albums in the late 1970s and early 1980s. Unfortunately, Peter was shot to death in his home in a robbery attempt just as he was gearing up to tour in support of his 1987 release *No More Nuclear War.*

4. Ian McCann, *Bob Marley: In His Own Words* (New York: Omnibus Press, 1993), 32.

5. Jimmy Cliff was born James Chambers in St. Catherine, Jamaica, on April 1, 1948. In his early teenage years, he began his singing career by moving to Kingston and auditioning for several studio heads. He had early success with Leslie Kong, but he signed with Chris Blackwell's Island Records. Cliff's popularity has come as the result of his 20-plus successful albums and his work as an actor and on the soundtrack for the cult film classic *The Harder They Come.*

6. McCann, *Bob Marley: In His Own Words*, 10.

7. Christopher Farley, *Before the Legend* (New York: HarperCollins, 2006), 53.

8. Davis, *Bob Marley*, 41.

9. Kevin Chang and Wayne Chen, "The Sounds of the Sixties," *Reggae Routes: The Story of Jamaican Music* (Philadelphia: Temple University Press, 1998), 92.

10. Roger Steffens, "Bob Marley: Rasta Warrior," *The Rastafari Reader: Chanting Down Babylon*, ed. Nathanial Murrell (Philadelphia: Temple University Press, 1998), 255.

11. The Skatalites started out as Dodd's studio band but eventually became a leg-endary group, part of which still performs to this time. The group consisted of Don Drummond on trombone, Roland Alphonso and Tommy McCook on tenor saxo-phone, Lester Sterling on alto saxophone, Johnny Moore and Leonard Dillon on trumpets, Jackie Mittoo on piano, Lloyd Brevett on bass, Lloyd Nibbs on drums, and Jah Jerry on guitar. The membership of the band was flexible, and several other members joined and left before the band broke up 14 months later. The group was instrumental in the creation of the ska sound and fostered the two-tone craze in the United Kingdom. In the early 1990, the band re-formed; it still uses several of its original members.

12. Kevin Chang and Wayne Chen, "Coxsone Dodd Reminisces about the Young Bob Marley," *Reggae Routes: The Story of Jamaican Music* (Philadelphia: Temple University Press, 1998), 93.

13. Davis, *Bob Marley*, 45.

14. The Uniques consisted of Keith "Slim" Smith, Roy Shirley, and Franklyn White.

15. Verena Reckford, "From Burru Drums to Reggae Ridims: The Evolution of Rasta Music," in *Chant Down Babylon: The Rastafari Reader*, ed. Nathanial Murrell (Philadelphia: Temple University Press, 1998), 247.

16. Davis, *Bob Marley*, 51.

17. McCann, *Bob Marley: In His Own Words*, 33.

18. Cedella Marley and Gerald Hausman, eds., *60 Visions: A Book of Prophesy by Bob Marley* (Miami, FL Tuff Gong Books, 2004), 37.

19. Rita was born Alpharita Anderson in Cuba, around 1950. As a youth, she relocated to Jamaica and began pursuing a music career with the Soulettes in Dodd's Studio One. Since her marriage, she has been the matron of the Marley family. Rita remains active with Marley family business and created the Rita Marley Foundation to supply and improve the infrastructure of underprivileged parts of Africa.

20. Davis, *Bob Marley*, 57.

21. Haile Selassie's name was Amharic for "power of the Trinity," and his common name was Tafari Makonnen. He was described as having descended from King David, the 225th ruler in the unbroken line of Ethiopian kings going back to the time of Solomon and Sheba.

22. Davis, *Bob Marley*, 65.

23. Davis, *Bob Marley*, 67.

24. The horn-driven ska style has enjoyed a rebirth in recent times with American and British bands such as the Mighty Might Bosstones, No Doubt, and the Specials.

25. Steffens, "Bob Marley: Rasta Warrior," 255.


# CHAPTER 3

1. Ian McCann, *Bob Marley: In His Own Words* (New York: Omnibus Press, 1993), 13.

2. In this case, the word "Nyabinghi" refers to Rastafarian music that consisted of chanting and drumming. It is typically used at meetings called grounations (also spelled "groundations").

3. Stephen Davis and Peter Simon, *Reggae Bloodlines: In Search of the Music and Culture of Jamaica* (New York: Da Capo Press, 1992), 35.

4. Clancey Eccles (1940–2005) was a well-known Jamaican record producer who was also an accomplished singer. Known for his rock steady and reggae productions, Eccles formed the Clandisc imprint and released the material of several rising stars, including Alton Ellis, Beres Hammond, and Joe Higgs. Bob and the Wailers were more comfortable working with Eccles, because he was also a Rastafarian whose hair was worn in dreadlocks.

5. McCann, *Bob Marley: In His Own Words*, 13.

6. Stephen Davis, *Bob Marley*, rev. ed. (Rochester, VT: Schenkman Books, 1990), 72.

7. Ziggy Marley and his band, the Melody Makers, consisting of several of his brothers and sisters, are no longer active. However, Ziggy continues to release new music, such as his *Dragonfly* album (2003) and *Love Is My Religion* (2006).

8. McCann, *Bob Marley: In His Own Words*, 19.

9. Many of these songs were rereleased in later Wailers albums. Because this release was not on the Island imprint, its coverage here is minimal.

10. Lee "Scratch" Perry was born Rainford Hugh Perry in St. Mary's, Jamaica, in 1936. After working for Coxsone Dodd, Perry worked for Joe Gibbs before starting his own Upsetter imprint in the late 1960s. During the 1970s, Perry's label was one of the most popular in Jamaica, and he recorded many perennial favorites such as the Wailers and the Congos. Aston "Family Man" Barrett and his brother Carlie were part of Perry's house band when he worked with Bob. As a result, Aston and Carlie went on to become the rhythm section of the Wailers band.

11. Davis, *Bob Marley*, 91.

12. Michael Norman Manley (1924–1997) was the fifth Prime Minister of Jamaica, elected in 1972, 1980, 1989, and 1992. He was the son of Jamaica's Premier Norman Manley and was the longtime leader of the People's National Party (PNP).

13. Timothy White, *Catch a Fire: The Life of Bob Marley* (New York: Henry Holt, 1983), 227.

14. McCann, *Bob Marley: In His Own Words*, 21.

15. The *akete* drum originated in Africa and was a high-pitched drum used in Rasta and reggae music. Also called the repeater, it normally functions as the lead drum in the three-drum group. Some disagreement exists about the term *"akete."* Some use the term to designate the three-drum set used in Rastafarian drumming. However, others consider the term synonymous with the high-pitched repeater.

16. The process of overdubbing was common in the recording industry. It is the addition of other tracks to those that are already recorded. In this case, Marley was overdubbing instrumental tracks to the existing vocal and rhythm tracks.

17. David Fricke, "Blackwell Remembers," *Rolling Stone* 969 (March 10, 2005), 78.

18. "Spliff" is the term for the large cone-shaped ganja cigarettes commonly smoked by Rastafarians and Jamaicans.

19. Maureen Sheridan, *The Story Behind Every Bob Marley Song, 1962–1981* (New York: Thunder's Mouth Press, 1999), 36.

20. In roots reggae music, the one-drop rhythm became quite popular in the mid-1970s. The rhythm was achieved by the drummer and had a distinct sound. In four/four time, one drop was achieved when the drummer was accenting only the third beat of the measure. Whereas European music most often accented the first and third beats and American rock and roll accented the second and fourth beats, reggae's

one-drop rhythm was unique. The rhythm was pioneered by the Wailers' rhythm section, Aston "Family Man" Barrett and his brother, Carlton "Carlie" Barrett. The Wailers used the rhythm extensively throughout the 1970s to the point that they wrote a song about it in 1979. Appearing on the *Survival* album, the song "One Drop" contained lyrics about the rhythm and how it fit into the sound of reggae music at the time.

21. In many of his songs, Peter Tosh referenced to the "youth." It was evident that he did not literally mean only young people but referred to all people who were forward looking and united against the system.

22. Kwame Dawes, *Bob Marley: Lyrical Genius* (London: Sanctuary, 2002), 68.

23. Dawes, *Bob Marley: Lyrical Genius,* 72.

24. Psalm 68: 16–18 states, "The chariots of God are tens of thousands and thousands of thousands; the Lord has come from Sinai into his sanctuary.

25. Davis, *Bob Marley,* 106.

26. A chalice was a ritual water pipe used in Rasta reasonings or grounations. It typically consists of a hollowed-out coconut filled with water and fitted with a large hardwood bowl, which held the marijuana.

27. Formed in the early 1970 as a studio band, the group was led by the keyboardist Geoffrey Chung and included Mikey Chung on lead guitar, Val Douglas on bass, Robert Lynn on keyboards, Earl "Wya" Lindo on organ, and Mikey "Boo" Richards on drums. Throughout the first half of the 1970s, the group played for all of the major Jamaican producers.

28. Because *Africa Herbsman* was not released on the Island imprint and was not an officially sanctioned release by the Wailers, coverage of the album in this work is minimal.

29. Ian McCann, *The Complete Guide to the Music of Bob Marley* (New York: Omnibus Press, 1994), 55.

30. McCann, *Bob Marley: In His Own Words,* 24.

31. McCann, *Bob Marley: In His Own Words,* 24.

32. Jean Watt was a known alias of the I-Threes member Judy Mowatt.

33. Dawes, *Bob Marley: Lyrical Genius,* 96.

34. McCann, *Bob Marley: In His Own Words,* 24.

35. McCann, *Bob Marley: In His Own Words,* 24.

36. McCann, *Bob Marley: In His Own Words,* 23.

37. Dawes, *Bob Marley: Lyrical Genius,* 98.

38. White, *Catch a Fire: The Life of Bob Marley,* 23.

39. Dawes, *Bob Marley: Lyrical Genius,* 95.

40. Dawes, *Bob Marley: Lyrical Genius,* 96.

41. Davis, *Bob Marley,* 130.

42. The Yoruba people are a large ethnolinguistic group in West Africa. They constitute about 30 percent of the population of Nigeria and number approximately 30 million throughout Western Africa. Most of the Yoruba people live in Nigeria, Benin, and Togo, but diasporic members are found in Trinidad and Puerto Rico and throughout the Caribbean.

43. McCann, *Bob Marley: In His Own Words,* 21.

44. McCann, *Bob Marley: In His Own Words,* 21.

45. McCann, *Bob Marley: In His Own Words,* 22.

46. Albert Anderson gained his early music experience at the Berklee School of Music, where he studied bass playing. He met Chris Wood of the rock band Traffic and through him came to know Chris Blackwell, the boss of Island Records. Through Blackwell, Anderson met and played with Bob Marley and worked with the group from 1974 to 1976, when he left to play with Peter Tosh's Word Sound & Power band. In 1979, he returned to the Wailers, where he played alongside the new lead guitarist Junior Marvin.

47. Don Taylor released his accounts of Bob's life in his book *Marley and Me: The Real Bob Marley Story* (New York: Barricade Books, 1995).

48. The house at 56 Hope Road is now the Bob Marley museum, where international visitors go on tours and learn more about Bob and the Wailers. A recording studio was built on the first floor and is still in use, and the rest of the house has been set up to give a brief history of Bob and the band. One of the upstairs bedrooms has been converted into a library lined with books on Rastafarianism, reggae, Bob, the Wailers, and all things associated with them. The rehearsal space in the back has been converted into a gallery that houses pictures of Bob and friends along with his signature Les Paul guitar.

49. McCann, *Bob Marley: In His Own Words*, 79.

50. Davis, *Bob Marley*, 144.

51. John Rockwell, "Marley, Wailers Dig into Reggae Roots," *New York Times* (June 20, 1975), 25.

52. Davis, *Bob Marley*, 145.

53. James E. Perone, *The Sound of Stevie Wonder: His Words and Music* (Westport, CT: Praeger, 2006), 129.

## CHAPTER 4

1. Smith had considerable rock steady and reggae experience with the Soul Syndicate, the Aggrovators, the Riddim Raiders, and the Professionals. After Bob's death, Smith went on to play with his son Ziggy in the Melody Makers and on material for another of Bob's sons, Julian.

2. Don Kinsey played with his father and brothers in Albert King's band. He had also played with Aerosmith, Yes, and Jethro Tull, among others.

3. Ian McCann, *Bob Marley: In His Own Words* (New York: Omnibus Press, 1993), 22.

4. McCann, *Bob Marley: In His Own Words*, 22.

5. Kwame Dawes, *Bob Marley: Lyrical Genius* (London: Sanctuary, 2002), 164.

6. Timothy White, *Catch a Fire: The Life of Bob* Marley (New York: Henry Holt, 1994), 24.

7. Compass Point has gone on to become a world-renowned studio with an impressive client list. The facility remains open and is available for booking.

8. Ackee is a Jamaica fruit that, when cooked, looks and tastes remarkably like scrambled eggs.

9. After leaving the Wailers, Peter Tosh formed the Word Sound & Power band, which accompanied him on all recordings except his first album, *Legalize It*.

10. The English punk band the Clash took its name from Culture's song and even periodically covered reggae songs. The connection between English punk and reggae music was very tight in the late 1970s.

11. Junior Murvin was born Murvin Junior Smith in Montego Bay, Jamaica. As a youth, he moved to Kingston and entered the music scene. He recorded with Sonja Pottinger, Derrick Harriott, and Mighty Two (Joe Gibbs and Errol Thompson), among others. He has enjoyed a long and successful career and was one of the few reggae legends to successfully make the transition to the more modern dancehall style.

12. McCann, *Bob Marley: In His Own Words,* 23.

13. McCann, *Bob Marley: In His Own Words,* 25.

14. Marcus Mosiah Garvey (1877–1940) established the Universal Negro Improvement Association, employed Ethiopianism to establish a sense of African identity in the African diaspora, paved the way for Rastafarianism, and admonished all black people to look to Africa for their roots or to repatriate to the mother country if possible. Paul Bogle (active c. 1855; hanged on the British ship HMS Wolverine on October 24, 1865) was the leader of a peasant revolt in Morant Bay, Jamaica, and a founding father of Pan-Africanism.

15. Dawes, *Bob Marley: Lyrical Genius,* 217.

16. Born Emmanual Rodriguez in 1934, "Rico" went on to become one of Jamaica's most famous trombone players. Through the course of a storied career, he has played with Clue J and his Blues Blasters, Rude Rich, and the Skatalites.

17. Davis, *Bob Marley,* 190.

# Chapter 5

1. Ian McCann, *Bob Marley: In His Own Words* (New York: Omnibus Press, 1993), 22.

2. Kwame Dawes, *Bob Marley: Lyrical Genius* (London: Sanctuary Publishing Limited, 2002), 222.

3. Bob Marley, "A Conversation with Bob Marley," reprinted as "Bob Marley 1979 Interview," *The Beat* 18, no. 3 (1999), 43.

4. Leroy Parks formed the We the People band in 1975. In addition to Parks on bass, the band included rock-solid drumming and an outstanding horn line. The We the People band backed notable artists such as Alton Ellis, John Holt, and the Mighty Diamonds.

5. The Maoris are a brown-skinned people, of Polynesian origin, native to New Zealand.

6. The struggle for power in Rhodesia began in 1890 when black nationalists started fighting the white minority government. The white British settlers, led by Cecil Rhodes, had gradually expanded their dominance by crushing African tribes in pursuit of their fertile land in Mashonland and Matabeleland. Rhodesia proclaimed its independence in 1965 but remained an apartheid state that endured periodic uprisings and guerrilla wars. In 1980, the country experienced its first free general election, and the ZANU leader Robert Mugabe was elected. The name of the country was officially changed to the Republic of Zimbabwe and its capital city renamed Harare.

7. The bands participating in the modern annual Reggae Sunsplash shows take the concert on tour after the show's performance in Jamaica and re-create the performance across the United States. Reggae Sunsplash continues today.

8. The word "Amandla" comes from the Shona language of Zimbabwe and is a shortening of the phrase "*amandle ngaweta*," meaning "power to the people."

9. Michael Babatunde "Baba" Olatunji died April 6, 1993, at age 75. During a long and storied career, Olatunji built a reputation as West Africa's most popular percussionist. In 1991, he was awarded a Grammy award for his work with Mickey Hard of the Grateful Dead.

10. Stephen Davis, *Bob Marley* (Rochester, VT: Schenkman Books, 1990), 216.

11. Ian McCann, *The Complete Guide to the Music of Bob Marley* (New York: Omnibus Press, 1994), 94.

## CHAPTER 6

1. El Hadj Omar Bono Ondimba was born Albert-Bernard Bongo in 1935. He became the president of Gabon at age 32 and continues to serve in that capacity. Bongo is the world's seventh-longest-serving ruler.

2. Stephen Davis, *Bob Marley* (Vermont: Schenkman Books, 1990), 222.

3. Don Taylor, *Marley and Me: The Real Bob Marley Story* (New York: Barricade Books, 1995), 184–185.

4. Ian McCann, *Bob Marley: In His Own Words* (New York: Omnibus Press, 1993), 23.

5. Cedella Marley and Gerald Hausman, eds., *60 Visions: A Book of Prophesy by Bob Marley* (Miami, FL: Tuff Gong Books, 2004), 24.

6. Kwame Dawes, *Bob Marley: Lyrical Genius* (London: Sanctuary, 2002), 295.

7. Ian McCann, *The Complete Guide to the Music of Bob Marley* (New York: Omnibus Press, 1994), 101.

8. Born Anthony Fairclough and Erroll Bennett, Papa Michigan and General Smiley were two of the first Jamaican DJs to unleash the rub-a-dub style. They had hits on several labels and appeared on Sunsplash from 1980 to 1985.

9. Davis, *Bob Marley*, 238.

10. Bad Wiessee is a spa town on Lake Tegernsee, in Bavaria, Germany.

11. Psalm 23 was David's acknowledgment that the Lord was his shepherd, and he did not fear evil or even death because he knew that he would dwell in the house of the Lord.

12. Mikal Gilmore, "The Life and Times of Bob Marley: How He Changed the World," *Rolling Stone* 969 (March 10, 2005), 74.

## CHAPTER 7

1. Howard Campbell, "Jamming with Jimmy Norman," *Jamaica Observer*, November 22, 2002, n.p.

2. St. George (died c. 304) was, among other things, the patron saint of Ethiopian farmers. The lore of George was that he slew a vicious dragon that had already claimed countless lives. He was rewarded by the king, but he distributed this wealth to the local poor. He is remembered as a soldier of Christ.

3. A suru board is a customized marijuana-cigarette rolling surface. Most are made of wood and have padding on the back, making it easier to keep them still by

them resting on the legs. The board face has several grooves cut in it and a shallow lip to hold the marijuana as it is being cleaned and rolled.

4. When discussing Haile Selassie I, one must remember that he was also referred to as Ras Tafari or Jah.

5. Although in Jamaican patois "mash up" means to destroy, in the contemporary American context it refers to the combining of two separate songs to create a new and distinct third song.

6. Bill Levenson has been an active music producer for years. His production credits include work on albums by Kiss, Eric Clapton, the Bee Gees, and Joe Cocker.

## CHAPTER 8

1. Tom Sinclair, "The Legend of Bob Marley," *Entertainment Weekly* 806 (February 11, 2005), 8.

2. Sinclair, "The Legend of Bob Marley," 8.

3. Bob Marley, "A Conversation with Bob Marley," reprinted as "Bob Marley 1979 Interview," *The Beat* 18, no. 3 (1999), 42.

# Bibliography

Austin, Diane. *Urban Life in Kingston, Jamaica*. New York: Gordon and Breach, 1984.

Backus, Leroy M., III. *Stylistic Development of Reggae Music*. M.A. thesis, University of Washington, 1976.

Balford, Henry. "Marley's legacy lives on, but. . . ." *Jamaica Observer*, February 26, 2004, n.p.

Barrett, Leonard. *The Rastafarians: The Dreadlocks of Jamaica*. Boston: Beacon Press, 1988.

Barrow, Steve, and Peter Dalton. *Reggae: The Rough Guide*. New York: Penguin Books, 1997.

Bennett, Scotty. *Bob Marley*. New York: Virgin, 1997.

Booker, Cedella, and Anthony Winker. *Bob Marley: An Intimate Portrait by His Mother*. New York: Viking, 1996.

Boot, Adrian, and Vivian Goldman. *Bob Marley—Soul Rebel—Natural Mystic*. London: Eel Pie, 1981.

Boot, Adrian, and Michael Thomas. *Jamaica: Babylon on a Thin Wire*. London: Thomas and Hudson, 1976.

Bordowitz, Hank, ed., *Every Little Thing Gonna Be Alright: The Bob Marley Reader*. Cambridge, MA: Da Capo Press, 2004.

Bradley, Lloyd. *Reggae on CD: The Essential Guide*. London: Kyle Cathie, 1996.

———. "Uprising." *Mojo*, March 2005, 69–81.

Bramwell, Osula. *"Redemption Song": Protest Reggae and Jamaica*. Ph.D. dissertation, University of Waterloo (Canada), 1984.

Burnett, Michael. *Jamaican Music*. London: Oxford University Press, 1982.

Campbell, Horace. *Rasta and Resistance: From Marcus Garvey to Walter Rodney*. Trenton, NJ: African World Press, 1987.

Campbell, Howard. "Jamming with Jimmy Norman." *Jamaica Observer,* November 22, 2002.

———. "Reggae Icon Remembered." *Jamaica Gleaner,* February 7, 2005.

———. "The Wailers Band: Still Rockin' in the Nineties." *Reggae Report* 14/4 (April 1996): 24–25.

Cassidy, Frederic Gomes, and R. B. Le Page. *Dictionary of Jamaican English.* 2nd ed. West Indies: University of the West Indies Press, 2003.

Chambers, Iain. *Urban Rhythms.* London: Macmillan, 1985.

Chevannes, Barry. *Rastafari: Roots and Ideology.* New York: Syracuse University Press, 1994.

Clarke, Colin. *Kingston, Jamaica: Urban Development and Social Change, 1692– 1962.* Berkeley: University of California Press, 1975.

Cooke, Mel. "Marley Museum Now Official Heritage Site." *Jamaica Gleaner,* February 7, 2005.

Cooper, Carolyn. "Chanting Down Babylon: Bob Marley's Song as Literary Text." *Jamaica Journal* 19/4 (November 1986): 2–8.

Dalrymple, Henderson. *Bob Marley: Music, Myth, and the Rastas.* Middlesex, England: Carib-Arawak Publishing, 1976.

Davis, Stephen. *Bob Marley.* New York: Doubleday, 1985.

———. *Bob Marley.* Rochester, VT: Schenkman. Reprint. 1990.

———. *Bob Marley: Conquering Lion of Reggae.* London: Plexus, 1994.

Davis, Stephen, and Peter Simon. *Reggae Bloodlines: In Search of the Music and Culture of Jamaica.* New York: Da Capo Press, 1992.

———. *Reggae International.* New York: Knopf, 1983.

Dawes, Kwame. *Bob Marley: Lyrical Genius.* Great Britain: Sanctuary, 2002.

Dolan, Sean. *Bob Marley.* Philadelphia: Chelsea House, 1996.

Farley, Christopher. *Before the Legend: The Rise of Bob Marley.* New York: HarperCollins, 2006.

———. "How Marley Caught Fire: Repackaging the Reggae King as a Rock Star Helped Sell His Music to the World." *The Wall Street Journal,* April 27, 2006.

Fricke, David. "Blackwell Remembers." *Rolling Stone* 969 (March 10, 2005), 78.

Furgusson, I. "'So Much Things to Say': The Journey of Bob Marley." *The Village Voice* 27 (May 18, 1982), 39–43.

Gilmore, Mikal. "The Life and Times of Bob Marley: How He Changed the World." *Rolling Stone* 969 (March 10, 2005), 68–78.

Goldman, Vivian. *The Book of Exodus: The Making and Meaning of Bob Marley's Album of the Century.* New York: Three Rivers Press, 2006.

Graham, Ronnie. *Stern's Guide to Contemporary African Music.* London: Zwan, 1988.

Gray, Obika. *Radicalism and Social Change in Jamaica, 1960–1972.* Knoxville: University of Tennessee Press, 1991.

Hausman, Gerald, ed. *The Kebra Nagast: The Lost Bible of Rastafarian Wisdom and Faith from Ethiopia and Jamaica.* New York: St. Martin's Press, 1997.

Henke, James. *Marley Legend: An Illustrated Life of Bob Marley.* San Francisco, CA: Chronicle Books, 2006.

Howard, Dennis. "Professor Rex Nettleford on the Creative Power of Bob Marley." *Reggae Report* 14/4 (April 1996): 20–21.

Jaffe, Lee. *One Love: Life with Bob Marley and the Wailers.* New York: Norton, 2003.

Jensen, Richard J. "Bob Marley's 'Redemption Song': The Rhetoric of Reggae and Rastafari." *Journal of Popular Culture* 29/3 (Winter 1995): 17–20.

Lacey, Terry. *Violence and Politics in Jamaica, 1960–1970.* Manchester, England: Manchester University Press, 1977.

Lee, Peter. "Glory to Jah: Remembering Bob Marley." *Guitar Player* 25/5 (May 1991): 82–87.

Lipsitz, George. *Dangerous Crossroads.* New York: Verso, 1994.

Manuel, Peter. *Caribbean Currents: Caribbean Music from Rumba to Reggae.* Philadelphia: Temple University Press, 1995.

Marley, Bob. "A Conversation with Bob Marley." Reprinted as "Bob Marley's 1979 Interview." *The Beat* 18, no. 3 (1999): 40–43.

Marley, Cedella, and Gerald Hausman, eds. *60 Visions: A Book of Prophesy by Bob Marley.* Miami, FL: Tuff Gong Books, 2004.

May, Chris. *Bob Marley.* London: Hamish, 1985.

McCann, Ian. *Bob Marley in His Own Words.* New York: Omnibus Press, 1993.

———. *The Complete Guide to the Music of Bob Marley.* New York: Omnibus Press, 1994.

McKenzie, Clyde. "Bob Marley: For the People." *Reggae Report* 14/4 (April 1996): 13.

Moskowitz, David. *Caribbean Popular Music: An Encyclopedia of Reggae, Mento, Ska, Rock Steady, and Dancehall.* Westport, CT: Greenwood Press, 2005.

Mulvaney, Rebekah M., and Carlos Nelson. *Rastafari and Reggae: A Dictionary and Source book.* Westport, CT: Greenwood Press, 1990.

Murrell, Nathanial, ed. *Chant Down Babylon: The Rastafari Reader.* Philadelphia: Temple University Press, 1998.

National Library of Jamaica. *Marley Bibliography.* Kingston, Jamaica: National Library of Jamaica, 1985.

Nettleford, Rex. *Caribbean Cultural Identity: An Essay in Cultural Dynamics.* Kingston, Jamaica: Ian Randle Publishers, 2003.

———. *Mirror Mirror: Identity, Race, and Protest in Jamaica.* Kingston, Jamaica: William Collins and Sangster, 1970.

Oumano, Elena. "Reggae: It's More Than the Riddim." *Billboard* 108/27 (July 6, 1996), 37–48.

Patterson, Orlando. *Children of Sisyphus.* London: Longman, 1964.

Perone, James. *The Key of Life: The Words and Music of Stevie Wonder.* Westport, CT: Praeger, 2006.

Potash, Chris. *Reggae, Rasta, Revolution: Jamaican Music from Ska to Dub.* New York: Schirmer Books, 1997.

Rockwell, John. "Marley, Wailers Dig into Reggae Roots." *New York Times,* June 20, 1975, 25.

Rodney, Walter. *The Groundings with My Brothers.* London: Bogle-L'Ouverture, 1969.

Rosen, Craig. "Marley's 'Legend' Lives on 1984 Island Set." *Billboard* 108/47 (November 23, 1996), 13–18.

Santoro, Gene. *Stir It Up: Musical Mixes from Roots to Jazz.* New York: Oxford University Press, 1997.

Sheridan, Maureen. *The Story behind Every Bob Marley Song: 1962–1981.* New York: Thunder's Mouth Press, 1999.

Sinclair, Tom. "The Legend of Bob Marley." *Entertainment Weekly* 806 (February 11, 2005), 6–10.

Smith, M. G. *Culture, Race, and Class in the Commonwealth Caribbean.* Kingston, Jamaica: University of the West Indies Press, 1984.

Stephens, Roger. "Bob Marley: Rasta Warrior." *The Rastafari Reader: Chant Down Babylon.* Philadelphia: Temple University Press, 1998.

Talamon, Bruce W. *Bob Marley: Spirit Dancer.* New York: Norton, 1994.

Taylor, Don. *Marley and Me: The Real Bob Marley Story.* New York: Barricade, 1995.

———. *So Much Things to Say: My Life as Bob Marley's Manager.* New York: Blake, 1995.

Wagner, Charles R. *Jah as Genre: The Interface of Reggae and American Popular Music.* Ph.D. dissertation, Bowling Green University, 1993.

Warner, Keith Q. "Calypso, Reggae, and Rastafarianism: Authentic Caribbean Voices." *Popular Music and Society* 12/1 (Spring 1988): 53–62.

White, Garth. *The Development of Jamaican Popular Music with Special Reference to the Music of Bob Marley.* Kingston: African-Caribbean Institute of Jamaica, 1982.

White, Timothy. *Catch a Fire: The Life of Bob Marley.* Rev. ed. New York: Henry Holt, 1994.

Whitney, Malika, and Dermott Hussey. *Bob Marley: Reggae King of the World.* Kingston, Jamaica: Kingston Publishers, 1984.

Winders, J. A. "Reggae, Rastafarians, and Revolution: Rock Music in the Third World." *Journal of Popular Culture* 17/1 (January 1983): 62.

# Index

## About the Author

DAVID MOSKOWITZ is Assistant Professor of Musicology at the University of South Dakota. He is the author of the Greenwood reference book, *The Encyclopedia of Reggae and Caribbean Music*.